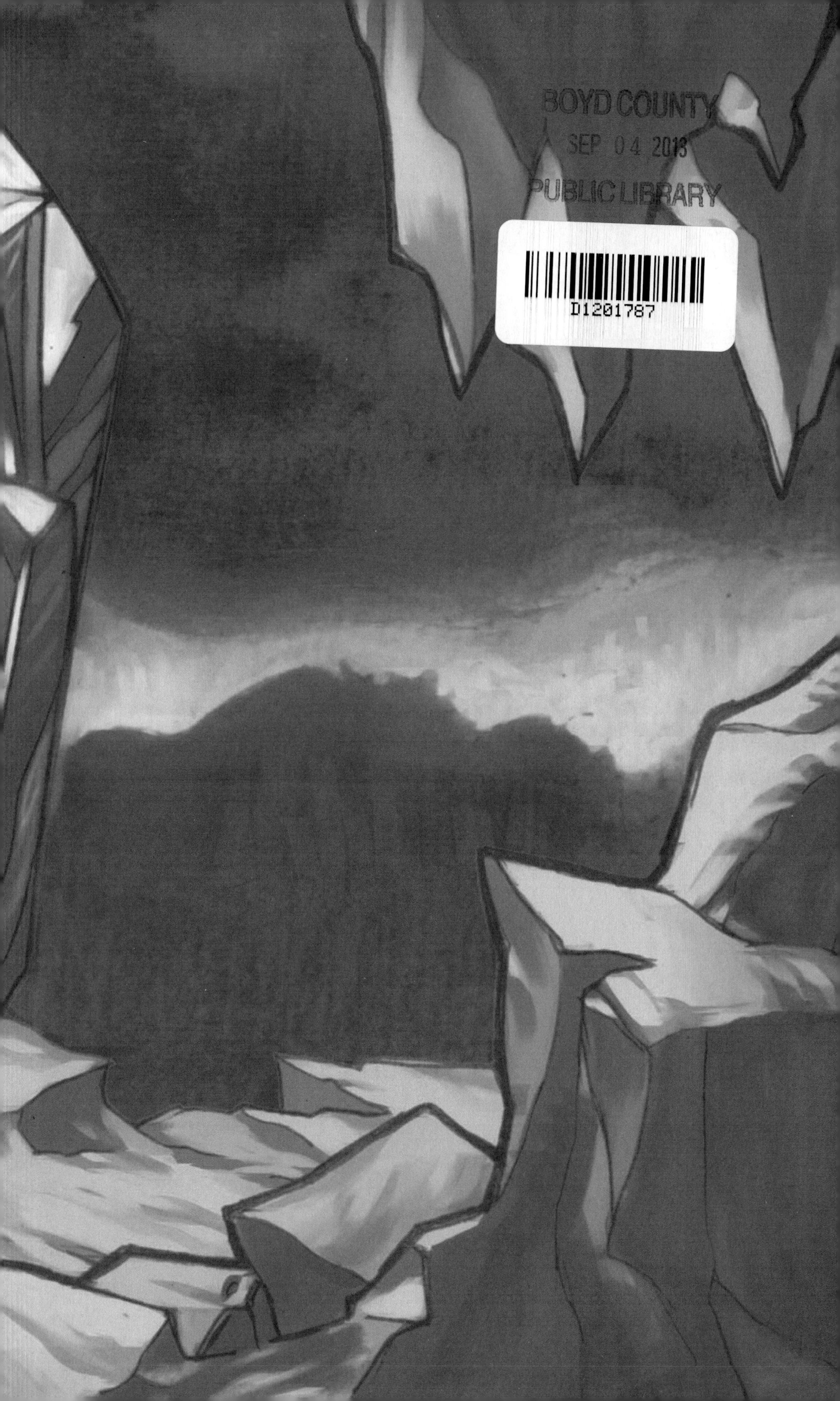

ANOTHER WORLD...
ANOTHER TIME...
IN THE AGE
OF WONDER

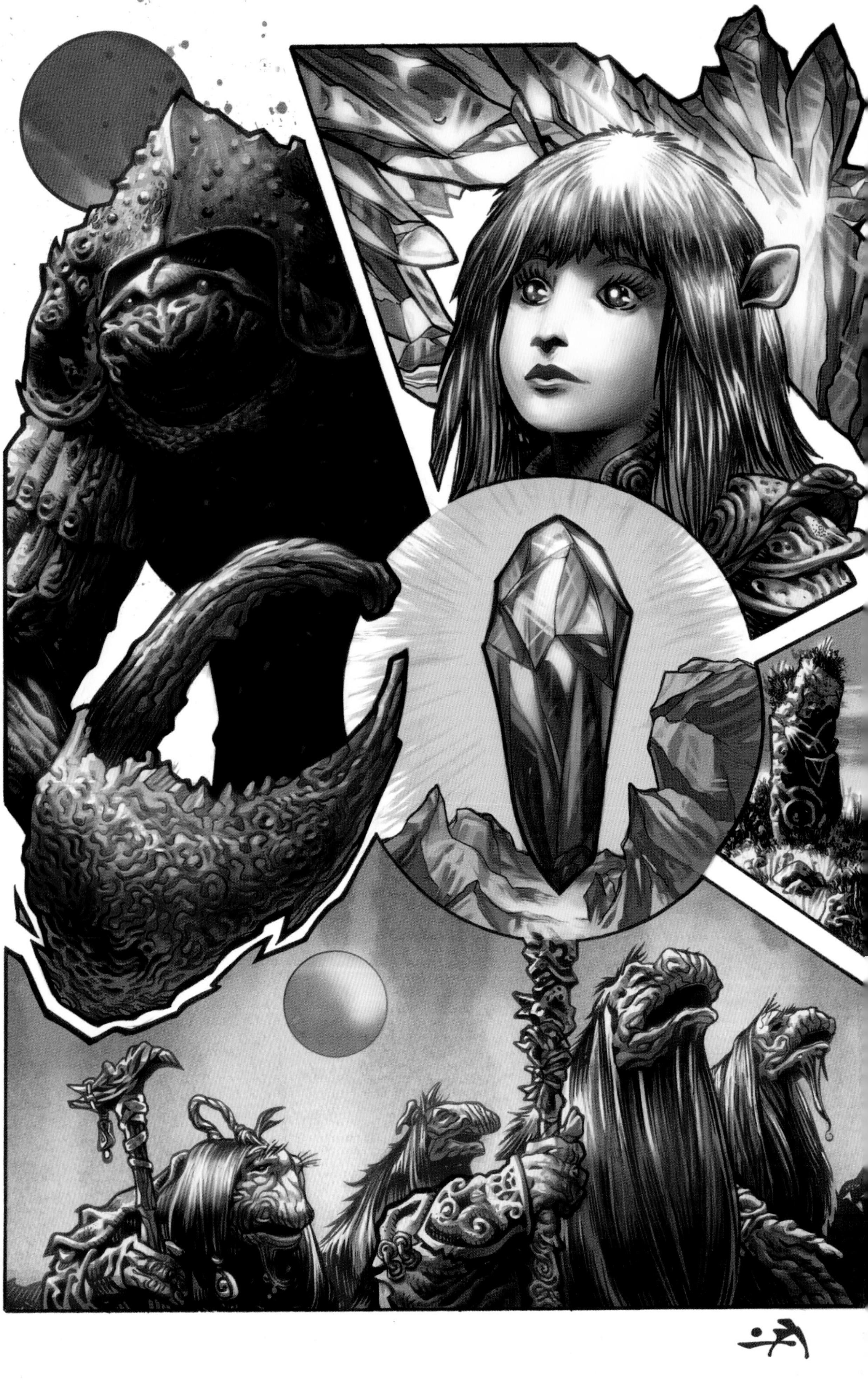

ARCHAIA™ AND *Jim Henson* THE JIM HENSON COMPANY PROUDLY PRESENT

THE DARK CRYSTAL CREATION MYTHS

VOLUME II

Concept, character designs and cover by
BRIAN FROUD

Written by JOSHUA DYSART

Illustrated by ALEX SHEIKMAN and LIZZY JOHN

Lettered by DERON BENNETT • Designed by FAWN LAU • Edited by TIM BEEDLE and STEPHEN CHRISTY

Based on the film by Jim Henson and Frank Oz • Written by David Odell • Conceptual Design by Brian Froud

Scott Newman, *Production Manager*

SPECIAL THANKS TO: Brian Henson, Lisa Henson, Jim Formanek, Nicole Goldman, Karen Falk, Maryanne Pittman, Melissa Segal, Hillary Howell, Jill Peterson, Ashley Griffis, Justin Hilden, Paul Morrissey, Robert Gould, Joe LeFavi, Luke Crane, Jared Sorensen, and the entire Jim Henson Company Team.

Archaia Entertainment LLC
PJ Bickett, *Chairman*
Jack Cummins, *President & COO*
Mark Smylie, *CCO*
Mike Kennedy, *Publisher*
Stephen Christy, *Editor-in-Chief*
Mel Caylo, *Marketing Manager*

Published by **Archaia**
Archaia Entertainment LLC
1680 Vine Street, Suite 1010
Los Angeles, California, 90028
WWW.ARCHAIA.COM

ISBN: 1-932386-80-0
ISBN 13: 978-1-932386-80-8

THE DARK CRYSTAL: CREATION MYTHS VOL. 2
February 2013 • FIRST PRINTING
10 9 8 7 6 5 4 3 2 1

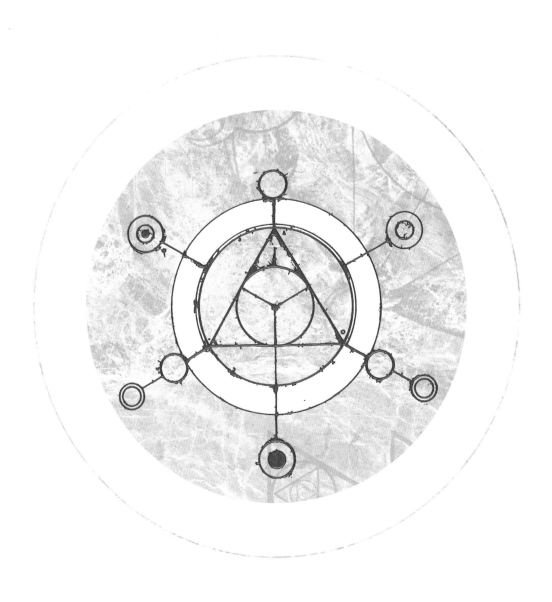

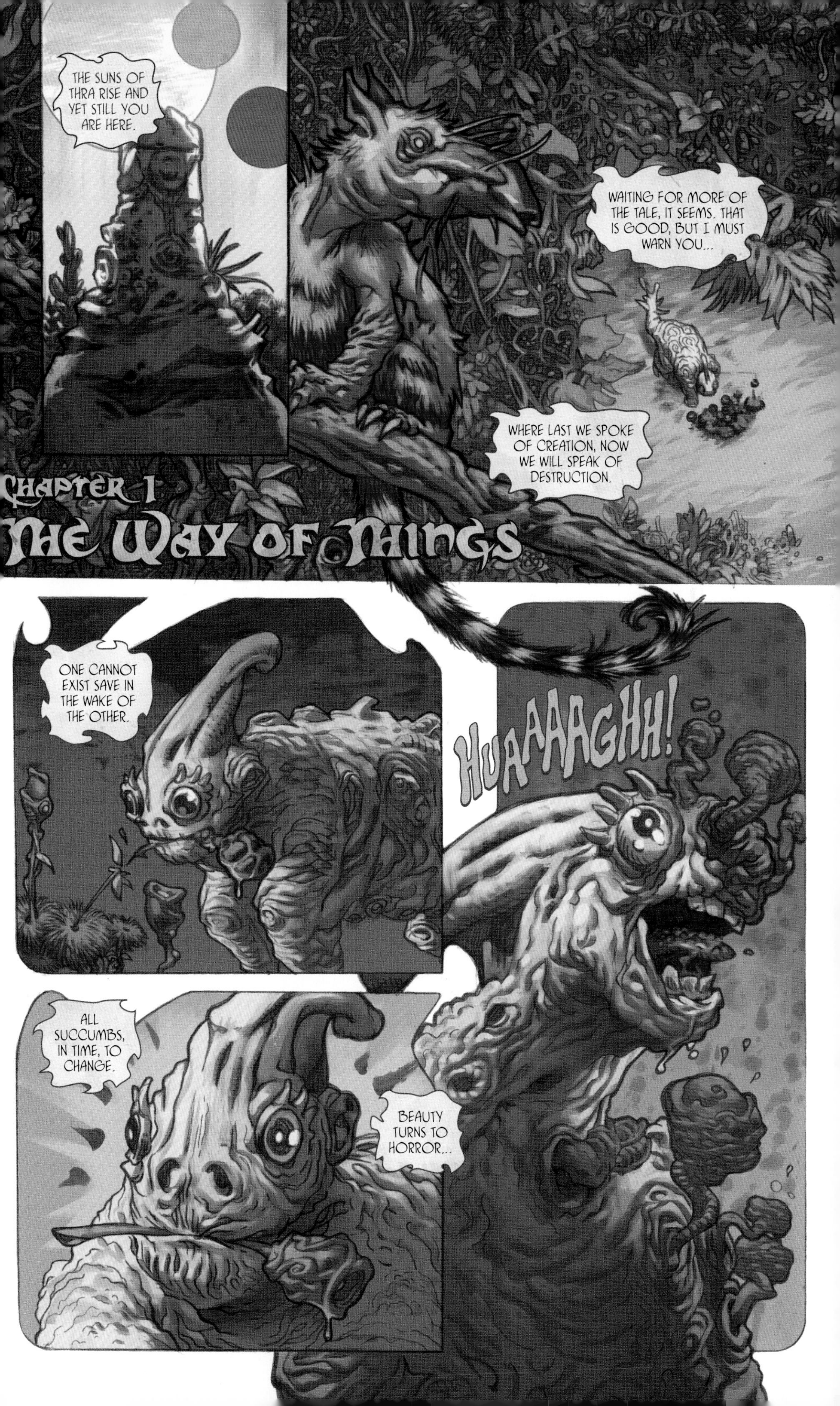
THE SUNS OF THRA RISE AND YET STILL YOU ARE HERE.
WAITING FOR MORE OF THE TALE, IT SEEMS. THAT IS GOOD, BUT I MUST WARN YOU...
WHERE LAST WE SPOKE OF CREATION, NOW WE WILL SPEAK OF DESTRUCTION.
CHAPTER 1
THE WAY OF THINGS
ONE CANNOT EXIST SAVE IN THE WAKE OF THE OTHER.
HUAAAAGHH!
ALL SUCCUMBS, IN TIME, TO CHANGE.
BEAUTY TURNS TO HORROR...

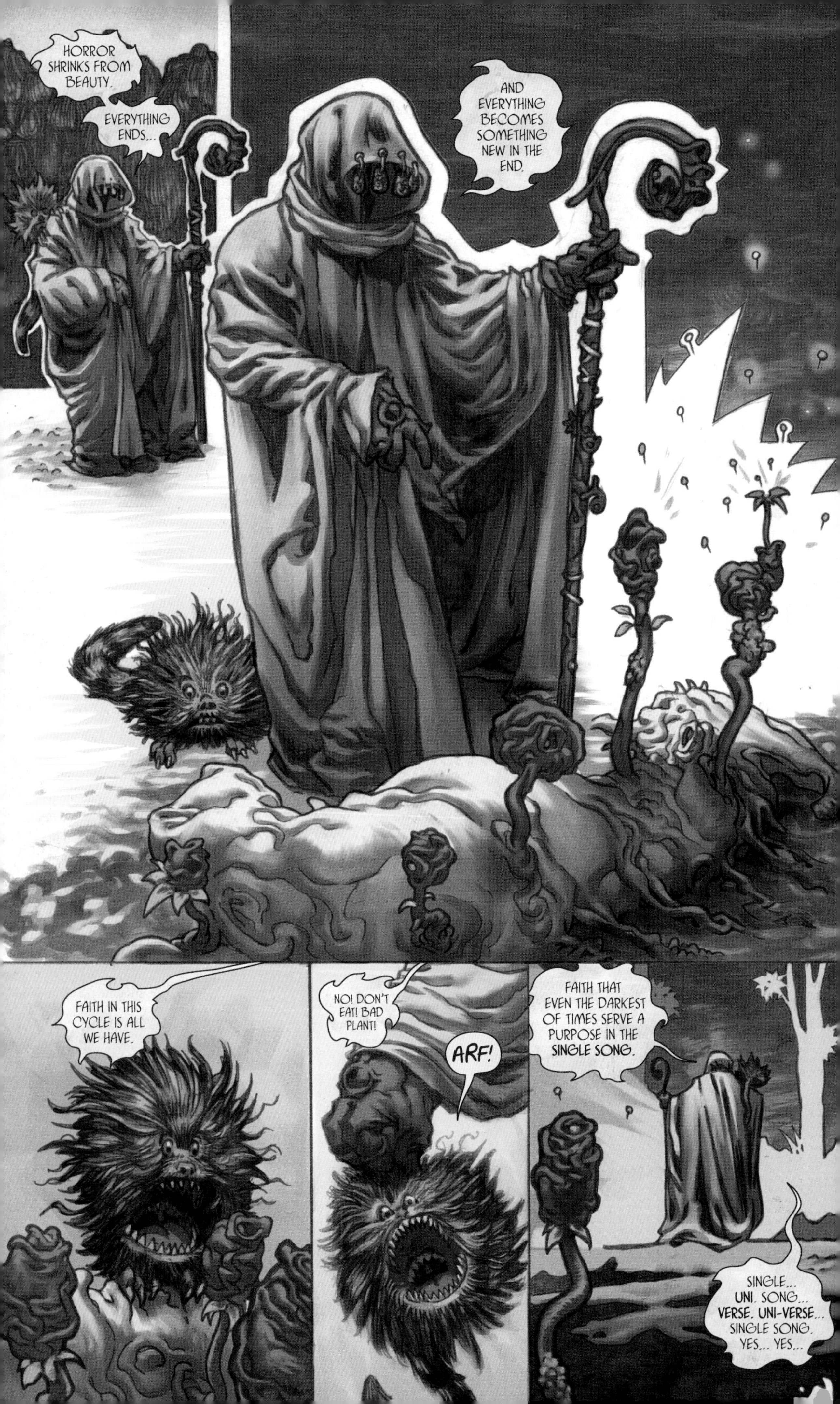
HORROR SHRINKS FROM BEAUTY.
EVERYTHING ENDS...
AND EVERYTHING BECOMES SOMETHING NEW IN THE END.
FAITH IN THIS CYCLE IS ALL WE HAVE.
NO! DON'T EAT! BAD PLANT!
ARF!
FAITH THAT EVEN THE DARKEST OF TIMES SERVE A PURPOSE IN THE SINGLE SONG.
SINGLE... UNI. SONG... VERSE. UNI-VERSE... SINGLE SONG. YES... YES...

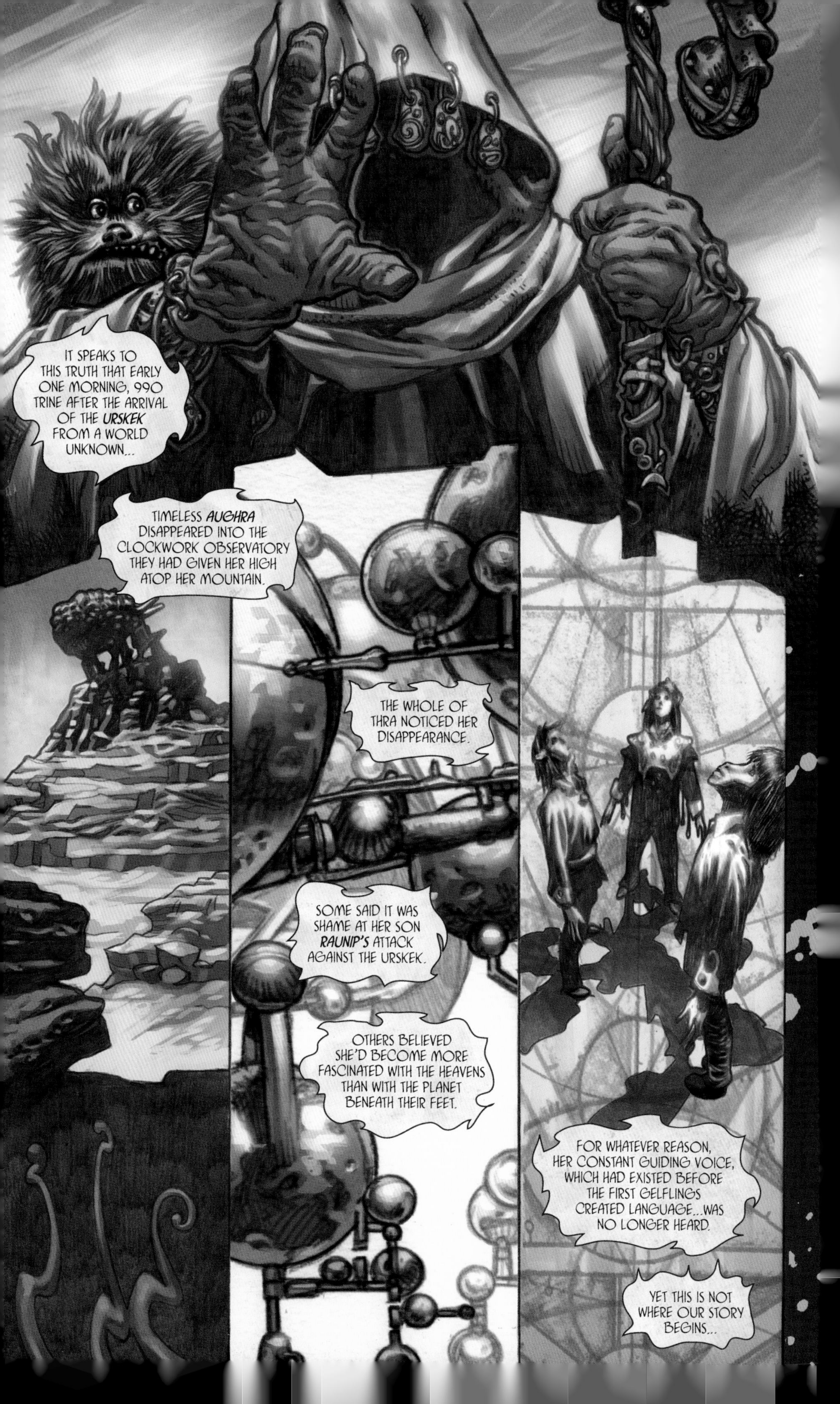

IT SPEAKS TO THIS TRUTH THAT EARLY ONE MORNING, 990 TRINE AFTER THE ARRIVAL OF THE URSKEK FROM A WORLD UNKNOWN...
TIMELESS AUGHRA DISAPPEARED INTO THE CLOCKWORK OBSERVATORY THEY HAD GIVEN HER HIGH ATOP HER MOUNTAIN.
THE WHOLE OF THRA NOTICED HER DISAPPEARANCE.
SOME SAID IT WAS SHAME AT HER SON RAUNIP'S ATTACK AGAINST THE URSKEK.
OTHERS BELIEVED SHE'D BECOME MORE FASCINATED WITH THE HEAVENS THAN WITH THE PLANET BENEATH THEIR FEET.
FOR WHATEVER REASON, HER CONSTANT GUIDING VOICE, WHICH HAD EXISTED BEFORE THE FIRST GELFLINGS CREATED LANGUAGE...WAS NO LONGER HEARD.
YET THIS IS NOT WHERE OUR STORY BEGINS...

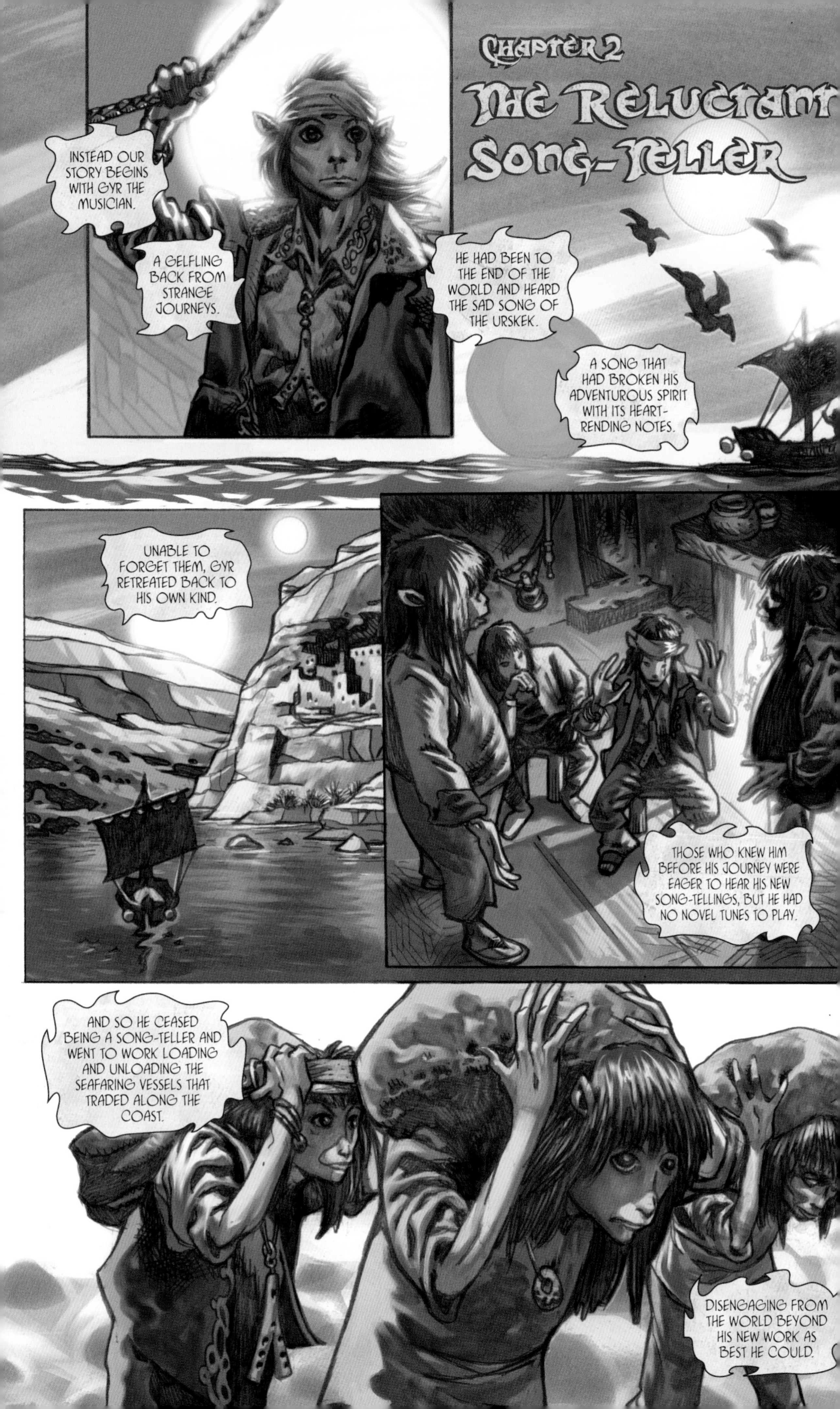

CHAPTER 2
THE RELUCTANT SONG-TELLER
INSTEAD OUR STORY BEGINS WITH GYR THE MUSICIAN.
A GELFLING BACK FROM STRANGE JOURNEYS.
HE HAD BEEN TO THE END OF THE WORLD AND HEARD THE SAD SONG OF THE URSKEK.
A SONG THAT HAD BROKEN HIS ADVENTUROUS SPIRIT WITH ITS HEART-RENDING NOTES.
UNABLE TO FORGET THEM, GYR RETREATED BACK TO HIS OWN KIND.
THOSE WHO KNEW HIM BEFORE HIS JOURNEY WERE EAGER TO HEAR HIS NEW SONG-TELLINGS, BUT HE HAD NO NOVEL TUNES TO PLAY.
AND SO HE CEASED BEING A SONG-TELLER AND WENT TO WORK LOADING AND UNLOADING THE SEAFARING VESSELS THAT TRADED ALONG THE COAST.
DISENGAGING FROM THE WORLD BEYOND HIS NEW WORK AS BEST HE COULD.

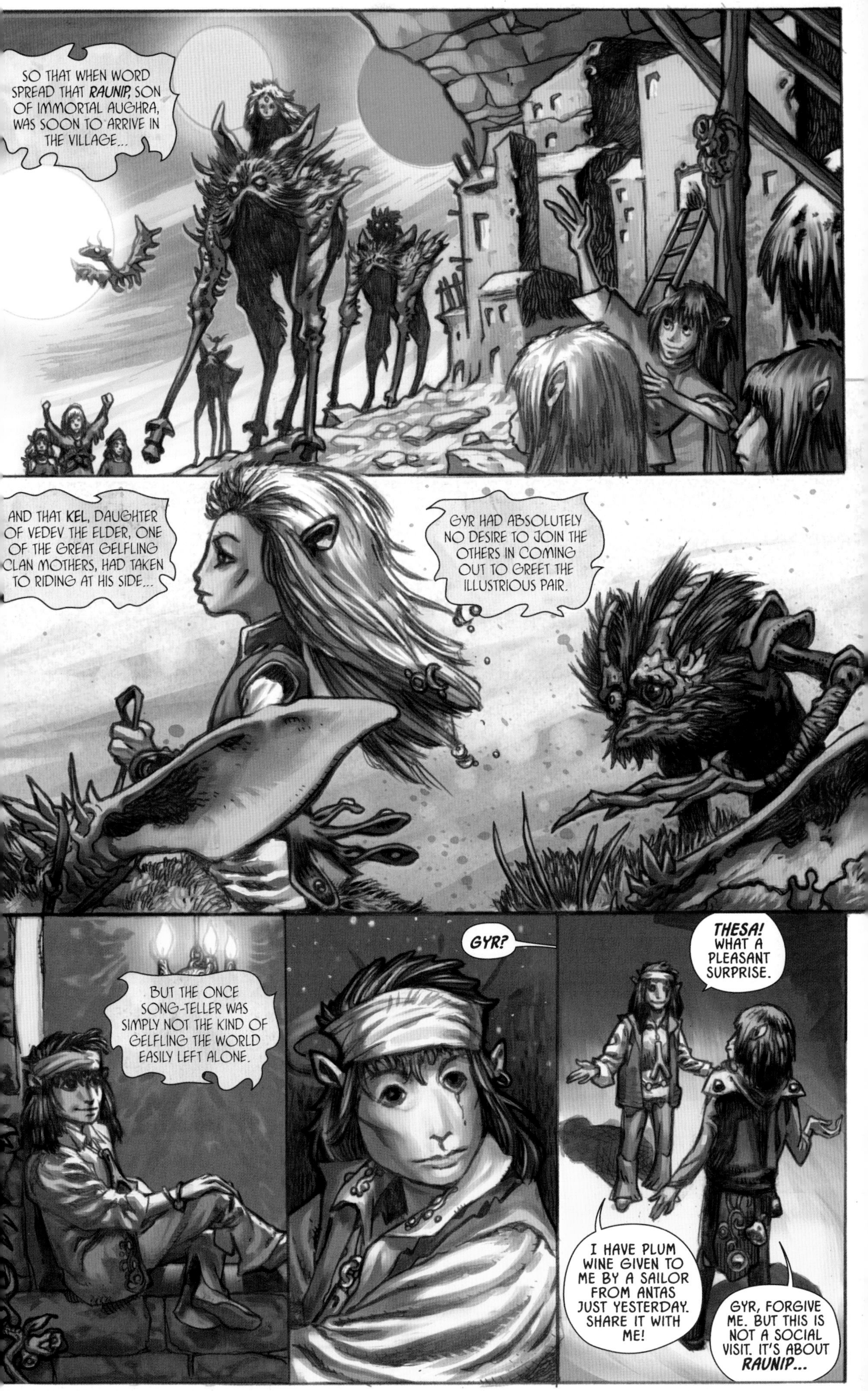
SO THAT WHEN WORD SPREAD THAT RAUNIP, SON OF IMMORTAL AUGHRA, WAS SOON TO ARRIVE IN THE VILLAGE...
AND THAT KEL, DAUGHTER OF VEDEV THE ELDER, ONE OF THE GREAT GELFLING CLAN MOTHERS, HAD TAKEN TO RIDING AT HIS SIDE...
GYR HAD ABSOLUTELY NO DESIRE TO JOIN THE OTHERS IN COMING OUT TO GREET THE ILLUSTRIOUS PAIR.
BUT THE ONCE SONG-TELLER WAS SIMPLY NOT THE KIND OF GELFLING THE WORLD EASILY LEFT ALONE.
GYR?
THESA! WHAT A PLEASANT SURPRISE.
I HAVE PLUM WINE GIVEN TO ME BY A SAILOR FROM ANTAS JUST YESTERDAY. SHARE IT WITH ME!
GYR, FORGIVE ME. BUT THIS IS NOT A SOCIAL VISIT. IT'S ABOUT RAUNIP...

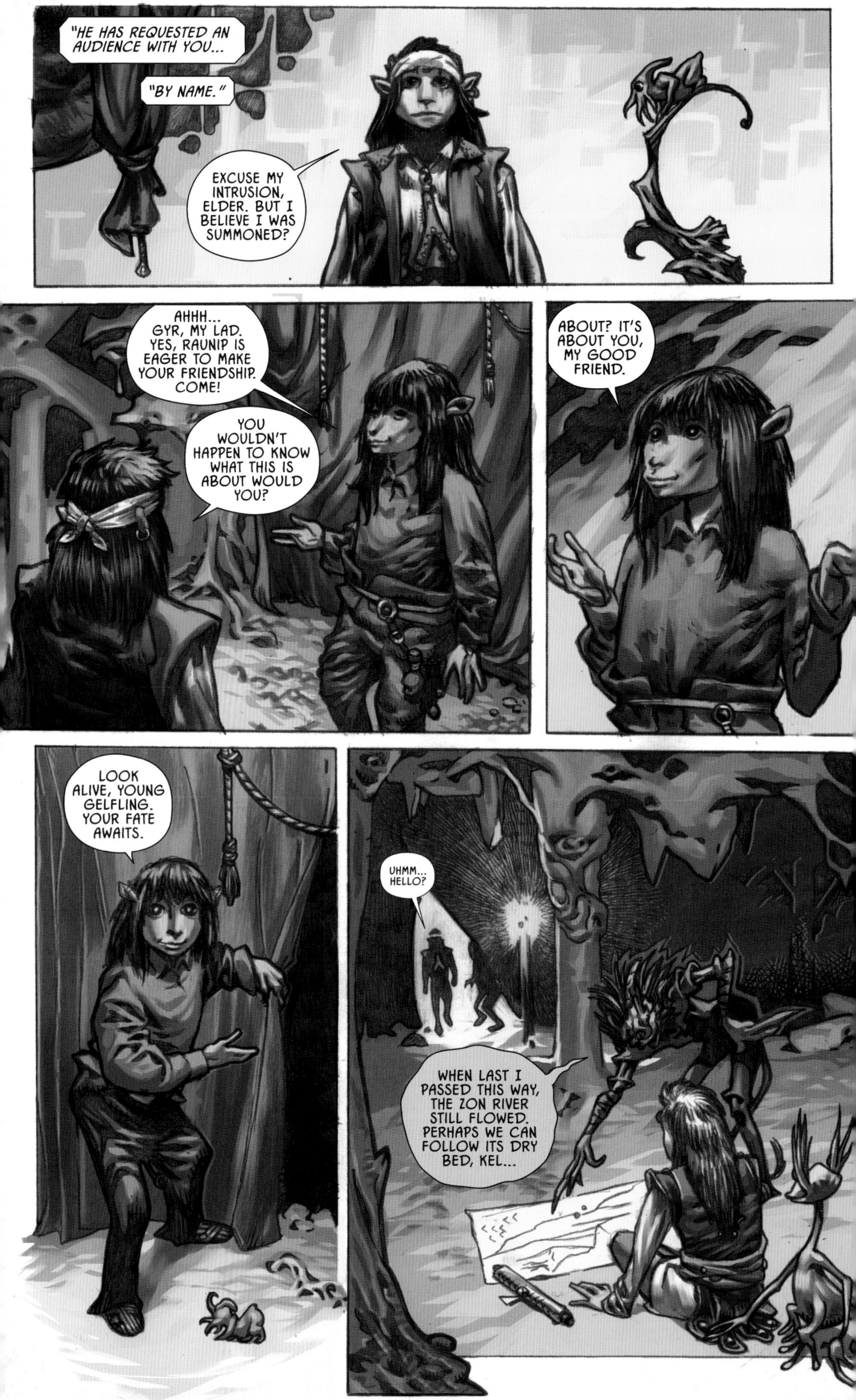
"HE HAS REQUESTED AN AUDIENCE WITH YOU...
"BY NAME."
EXCUSE MY INTRUSION, ELDER. BUT I BELIEVE I WAS SUMMONED?
AHHH... GYR, MY LAD. YES, RAUNIP IS EAGER TO MAKE YOUR FRIENDSHIP. COME!
YOU WOULDN'T HAPPEN TO KNOW WHAT THIS IS ABOUT WOULD YOU?
ABOUT? IT'S ABOUT YOU, MY GOOD FRIEND.
LOOK ALIVE, YOUNG GELFLING. YOUR FATE AWAITS.
UHMM... HELLO?
WHEN LAST I PASSED THIS WAY, THE ZON RIVER STILL FLOWED. PERHAPS WE CAN FOLLOW ITS DRY BED, KEL...

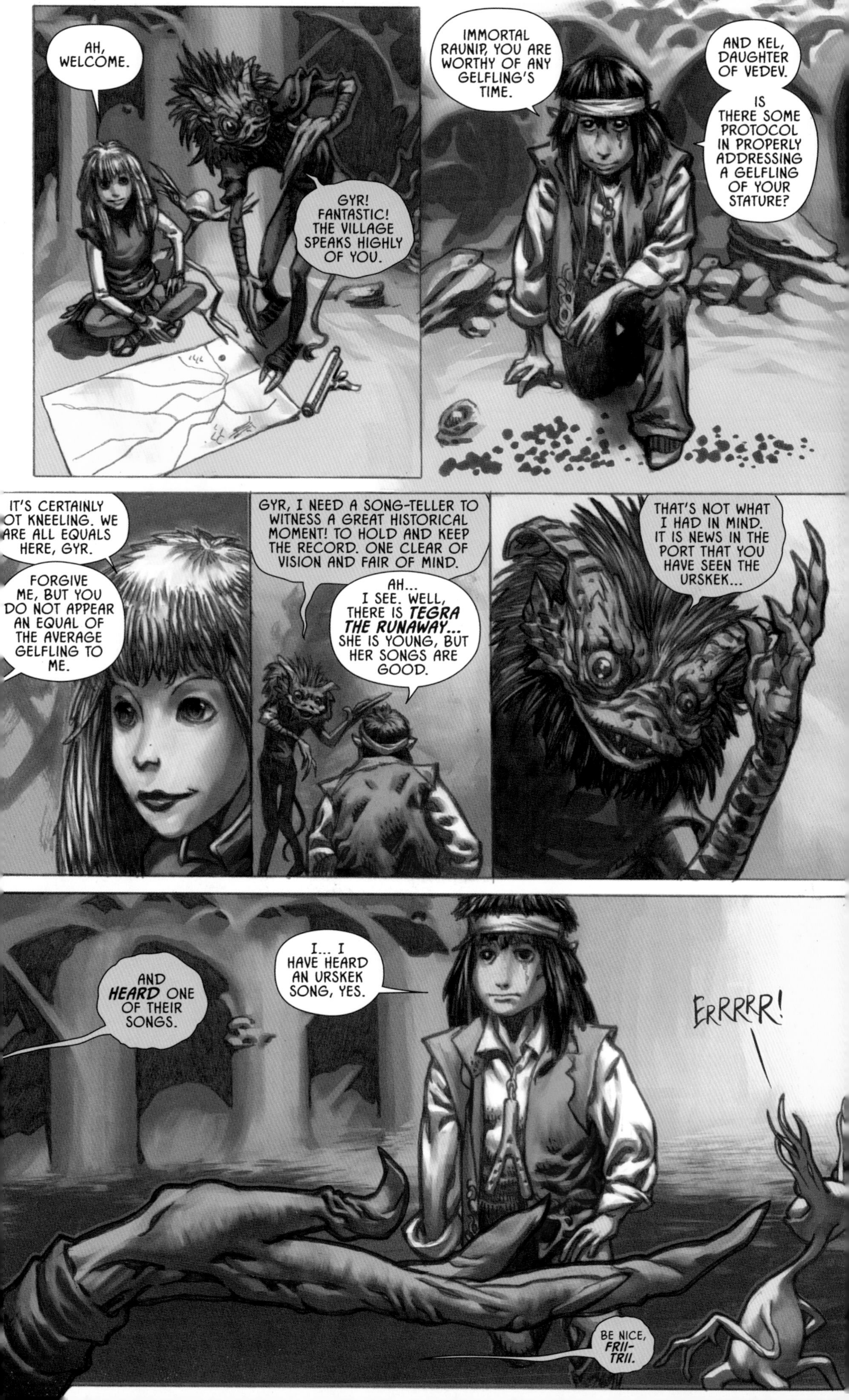
AH, WELCOME.
GYR! FANTASTIC! THE VILLAGE SPEAKS HIGHLY OF YOU.
IMMORTAL RAUNIP, YOU ARE WORTHY OF ANY GELFLING'S TIME.
AND KEL, DAUGHTER OF VEDEV.
IS THERE SOME PROTOCOL IN PROPERLY ADDRESSING A GELFLING OF YOUR STATURE?
IT'S CERTAINLY OT KNEELING. WE ARE ALL EQUALS HERE, GYR.
FORGIVE ME, BUT YOU DO NOT APPEAR AN EQUAL OF THE AVERAGE GELFLING TO ME.
GYR, I NEED A SONG-TELLER TO WITNESS A GREAT HISTORICAL MOMENT! TO HOLD AND KEEP THE RECORD. ONE CLEAR OF VISION AND FAIR OF MIND.
AH... I SEE. WELL, THERE IS **TEGRA THE RUNAWAY...** SHE IS YOUNG, BUT HER SONGS ARE GOOD.
THAT'S NOT WHAT I HAD IN MIND. IT IS NEWS IN THE PORT THAT YOU HAVE SEEN THE URSKEK...
AND **HEARD** ONE OF THEIR SONGS.
I... I HAVE HEARD AN URSKEK SONG, YES.
ERRRRR!
BE NICE, **FRII-TRII.**

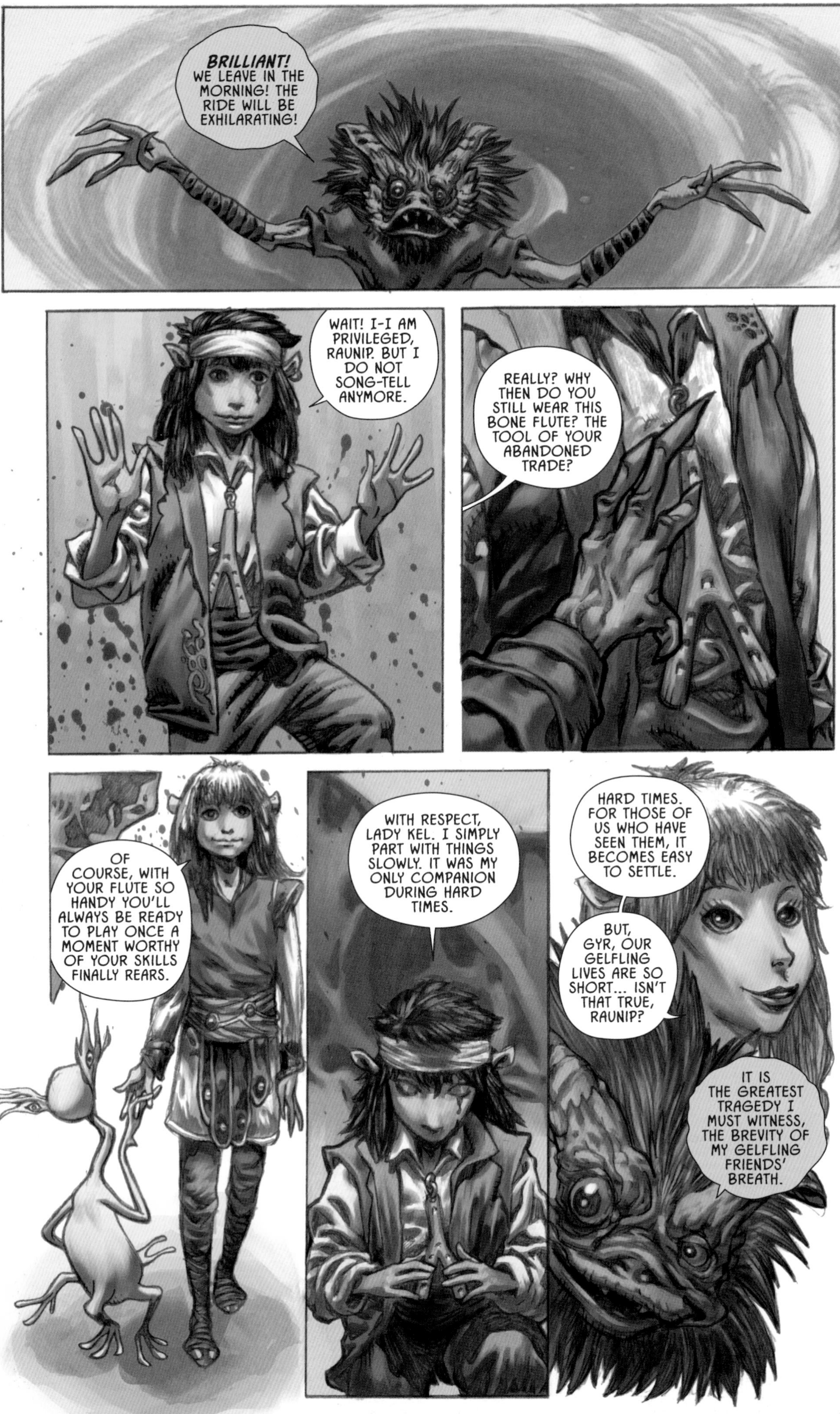
BRILLIANT! WE LEAVE IN THE MORNING! THE RIDE WILL BE EXHILARATING!
WAIT! I-I AM PRIVILEGED, RAUNIP. BUT I DO NOT SONG-TELL ANYMORE.
REALLY? WHY THEN DO YOU STILL WEAR THIS BONE FLUTE? THE TOOL OF YOUR ABANDONED TRADE?
OF COURSE, WITH YOUR FLUTE SO HANDY YOU'LL ALWAYS BE READY TO PLAY ONCE A MOMENT WORTHY OF YOUR SKILLS FINALLY REARS.
WITH RESPECT, LADY KEL. I SIMPLY PART WITH THINGS SLOWLY. IT WAS MY ONLY COMPANION DURING HARD TIMES.
HARD TIMES. FOR THOSE OF US WHO HAVE SEEN THEM, IT BECOMES EASY TO SETTLE.
BUT, GYR, OUR GELFLING LIVES ARE SO SHORT... ISN'T THAT TRUE, RAUNIP?
IT IS THE GREATEST TRAGEDY I MUST WITNESS, THE BREVITY OF MY GELFLING FRIENDS' BREATH.

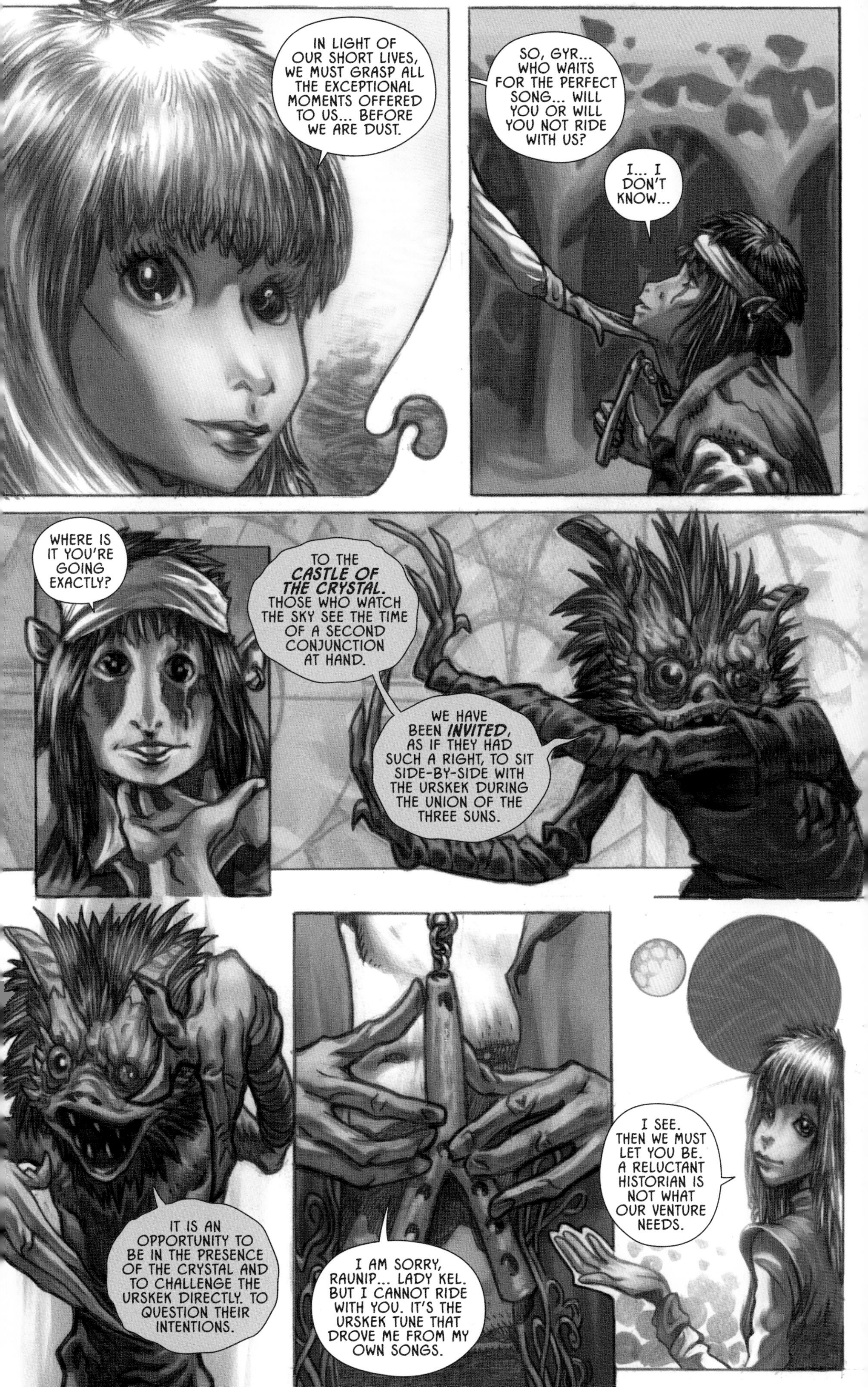
IN LIGHT OF OUR SHORT LIVES, WE MUST GRASP ALL THE EXCEPTIONAL MOMENTS OFFERED TO US... BEFORE WE ARE DUST.
SO, GYR... WHO WAITS FOR THE PERFECT SONG... WILL YOU OR WILL YOU NOT RIDE WITH US?
I... I DON'T KNOW...
WHERE IS IT YOU'RE GOING EXACTLY?
TO THE *CASTLE OF THE CRYSTAL.* THOSE WHO WATCH THE SKY SEE THE TIME OF A SECOND CONJUNCTION AT HAND.
WE HAVE BEEN *INVITED,* AS IF THEY HAD SUCH A RIGHT, TO SIT SIDE-BY-SIDE WITH THE URSKEK DURING THE UNION OF THE THREE SUNS.
IT IS AN OPPORTUNITY TO BE IN THE PRESENCE OF THE CRYSTAL AND TO CHALLENGE THE URSKEK DIRECTLY. TO QUESTION THEIR INTENTIONS.
I AM SORRY, RAUNIP... LADY KEL. BUT I CANNOT RIDE WITH YOU. IT'S THE URSKEK TUNE THAT DROVE ME FROM MY OWN SONGS.
I SEE. THEN WE MUST LET YOU BE. A RELUCTANT HISTORIAN IS NOT WHAT OUR VENTURE NEEDS.

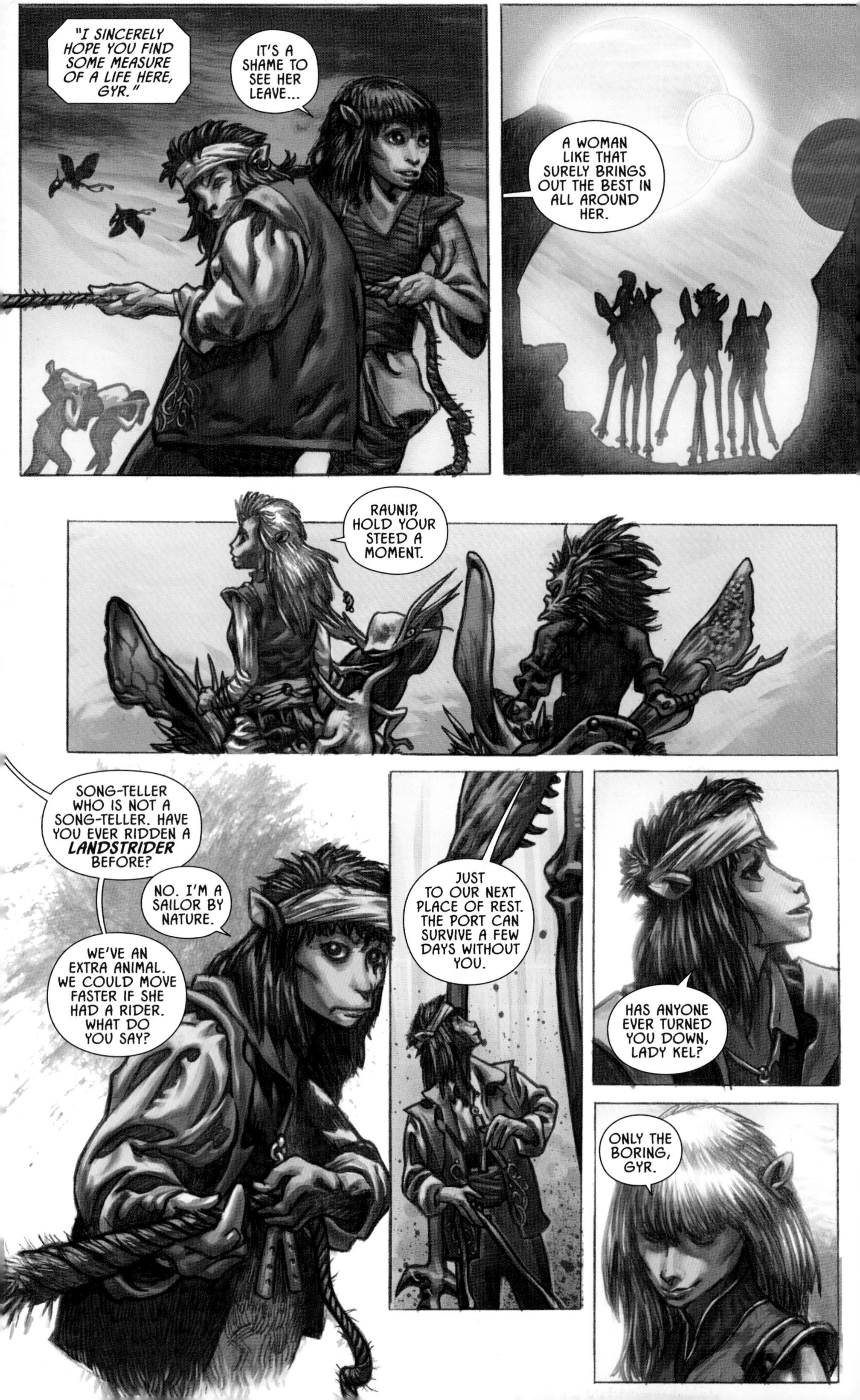
"I SINCERELY HOPE YOU FIND SOME MEASURE OF A LIFE HERE, GYR."
IT'S A SHAME TO SEE HER LEAVE...
A WOMAN LIKE THAT SURELY BRINGS OUT THE BEST IN ALL AROUND HER.
RAUNIP, HOLD YOUR STEED A MOMENT.
SONG-TELLER WHO IS NOT A SONG-TELLER. HAVE YOU EVER RIDDEN A ***LANDSTRIDER*** BEFORE?
NO. I'M A SAILOR BY NATURE.
WE'VE AN EXTRA ANIMAL. WE COULD MOVE FASTER IF SHE HAD A RIDER. WHAT DO YOU SAY?
JUST TO OUR NEXT PLACE OF REST. THE PORT CAN SURVIVE A FEW DAYS WITHOUT YOU.
HAS ANYONE EVER TURNED YOU DOWN, LADY KEL?
ONLY THE BORING, GYR.

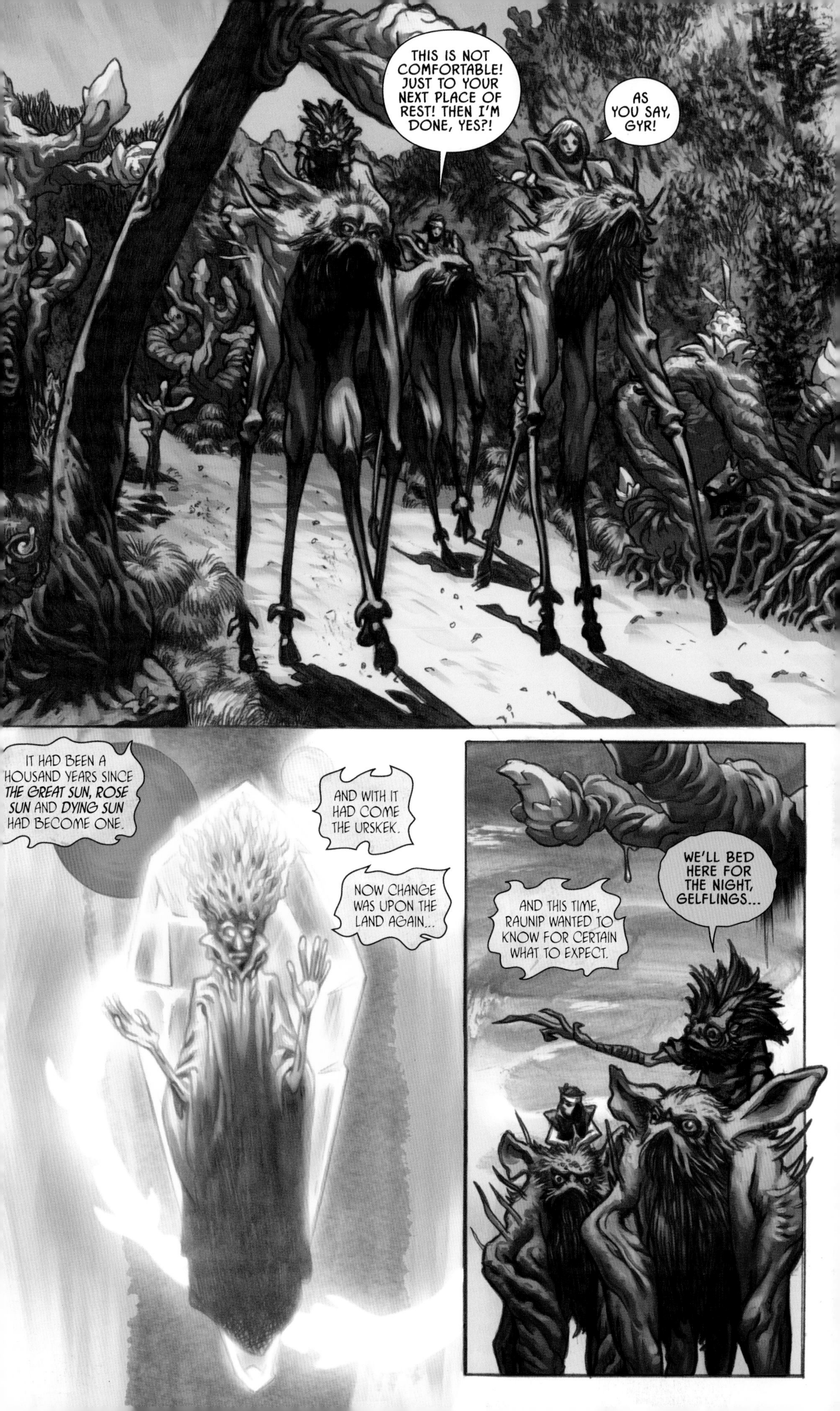
THIS IS NOT COMFORTABLE! JUST TO YOUR NEXT PLACE OF REST! THEN I'M DONE, YES?!
AS YOU SAY, GYR!
IT HAD BEEN A HOUSAND YEARS SINCE *THE GREAT SUN, ROSE SUN* AND *DYING SUN* HAD BECOME ONE.
AND WITH IT HAD COME THE URSKEK.
NOW CHANGE WAS UPON THE LAND AGAIN...
AND THIS TIME, RAUNIP WANTED TO KNOW FOR CERTAIN WHAT TO EXPECT.
WE'LL BED HERE FOR THE NIGHT, GELFLINGS...

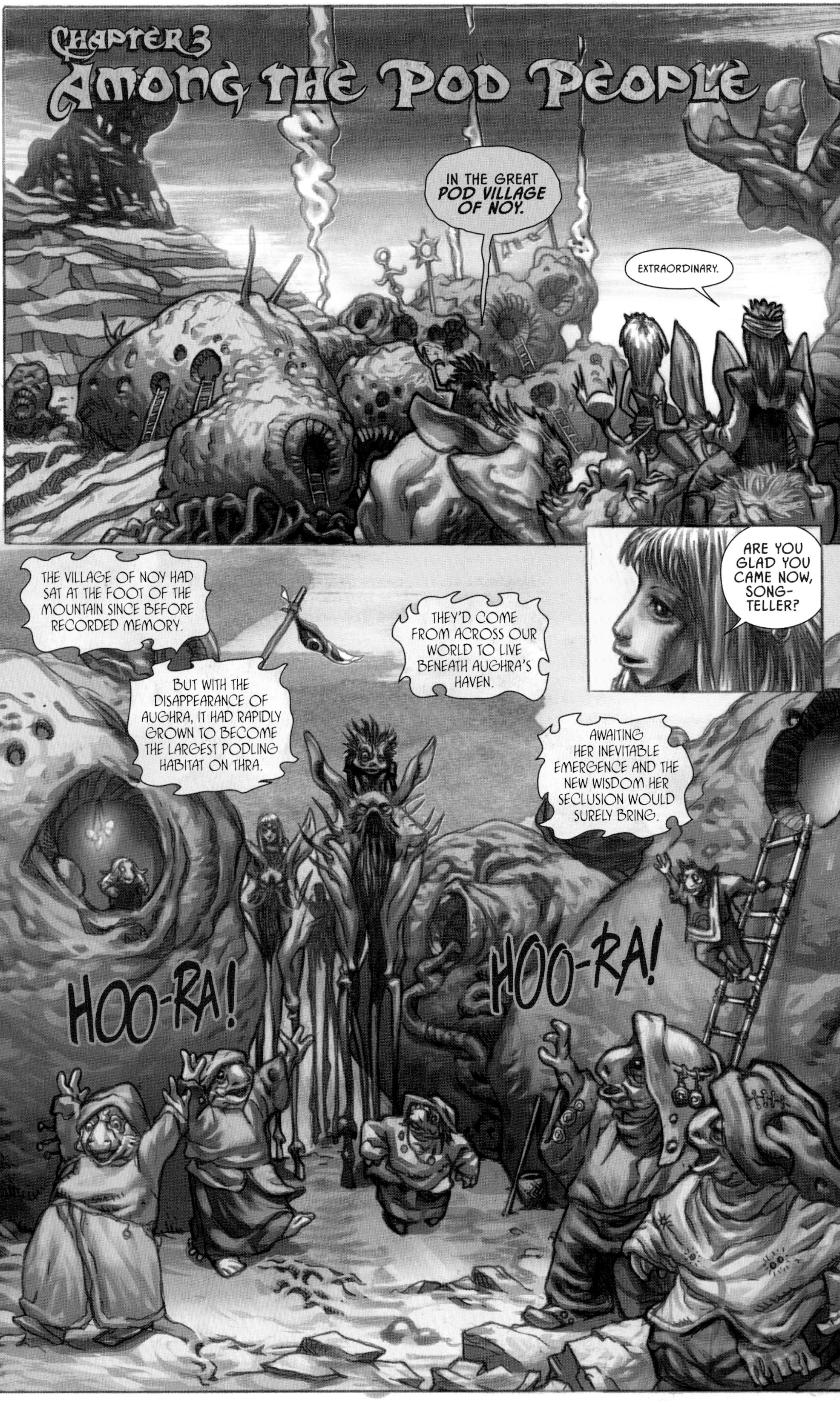

CHAPTER 3
AMONG THE POD PEOPLE
IN THE GREAT POD VILLAGE OF NOY.
EXTRAORDINARY.
ARE YOU GLAD YOU CAME NOW, SONG-TELLER?
THE VILLAGE OF NOY HAD SAT AT THE FOOT OF THE MOUNTAIN SINCE BEFORE RECORDED MEMORY.
THEY'D COME FROM ACROSS OUR WORLD TO LIVE BENEATH AUGHRA'S HAVEN.
BUT WITH THE DISAPPEARANCE OF AUGHRA, IT HAD RAPIDLY GROWN TO BECOME THE LARGEST PODLING HABITAT ON THRA.
AWAITING HER INEVITABLE EMERGENCE AND THE NEW WISDOM HER SECLUSION WOULD SURELY BRING.
HOO-RA!
HOO-RA!

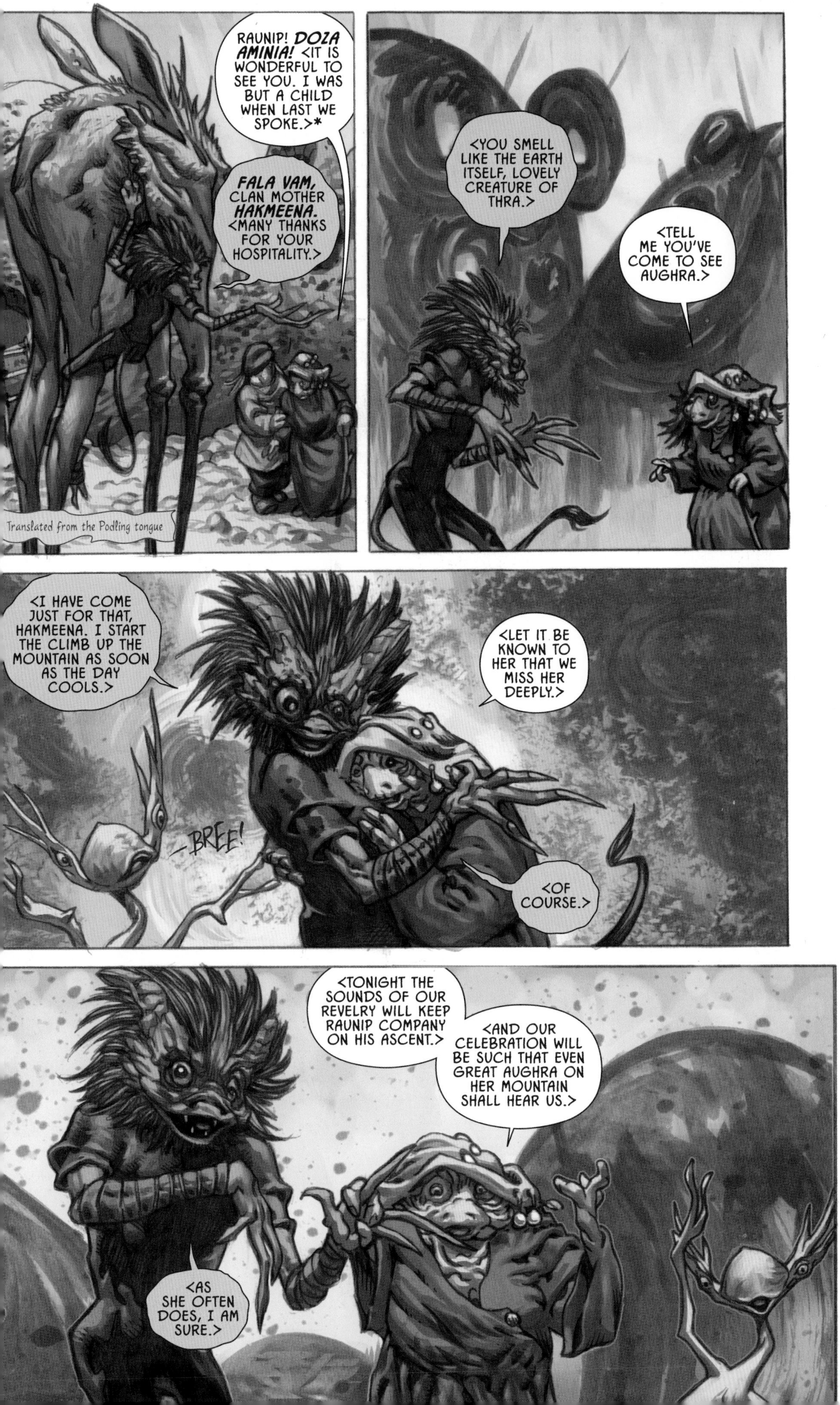
RAUNIP! DOZA AMINIA! <IT IS WONDERFUL TO SEE YOU. I WAS BUT A CHILD WHEN LAST WE SPOKE.>*
FALA VAM, CLAN MOTHER HAKMEENA. <MANY THANKS FOR YOUR HOSPITALITY.>
Translated from the Podling tongue
<YOU SMELL LIKE THE EARTH ITSELF, LOVELY CREATURE OF THRA.>
<TELL ME YOU'VE COME TO SEE AUGHRA.>
<I HAVE COME JUST FOR THAT, HAKMEENA. I START THE CLIMB UP THE MOUNTAIN AS SOON AS THE DAY COOLS.>
<LET IT BE KNOWN TO HER THAT WE MISS HER DEEPLY.>
-BREE!
<OF COURSE.>
<TONIGHT THE SOUNDS OF OUR REVELRY WILL KEEP RAUNIP COMPANY ON HIS ASCENT.>
<AND OUR CELEBRATION WILL BE SUCH THAT EVEN GREAT AUGHRA ON HER MOUNTAIN SHALL HEAR US.>
<AS SHE OFTEN DOES, I AM SURE.>

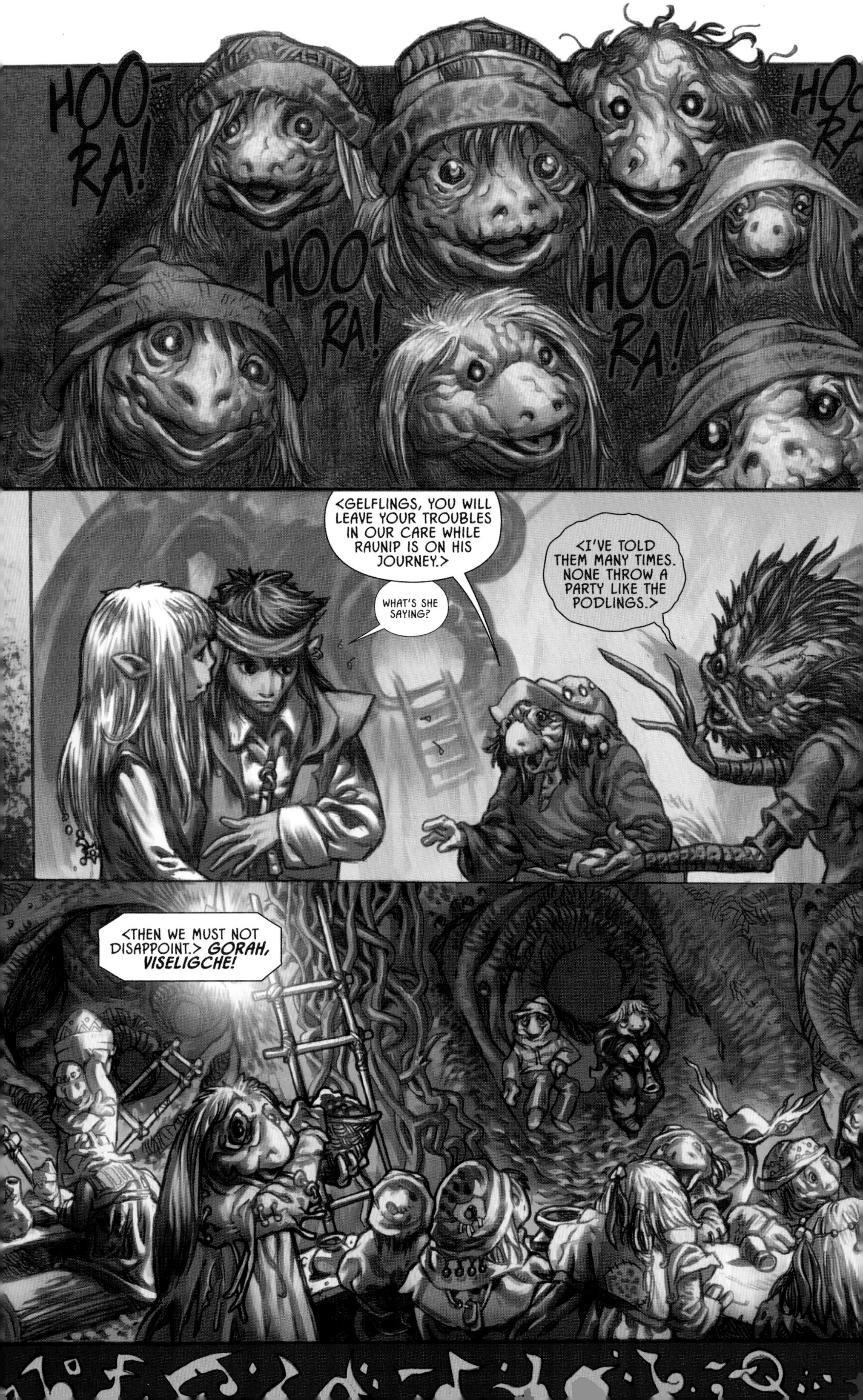
HOO-RA!
HOO-RA!
HOO-RA!
HOO-RA!
<GELFLINGS, YOU WILL LEAVE YOUR TROUBLES IN OUR CARE WHILE RAUNIP IS ON HIS JOURNEY.>
WHAT'S SHE SAYING?
<I'VE TOLD THEM MANY TIMES. NONE THROW A PARTY LIKE THE PODLINGS.>
<THEN WE MUST NOT DISAPPOINT.> *GORAH, VISELIGCHE!*

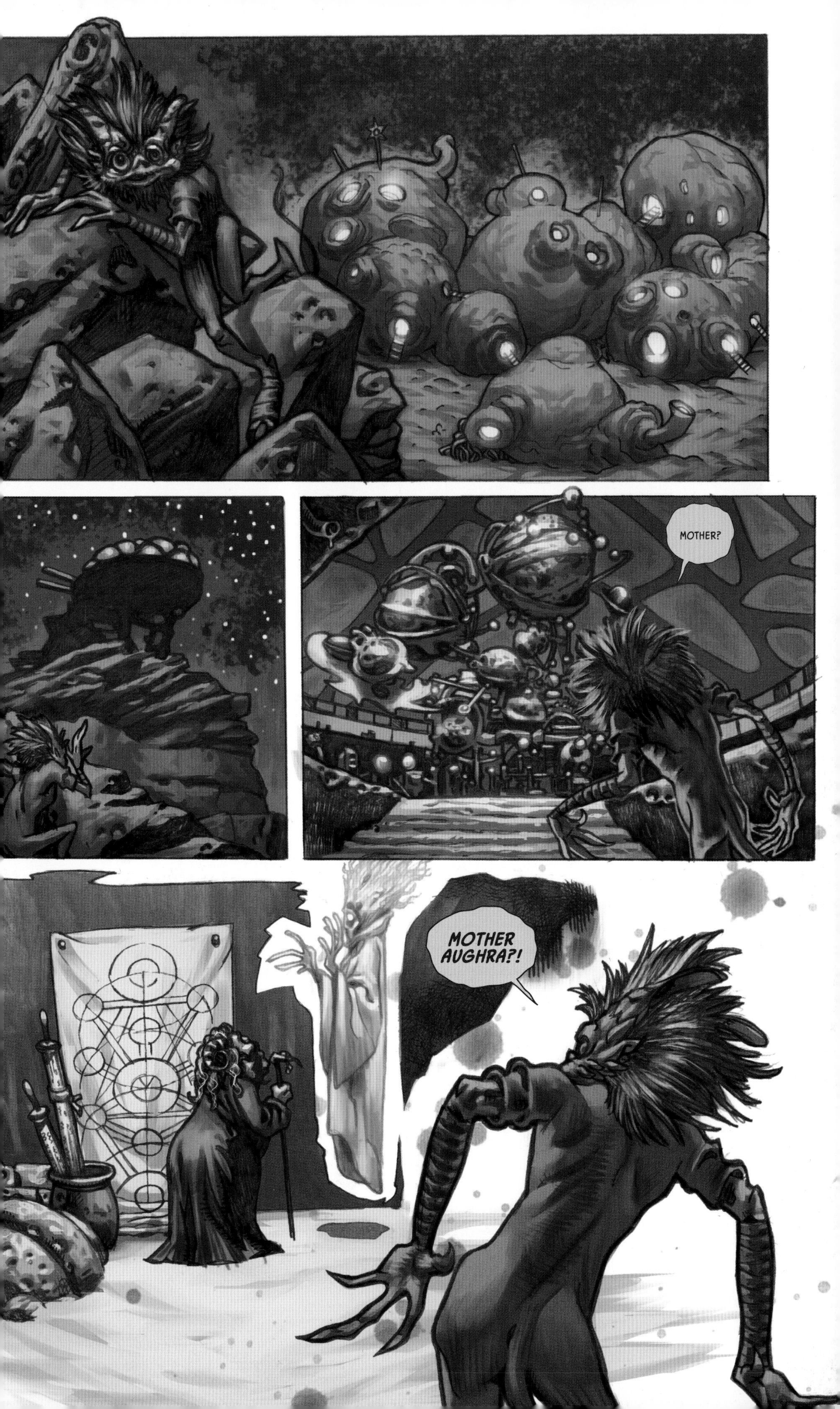
MOTHER?
MOTHER AUGHRA?!

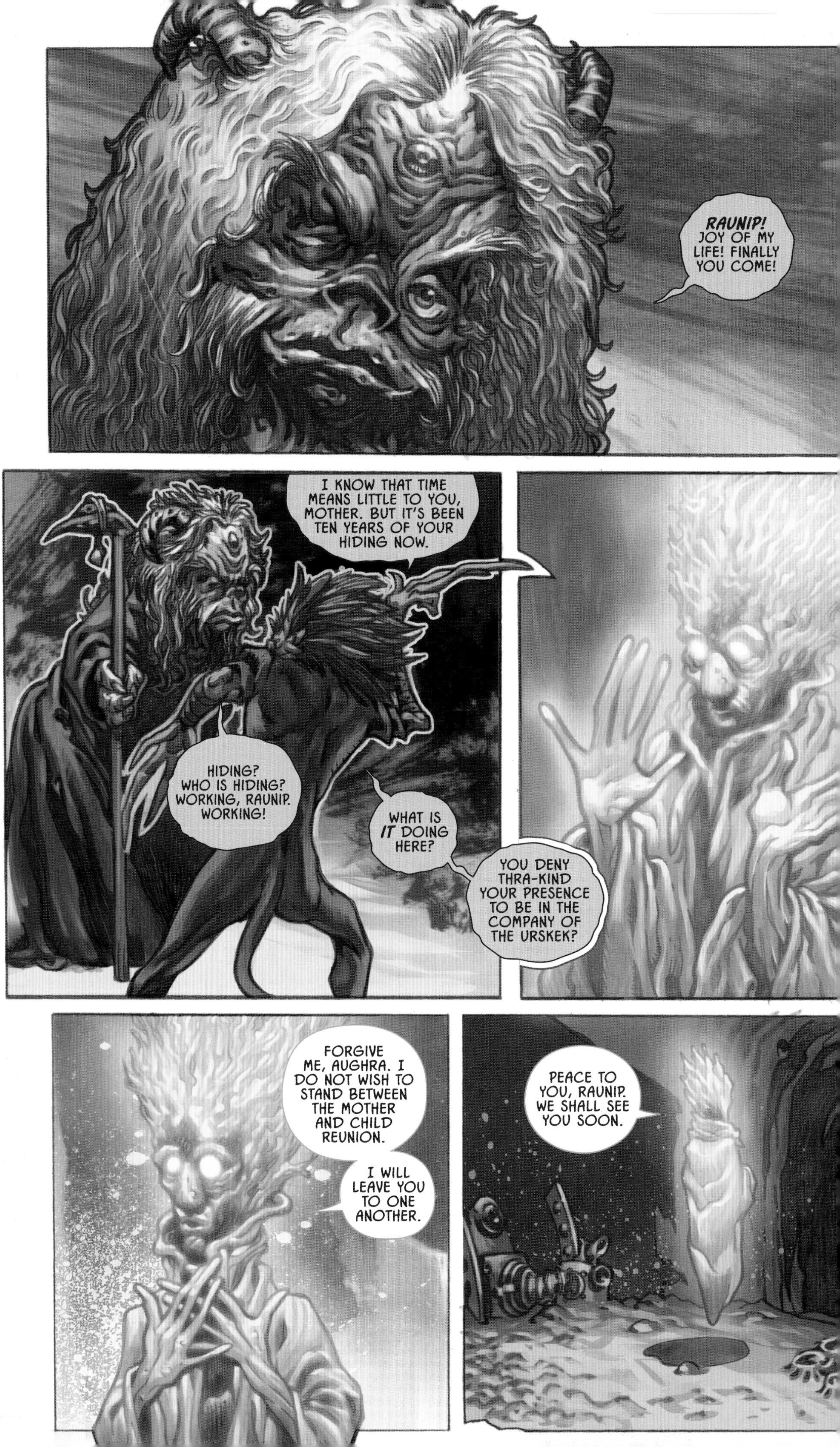

RAUNIP! JOY OF MY LIFE! FINALLY YOU COME!
I KNOW THAT TIME MEANS LITTLE TO YOU, MOTHER. BUT IT'S BEEN TEN YEARS OF YOUR HIDING NOW.
HIDING? WHO IS HIDING? WORKING, RAUNIP. WORKING!
WHAT IS *IT* DOING HERE?
YOU DENY THRA-KIND YOUR PRESENCE TO BE IN THE COMPANY OF THE URSKEK?
FORGIVE ME, AUGHRA. I DO NOT WISH TO STAND BETWEEN THE MOTHER AND CHILD REUNION.
I WILL LEAVE YOU TO ONE ANOTHER.
PEACE TO YOU, RAUNIP. WE SHALL SEE YOU SOON.

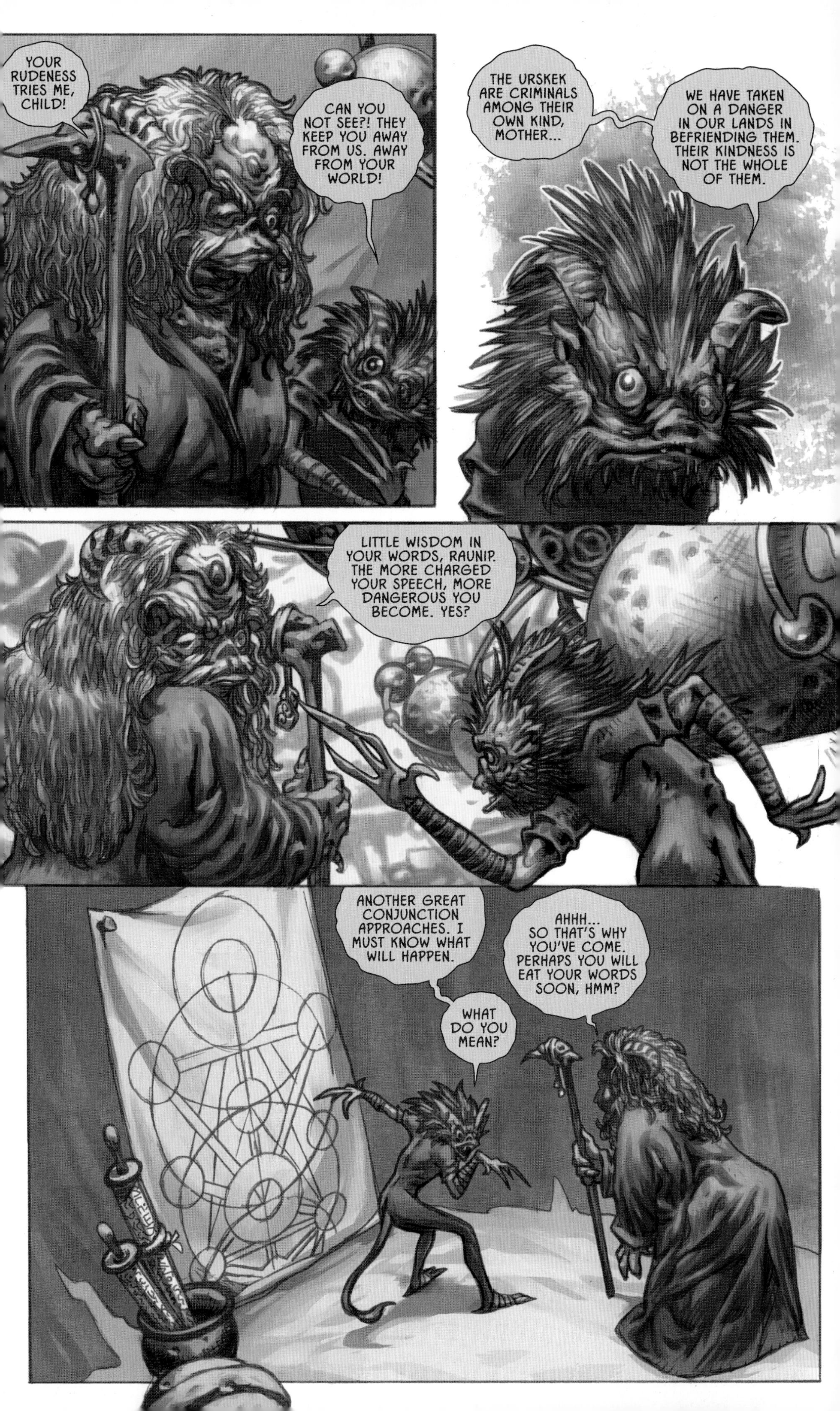
YOUR RUDENESS TRIES ME, CHILD!
CAN YOU NOT SEE?! THEY KEEP YOU AWAY FROM US. AWAY FROM YOUR WORLD!
THE URSKEK ARE CRIMINALS AMONG THEIR OWN KIND, MOTHER...
WE HAVE TAKEN ON A DANGER IN OUR LANDS IN BEFRIENDING THEM. THEIR KINDNESS IS NOT THE WHOLE OF THEM.
LITTLE WISDOM IN YOUR WORDS, RAUNIP. THE MORE CHARGED YOUR SPEECH, MORE DANGEROUS YOU BECOME. YES?
ANOTHER GREAT CONJUNCTION APPROACHES. I MUST KNOW WHAT WILL HAPPEN.
WHAT DO YOU MEAN?
AHHH... SO THAT'S WHY YOU'VE COME. PERHAPS YOU WILL EAT YOUR WORDS SOON, HMM?

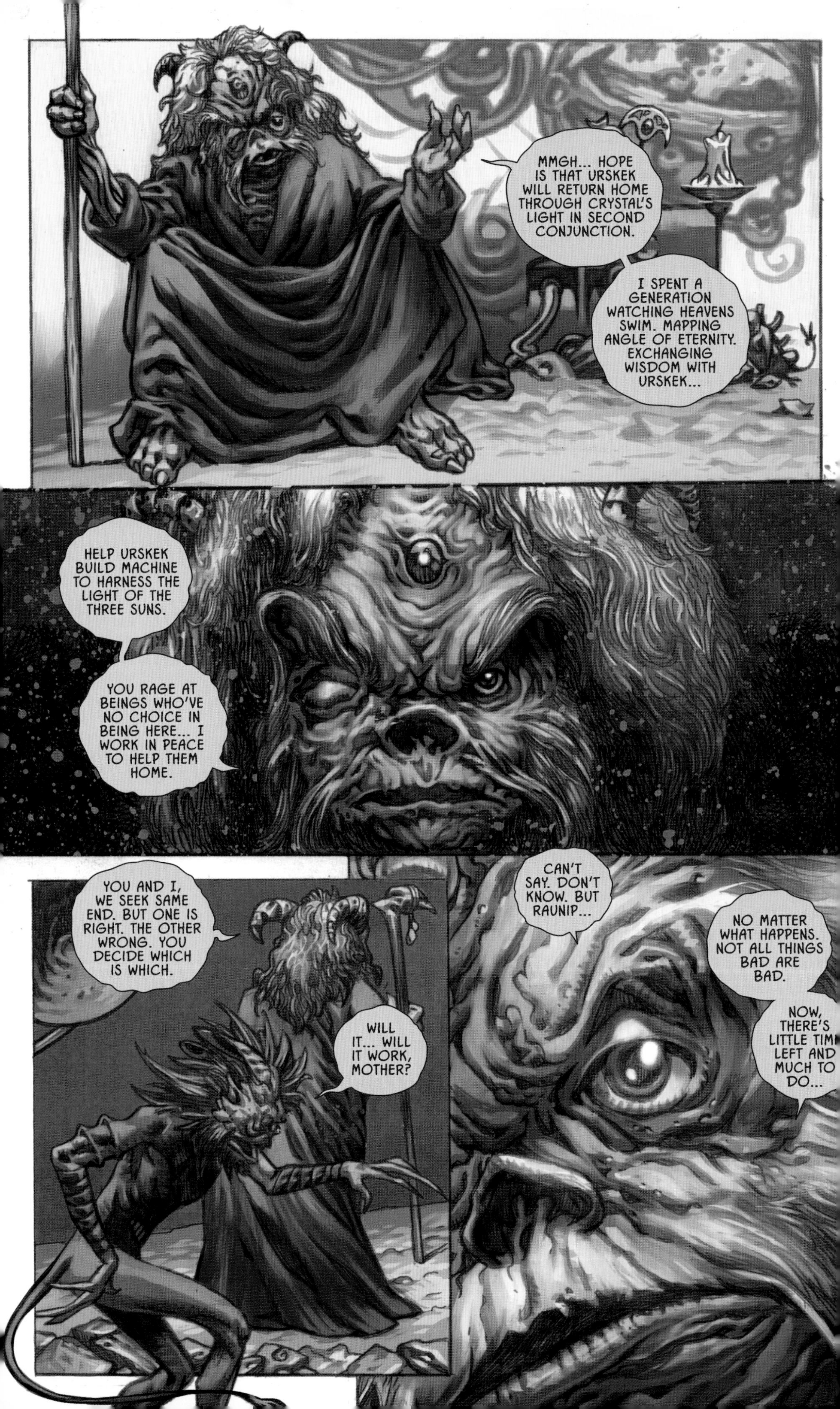
MMGH... HOPE IS THAT URSKEK WILL RETURN HOME THROUGH CRYSTAL'S LIGHT IN SECOND CONJUNCTION.
I SPENT A GENERATION WATCHING HEAVENS SWIM. MAPPING ANGLE OF ETERNITY. EXCHANGING WISDOM WITH URSKEK...
HELP URSKEK BUILD MACHINE TO HARNESS THE LIGHT OF THE THREE SUNS.
YOU RAGE AT BEINGS WHO'VE NO CHOICE IN BEING HERE... I WORK IN PEACE TO HELP THEM HOME.
YOU AND I, WE SEEK SAME END. BUT ONE IS RIGHT. THE OTHER WRONG. YOU DECIDE WHICH IS WHICH.
WILL IT... WILL IT WORK, MOTHER?
CAN'T SAY. DON'T KNOW. BUT RAUNIP...
NO MATTER WHAT HAPPENS. NOT ALL THINGS BAD ARE BAD.
NOW, THERE'S LITTLE TIM LEFT AND MUCH TO DO...

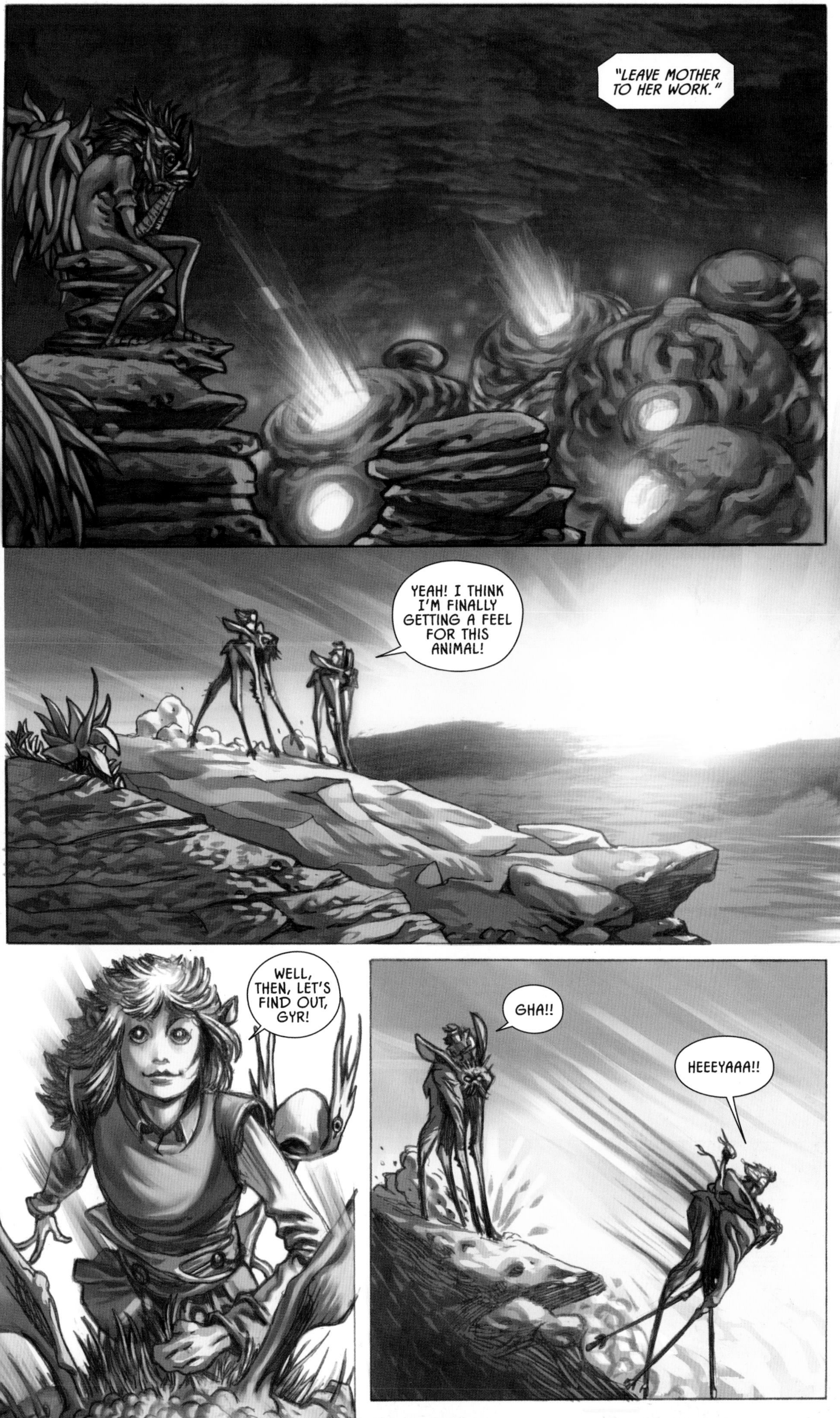
"LEAVE MOTHER TO HER WORK."
YEAH! I THINK I'M FINALLY GETTING A FEEL FOR THIS ANIMAL!
WELL, THEN, LET'S FIND OUT, GYR!
GHA!!
HEEEYAAA!!

QUEEEEE!!

HAHA!

GYR?

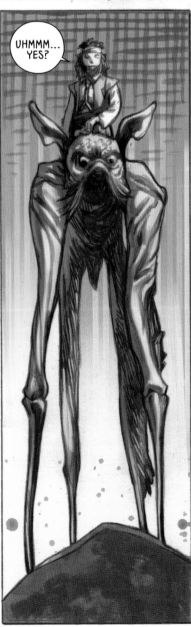

UHMMM... YES?

COME ON DOWN! TRUST IN YOUR MOUNT.

THE FEMALE STRIDER IS STRONGER IN INTUITION THAN THE MALE. SHE'LL TAKE CARE OF YOU!

BUT DON'T TRY TO STEER HER! JUST RIDE HER!

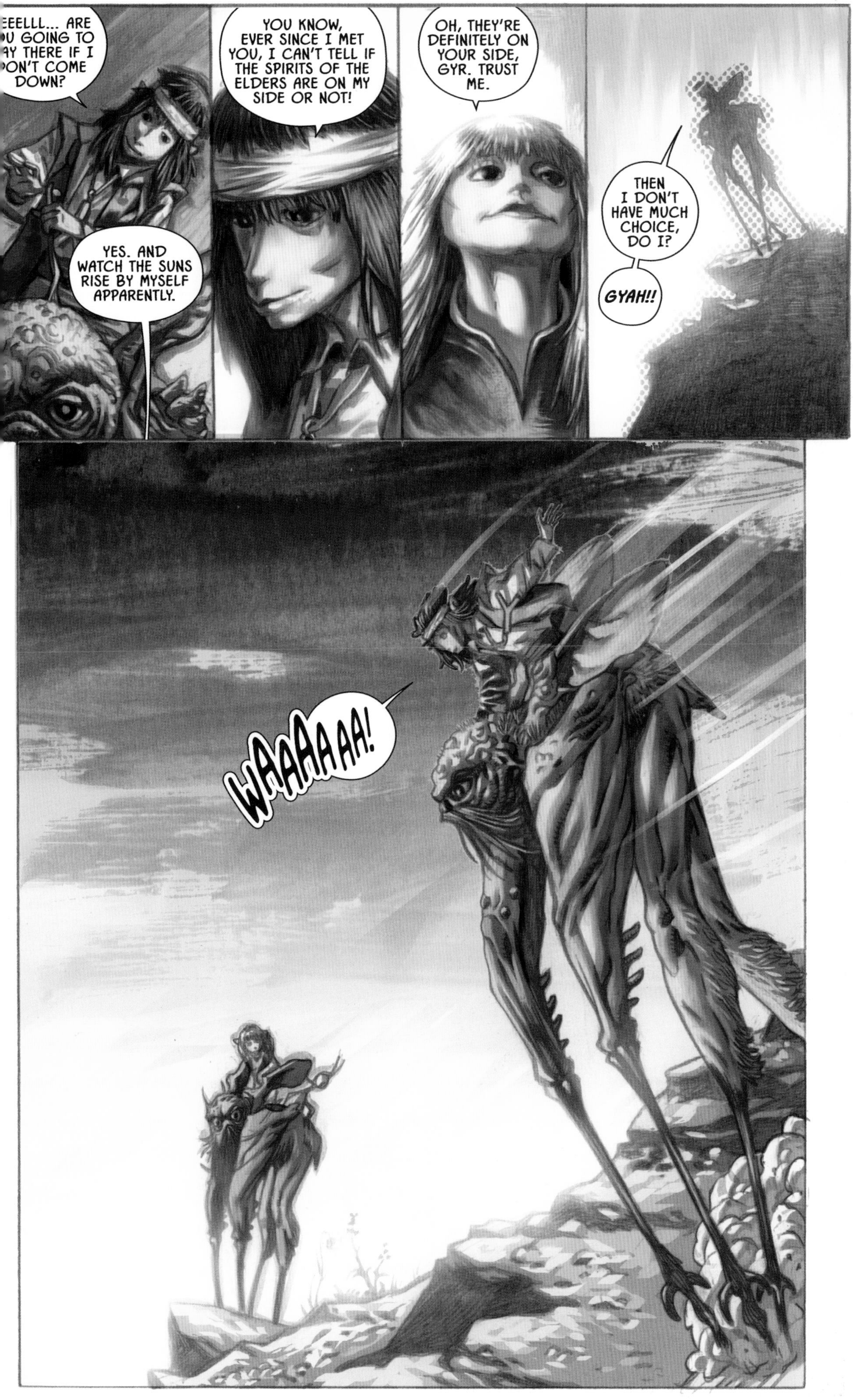
EEELLL... ARE
OU GOING TO
AY THERE IF I
ON'T COME
DOWN?
YES. AND WATCH THE SUNS RISE BY MYSELF APPARENTLY.
YOU KNOW, EVER SINCE I MET YOU, I CAN'T TELL IF THE SPIRITS OF THE ELDERS ARE ON MY SIDE OR NOT!
OH, THEY'RE DEFINITELY ON YOUR SIDE, GYR. TRUST ME.
THEN I DON'T HAVE MUCH CHOICE, DO I?
GYAH!!
WAAAAAA!

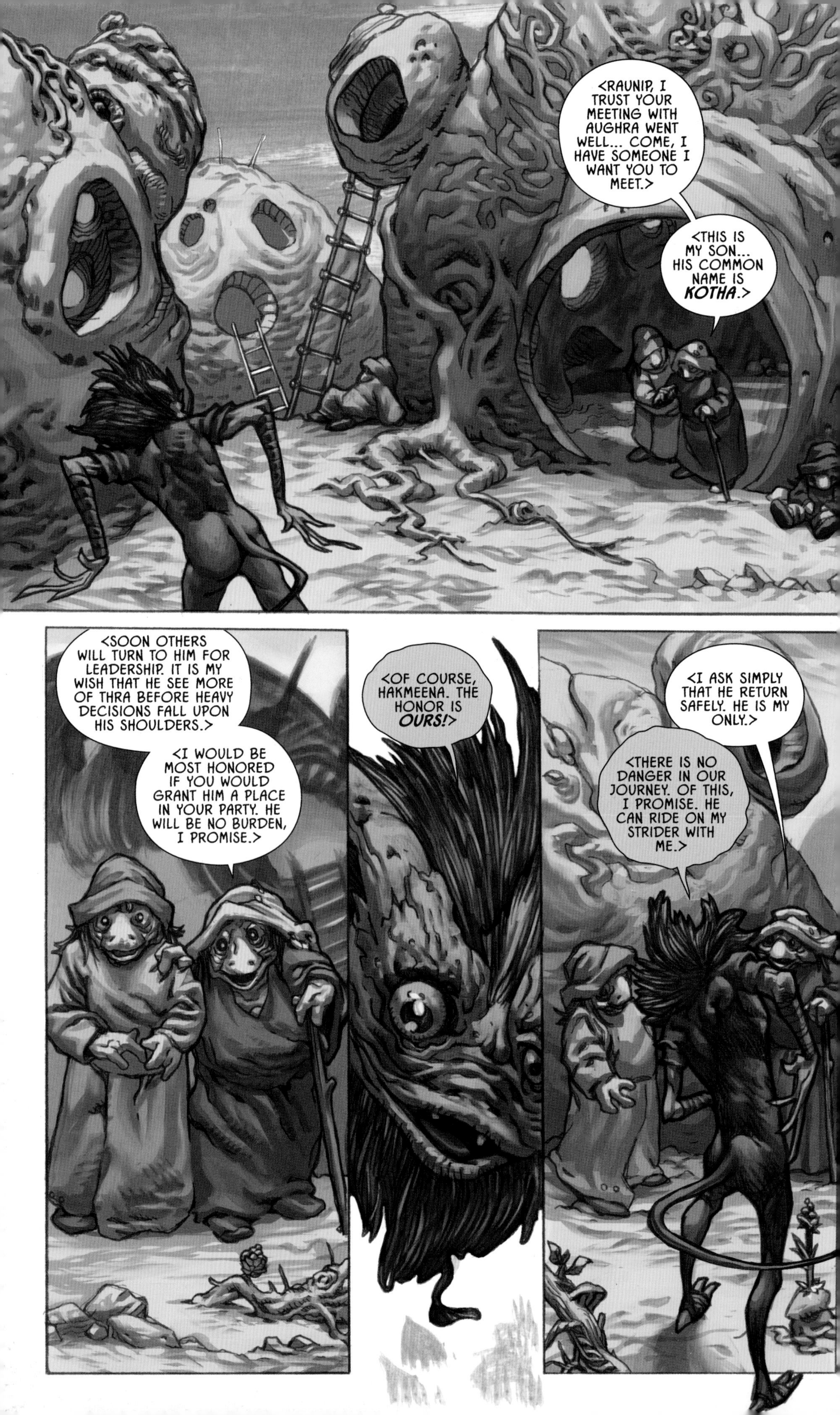
<RAUNIP, I TRUST YOUR MEETING WITH AUGHRA WENT WELL... COME, I HAVE SOMEONE I WANT YOU TO MEET.>
<THIS IS MY SON... HIS COMMON NAME IS ***KOTHA***.>
<SOON OTHERS WILL TURN TO HIM FOR LEADERSHIP. IT IS MY WISH THAT HE SEE MORE OF THRA BEFORE HEAVY DECISIONS FALL UPON HIS SHOULDERS.>
<I WOULD BE MOST HONORED IF YOU WOULD GRANT HIM A PLACE IN YOUR PARTY. HE WILL BE NO BURDEN, I PROMISE.>
<OF COURSE, HAKMEENA. THE HONOR IS ***OURS!***>
<I ASK SIMPLY THAT HE RETURN SAFELY. HE IS MY ONLY.>
<THERE IS NO DANGER IN OUR JOURNEY. OF THIS, I PROMISE. HE CAN RIDE ON MY STRIDER WITH ME.>

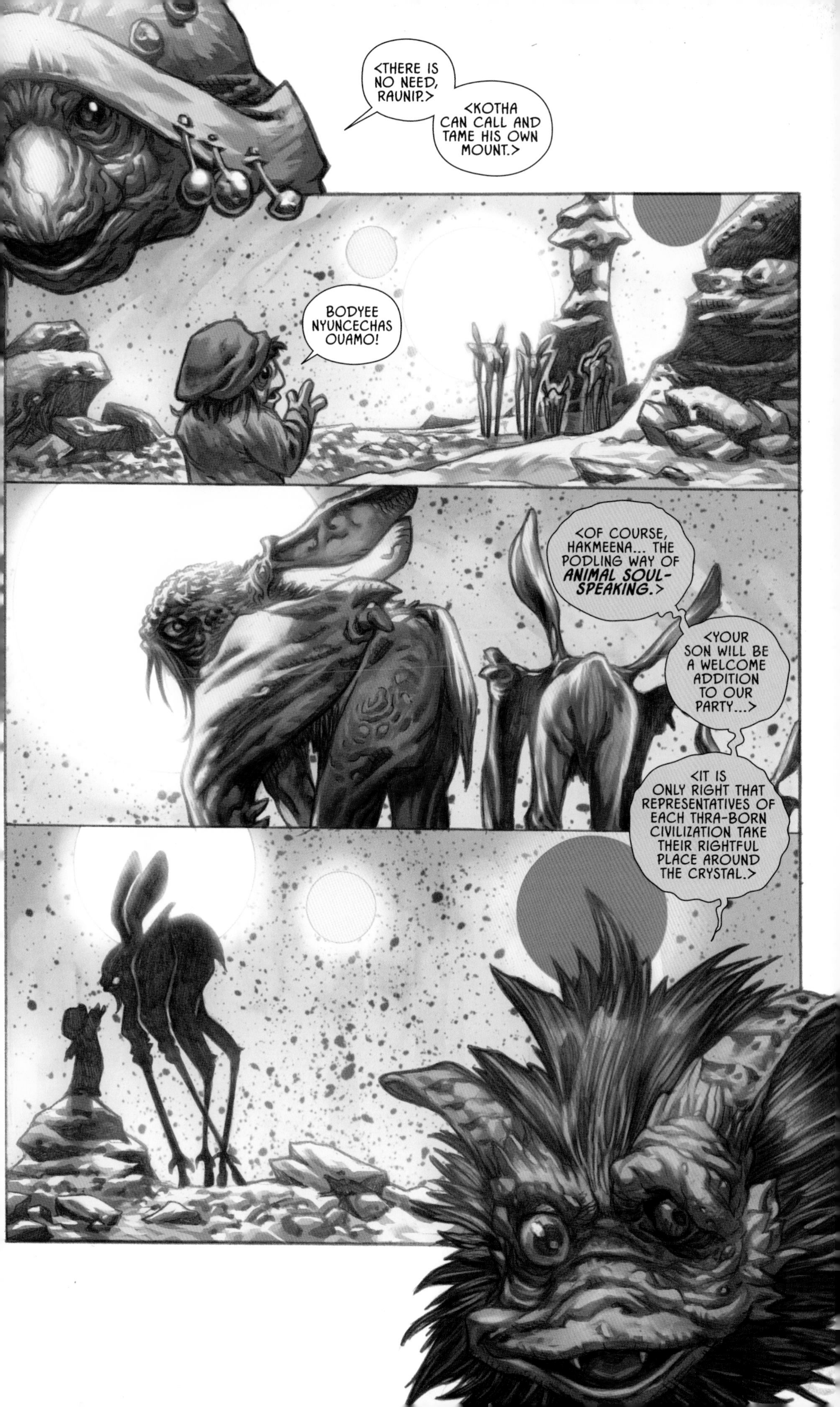

<THERE IS NO NEED, RAUNIP.>
<KOTHA CAN CALL AND TAME HIS OWN MOUNT.>
BODYEE NYUNCECHAS OUAMO!
<OF COURSE, HAKMEENA... THE PODLING WAY OF *ANIMAL SOUL-SPEAKING.*>
<YOUR SON WILL BE A WELCOME ADDITION TO OUR PARTY...>
<IT IS ONLY RIGHT THAT REPRESENTATIVES OF EACH THRA-BORN CIVILIZATION TAKE THEIR RIGHTFUL PLACE AROUND THE CRYSTAL.>

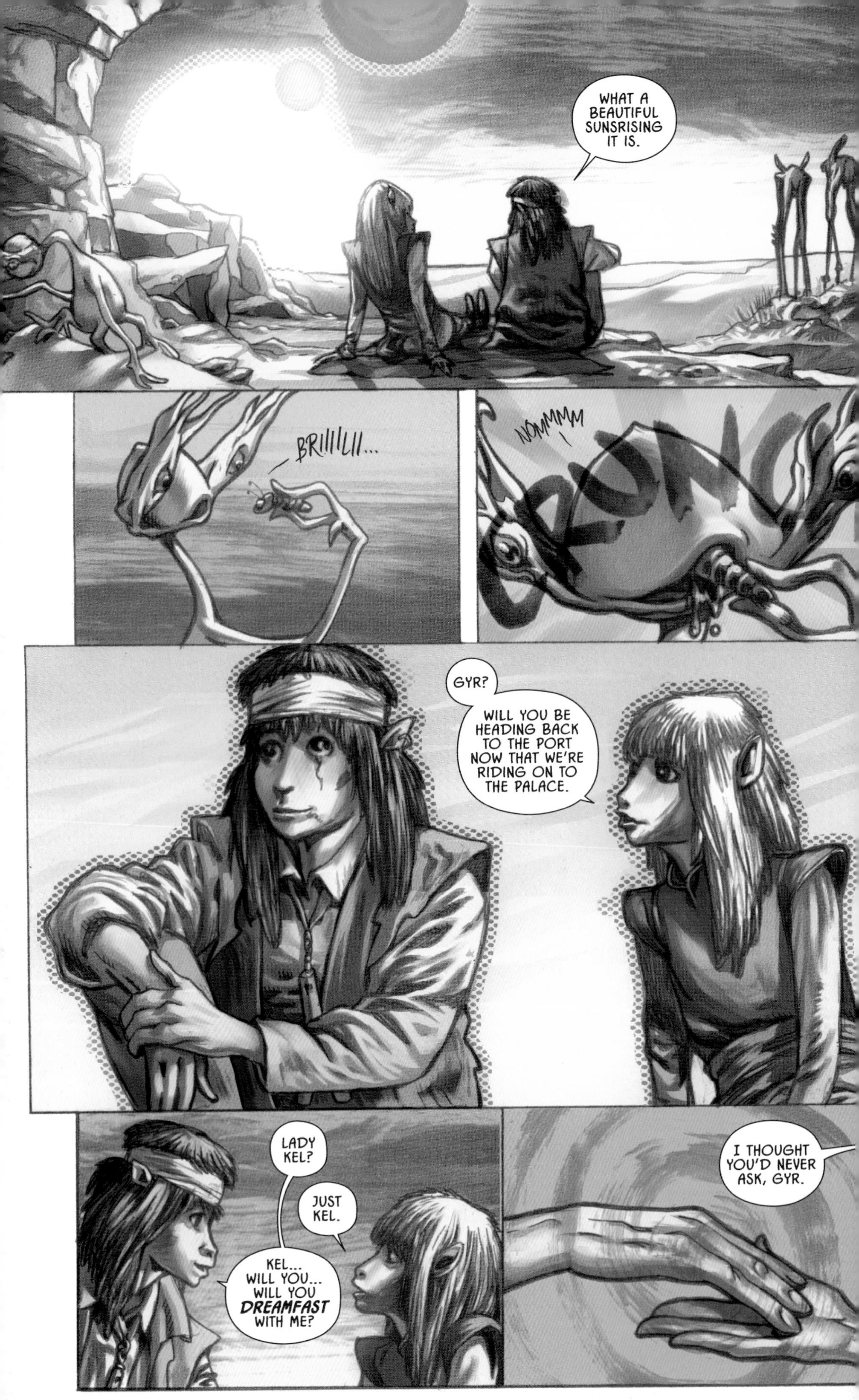
WHAT A BEAUTIFUL SUNSRISING IT IS.
BRIIIILII...
NOMMMM
GYR?
WILL YOU BE HEADING BACK TO THE PORT NOW THAT WE'RE RIDING ON TO THE PALACE.
LADY KEL?
JUST KEL.
KEL... WILL YOU... WILL YOU *DREAMFAST* WITH ME?
I THOUGHT YOU'D NEVER ASK, GYR.

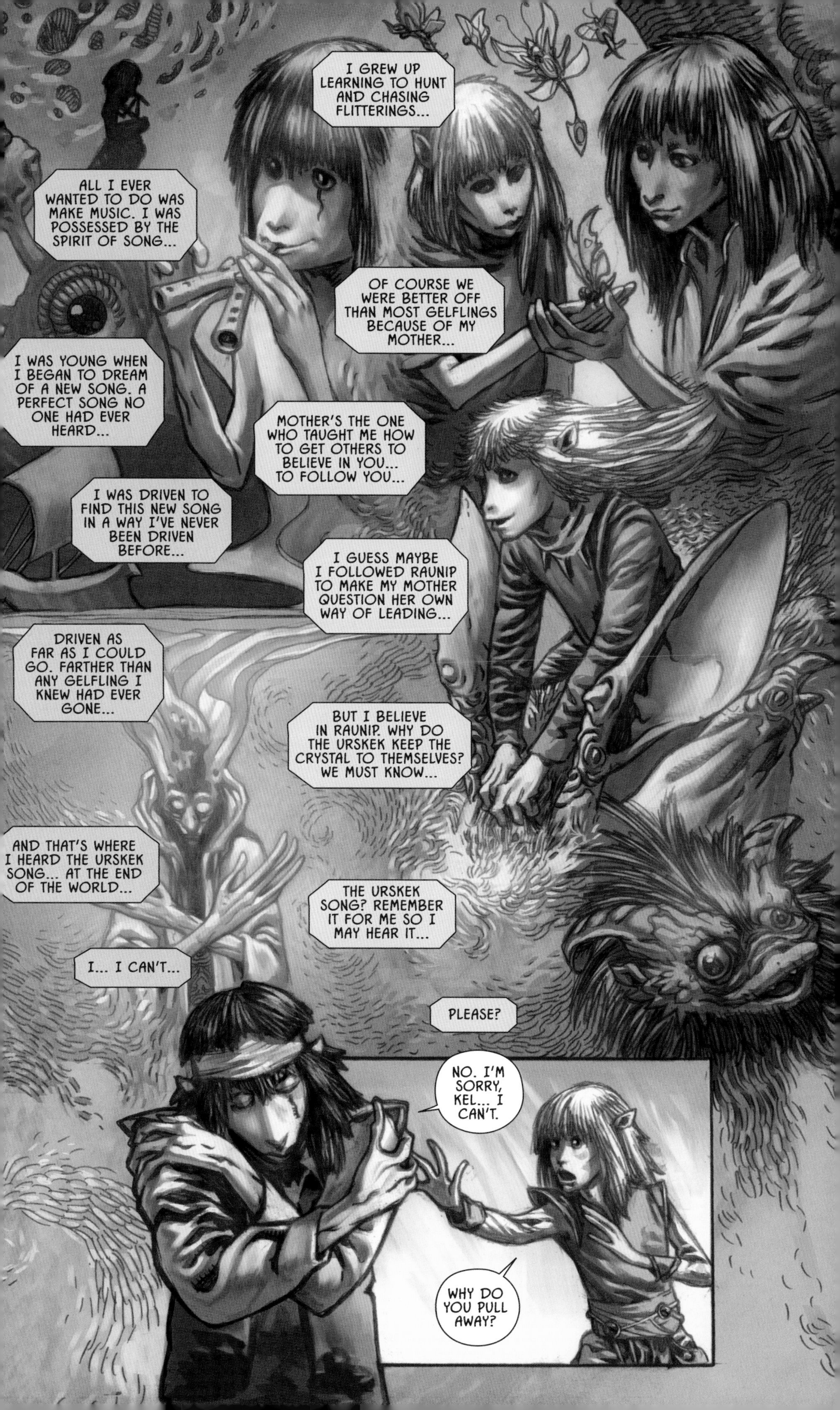
ALL I EVER WANTED TO DO WAS MAKE MUSIC. I WAS POSSESSED BY THE SPIRIT OF SONG...
I GREW UP LEARNING TO HUNT AND CHASING FLITTERINGS...
OF COURSE WE WERE BETTER OFF THAN MOST GELFLINGS BECAUSE OF MY MOTHER...
I WAS YOUNG WHEN I BEGAN TO DREAM OF A NEW SONG. A PERFECT SONG NO ONE HAD EVER HEARD...
MOTHER'S THE ONE WHO TAUGHT ME HOW TO GET OTHERS TO BELIEVE IN YOU... TO FOLLOW YOU...
I WAS DRIVEN TO FIND THIS NEW SONG IN A WAY I'VE NEVER BEEN DRIVEN BEFORE...
I GUESS MAYBE I FOLLOWED RAUNIP TO MAKE MY MOTHER QUESTION HER OWN WAY OF LEADING...
DRIVEN AS FAR AS I COULD GO. FARTHER THAN ANY GELFLING I KNEW HAD EVER GONE...
BUT I BELIEVE IN RAUNIP. WHY DO THE URSKEK KEEP THE CRYSTAL TO THEMSELVES? WE MUST KNOW...
AND THAT'S WHERE I HEARD THE URSKEK SONG... AT THE END OF THE WORLD...
THE URSKEK SONG? REMEMBER IT FOR ME SO I MAY HEAR IT...
I... I CAN'T...
PLEASE?
NO. I'M SORRY, KEL... I CAN'T.
WHY DO YOU PULL AWAY?

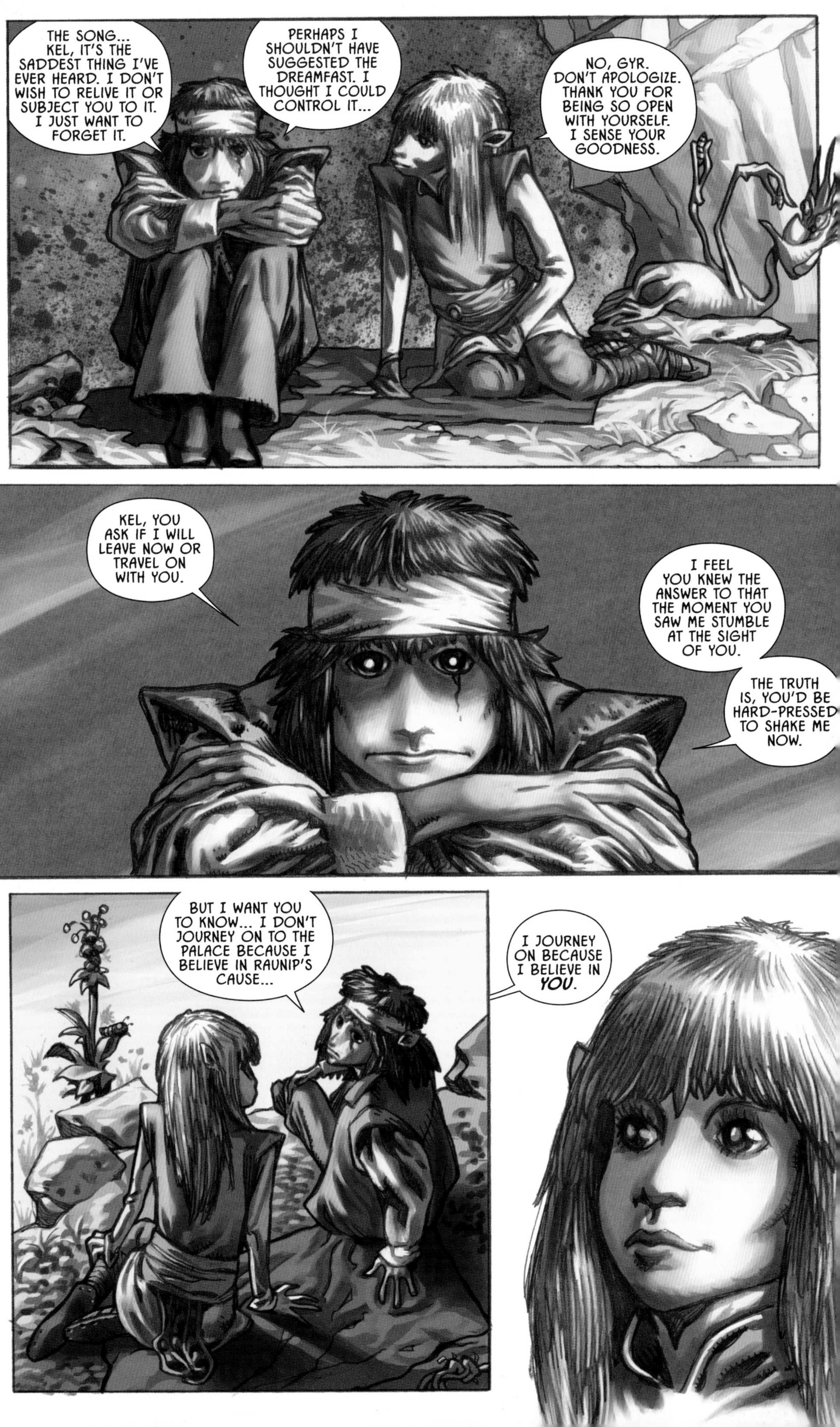
THE SONG... KEL, IT'S THE SADDEST THING I'VE EVER HEARD. I DON'T WISH TO RELIVE IT OR SUBJECT YOU TO IT. I JUST WANT TO FORGET IT.
PERHAPS I SHOULDN'T HAVE SUGGESTED THE DREAMFAST. I THOUGHT I COULD CONTROL IT...
NO, GYR. DON'T APOLOGIZE. THANK YOU FOR BEING SO OPEN WITH YOURSELF. I SENSE YOUR GOODNESS.
KEL, YOU ASK IF I WILL LEAVE NOW OR TRAVEL ON WITH YOU.
I FEEL YOU KNEW THE ANSWER TO THAT THE MOMENT YOU SAW ME STUMBLE AT THE SIGHT OF YOU.
THE TRUTH IS, YOU'D BE HARD-PRESSED TO SHAKE ME NOW.
BUT I WANT YOU TO KNOW... I DON'T JOURNEY ON TO THE PALACE BECAUSE I BELIEVE IN RAUNIP'S CAUSE...
I JOURNEY ON BECAUSE I BELIEVE IN *YOU*.

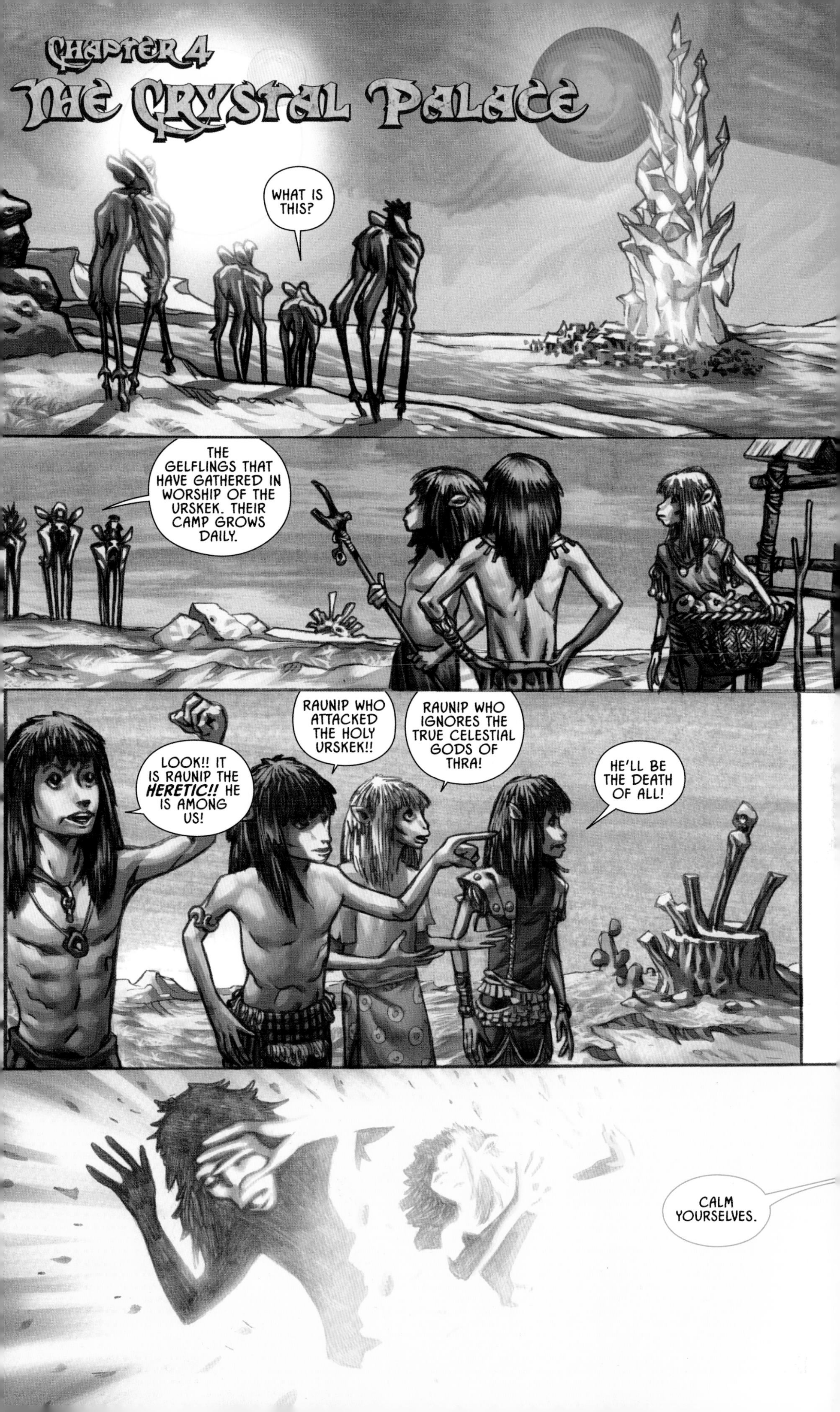
CHAPTER 4
THE CRYSTAL PALACE
WHAT IS THIS?
THE GELFLINGS THAT HAVE GATHERED IN WORSHIP OF THE URSKEK. THEIR CAMP GROWS DAILY.
LOOK!! IT IS RAUNIP THE *HERETIC!!* HE IS AMONG US!
RAUNIP WHO ATTACKED THE HOLY URSKEK!!
RAUNIP WHO IGNORES THE TRUE CELESTIAL GODS OF THRA!
HE'LL BE THE DEATH OF ALL!
CALM YOURSELVES.

THESE ARE INVITED GUESTS OF THE CRYSTAL PALACE.

RAUNIP, WE BEG YOU FORGIVE THE INSULTS OF THOSE WHO HAVE GATHERED IN OUR NAME.

WE DID NOT ASK FOR THEIR ADORATION.

AS LONG AS YOU CONTROL THE CRYSTAL, YOU WILL BE A DIVISIVE FORCE AMONG US, URSKEK.

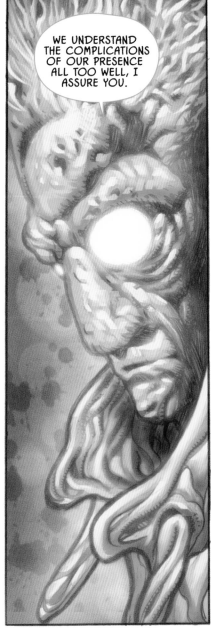

WE UNDERSTAND THE COMPLICATIONS OF OUR PRESENCE ALL TOO WELL, I ASSURE YOU.

COME. THE PALACE AWAITS.

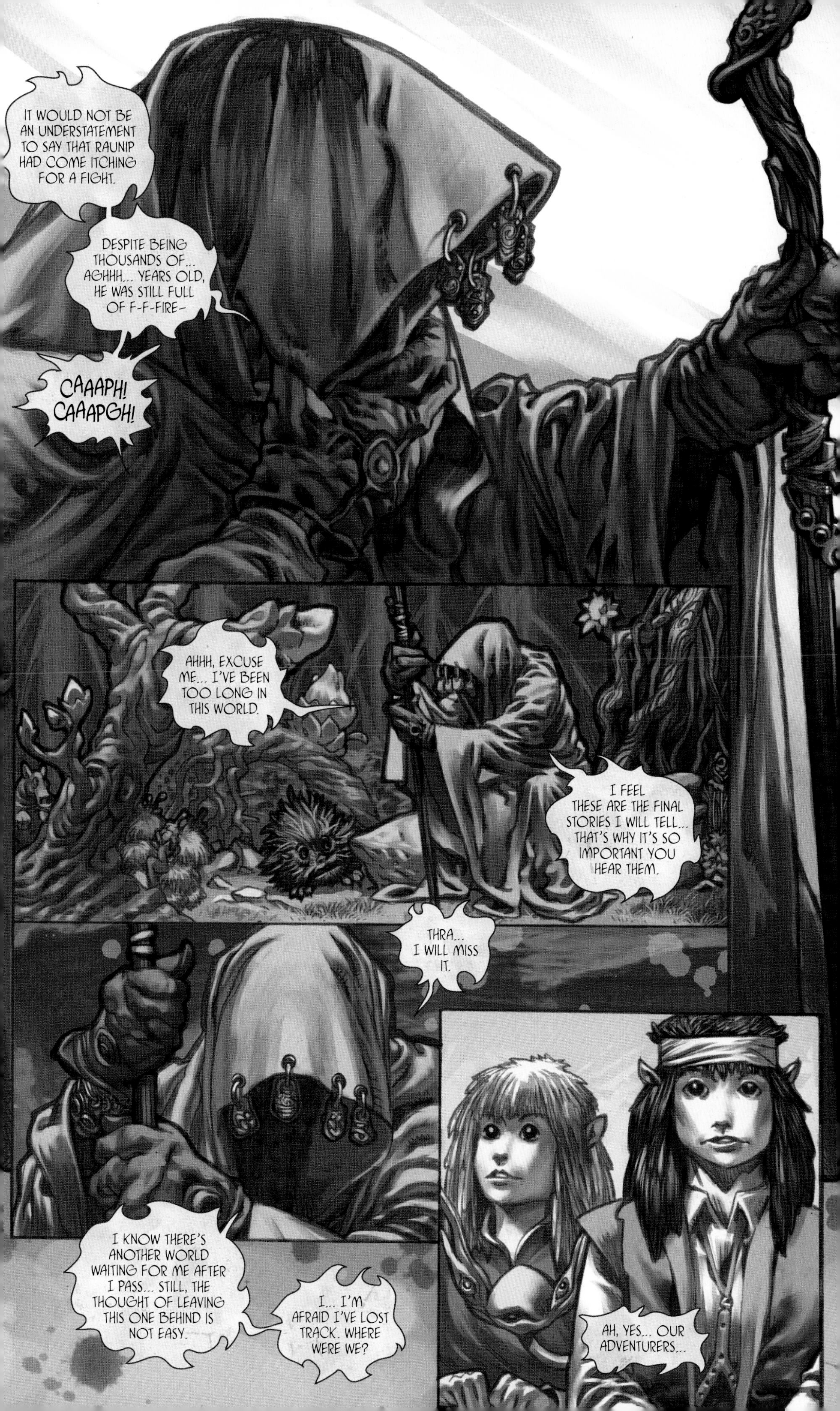
IT WOULD NOT BE AN UNDERSTATEMENT TO SAY THAT RAUNIP HAD COME ITCHING FOR A FIGHT.
DESPITE BEING THOUSANDS OF... AGHHH... YEARS OLD, HE WAS STILL FULL OF F-F-FIRE–
CAAAPH! CAAAPGH!
AHHH, EXCUSE ME... I'VE BEEN TOO LONG IN THIS WORLD.
I FEEL THESE ARE THE FINAL STORIES I WILL TELL... THAT'S WHY IT'S SO IMPORTANT YOU HEAR THEM.
THRA... I WILL MISS IT.
I KNOW THERE'S ANOTHER WORLD WAITING FOR ME AFTER I PASS... STILL, THE THOUGHT OF LEAVING THIS ONE BEHIND IS NOT EASY.
I... I'M AFRAID I'VE LOST TRACK. WHERE WERE WE?
AH, YES... OUR ADVENTURERS...

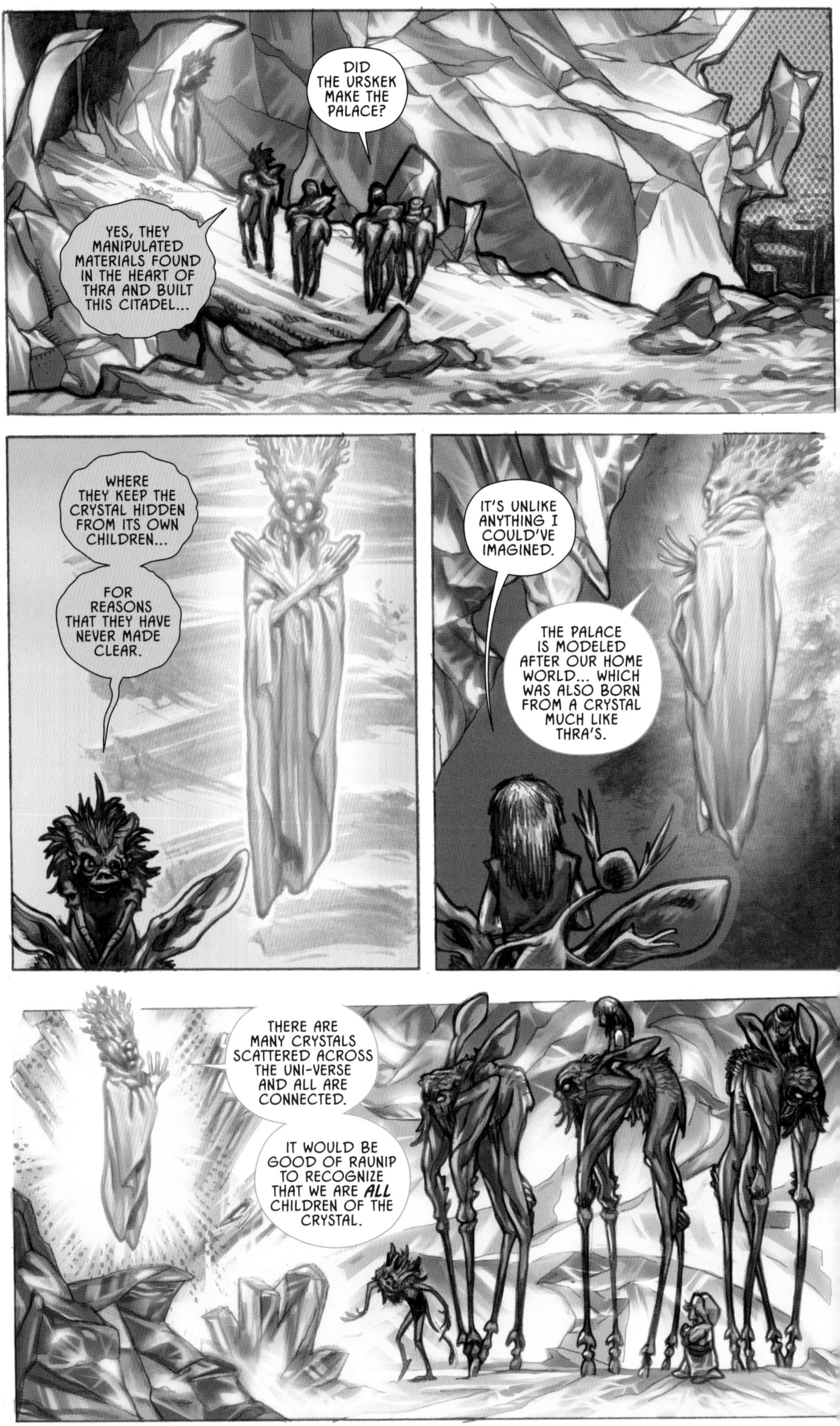
DID THE URSKEK MAKE THE PALACE?
YES, THEY MANIPULATED MATERIALS FOUND IN THE HEART OF THRA AND BUILT THIS CITADEL...
WHERE THEY KEEP THE CRYSTAL HIDDEN FROM ITS OWN CHILDREN...
FOR REASONS THAT THEY HAVE NEVER MADE CLEAR.
IT'S UNLIKE ANYTHING I COULD'VE IMAGINED.
THE PALACE IS MODELED AFTER OUR HOME WORLD... WHICH WAS ALSO BORN FROM A CRYSTAL MUCH LIKE THRA'S.
THERE ARE MANY CRYSTALS SCATTERED ACROSS THE UNI-VERSE AND ALL ARE CONNECTED.
IT WOULD BE GOOD OF RAUNIP TO RECOGNIZE THAT WE ARE *ALL* CHILDREN OF THE CRYSTAL.

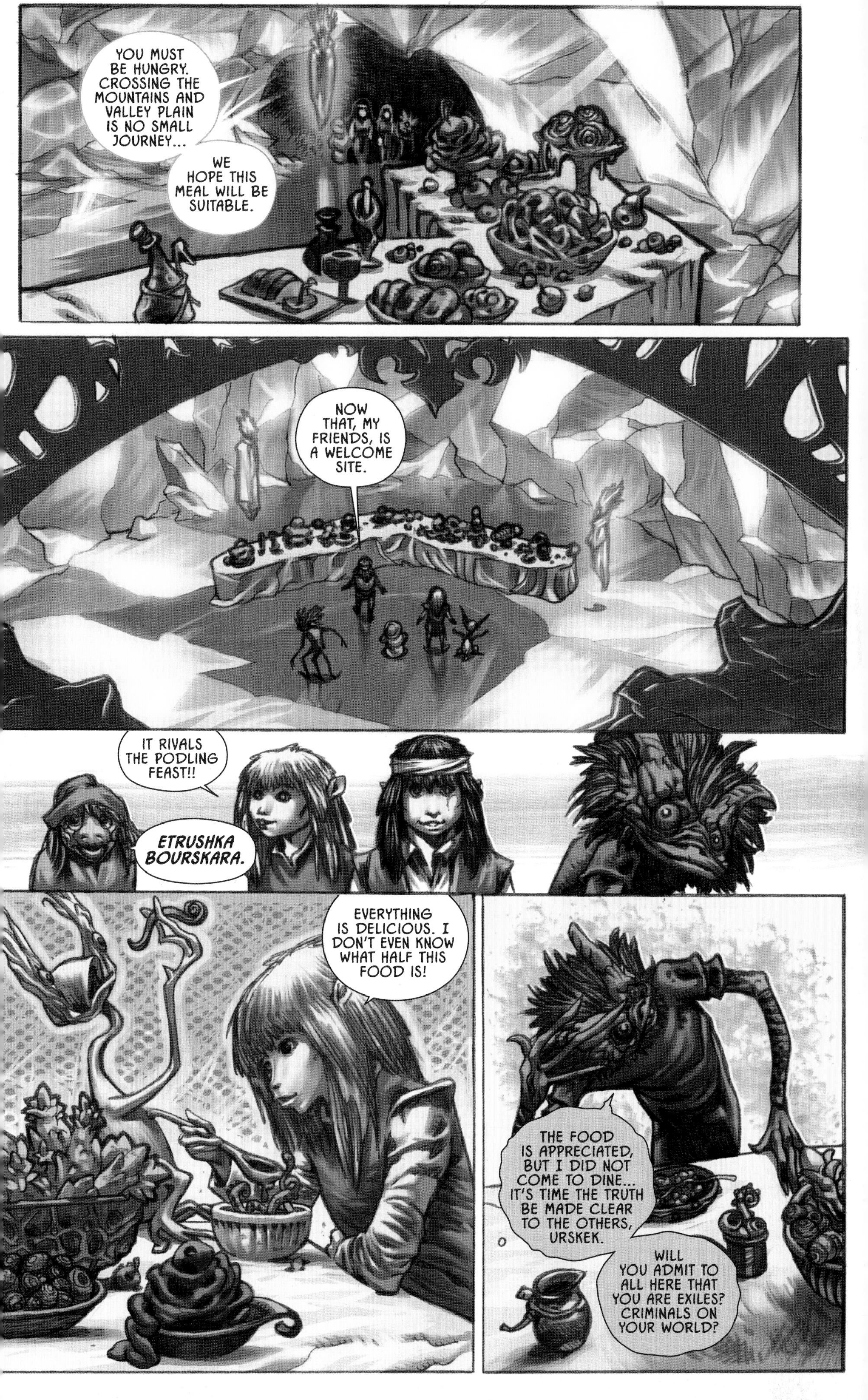
YOU MUST BE HUNGRY. CROSSING THE MOUNTAINS AND VALLEY PLAIN IS NO SMALL JOURNEY...
WE HOPE THIS MEAL WILL BE SUITABLE.
NOW THAT, MY FRIENDS, IS A WELCOME SITE.
IT RIVALS THE PODLING FEAST!!
ETRUSHKA BOURSKARA.
EVERYTHING IS DELICIOUS. I DON'T EVEN KNOW WHAT HALF THIS FOOD IS!
THE FOOD IS APPRECIATED, BUT I DID NOT COME TO DINE... IT'S TIME THE TRUTH BE MADE CLEAR TO THE OTHERS, URSKEK.
WILL YOU ADMIT TO ALL HERE THAT YOU ARE EXILES? CRIMINALS ON YOUR WORLD?

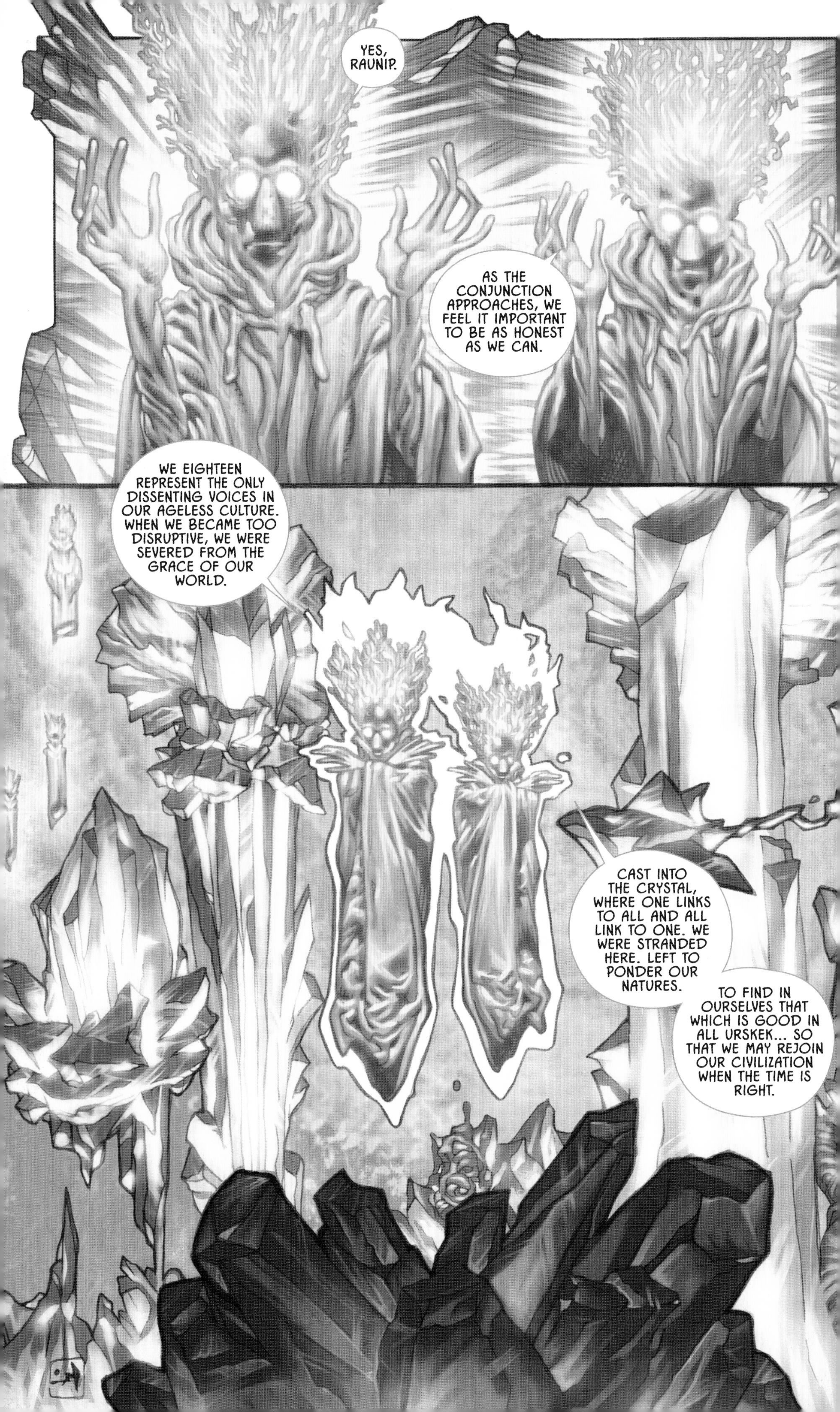
YES, RAUNIP.
AS THE CONJUNCTION APPROACHES, WE FEEL IT IMPORTANT TO BE AS HONEST AS WE CAN.
WE EIGHTEEN REPRESENT THE ONLY DISSENTING VOICES IN OUR AGELESS CULTURE. WHEN WE BECAME TOO DISRUPTIVE, WE WERE SEVERED FROM THE GRACE OF OUR WORLD.
CAST INTO THE CRYSTAL, WHERE ONE LINKS TO ALL AND ALL LINK TO ONE. WE WERE STRANDED HERE. LEFT TO PONDER OUR NATURES.
TO FIND IN OURSELVES THAT WHICH IS GOOD IN ALL URSKEK... SO THAT WE MAY REJOIN OUR CIVILIZATION WHEN THE TIME IS RIGHT.

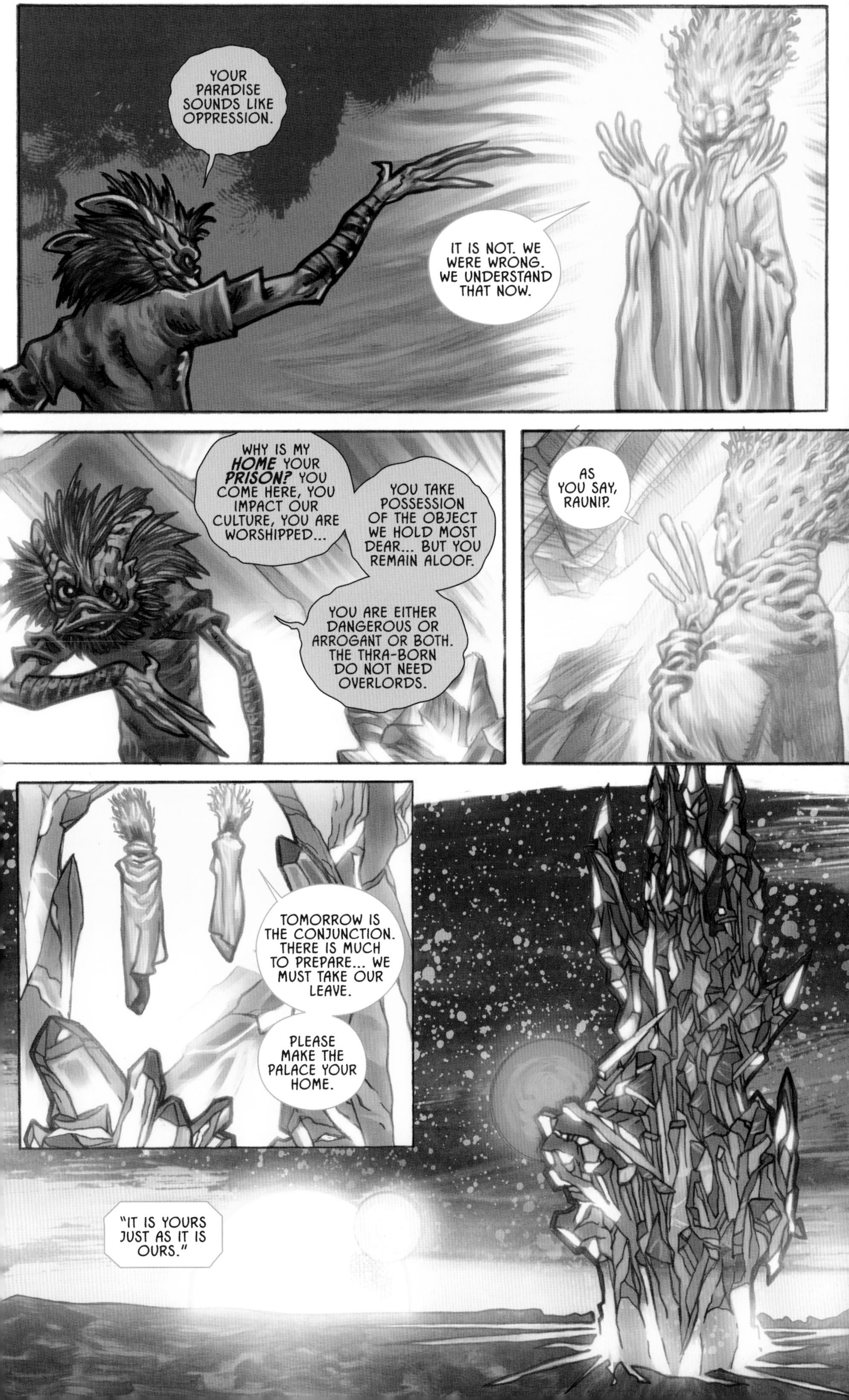
YOUR PARADISE SOUNDS LIKE OPPRESSION.
IT IS NOT. WE WERE WRONG. WE UNDERSTAND THAT NOW.
WHY IS MY **HOME** YOUR **PRISON?** YOU COME HERE, YOU IMPACT OUR CULTURE, YOU ARE WORSHIPPED...
YOU TAKE POSSESSION OF THE OBJECT WE HOLD MOST DEAR... BUT YOU REMAIN ALOOF.
YOU ARE EITHER DANGEROUS OR ARROGANT OR BOTH. THE THRA-BORN DO NOT NEED OVERLORDS.
AS YOU SAY, RAUNIP.
TOMORROW IS THE CONJUNCTION. THERE IS MUCH TO PREPARE... WE MUST TAKE OUR LEAVE.
PLEASE MAKE THE PALACE YOUR HOME.
"IT IS YOURS JUST AS IT IS OURS."

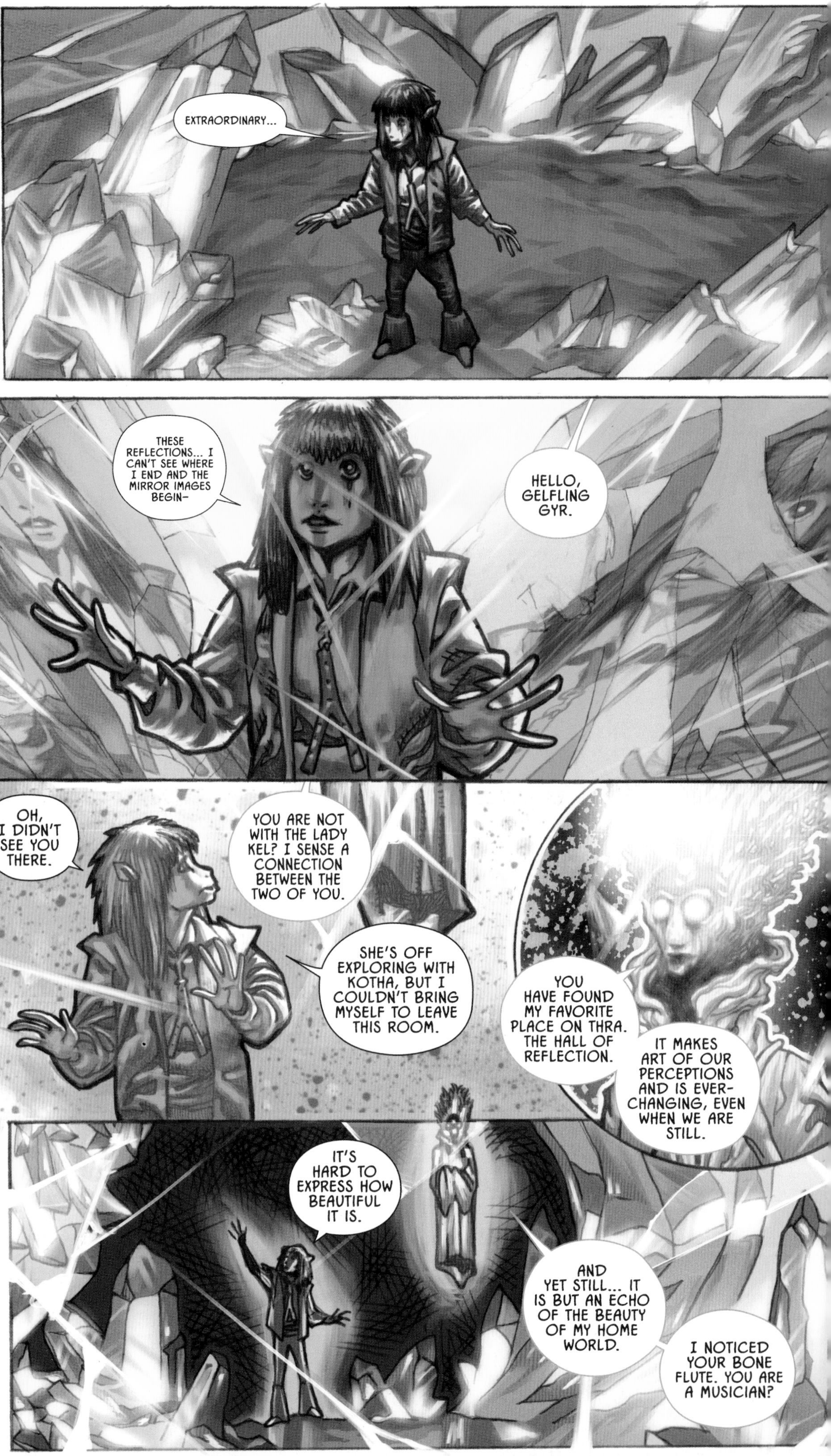

EXTRAORDINARY...
THESE REFLECTIONS... I CAN'T SEE WHERE I END AND THE MIRROR IMAGES BEGIN–
HELLO, GELFLING GYR.
OH, I DIDN'T SEE YOU THERE.
YOU ARE NOT WITH THE LADY KEL? I SENSE A CONNECTION BETWEEN THE TWO OF YOU.
SHE'S OFF EXPLORING WITH KOTHA, BUT I COULDN'T BRING MYSELF TO LEAVE THIS ROOM.
YOU HAVE FOUND MY FAVORITE PLACE ON THRA. THE HALL OF REFLECTION.
IT MAKES ART OF OUR PERCEPTIONS AND IS EVER-CHANGING, EVEN WHEN WE ARE STILL.
IT'S HARD TO EXPRESS HOW BEAUTIFUL IT IS.
AND YET STILL... IT IS BUT AN ECHO OF THE BEAUTY OF MY HOME WORLD.
I NOTICED YOUR BONE FLUTE. YOU ARE A MUSICIAN?

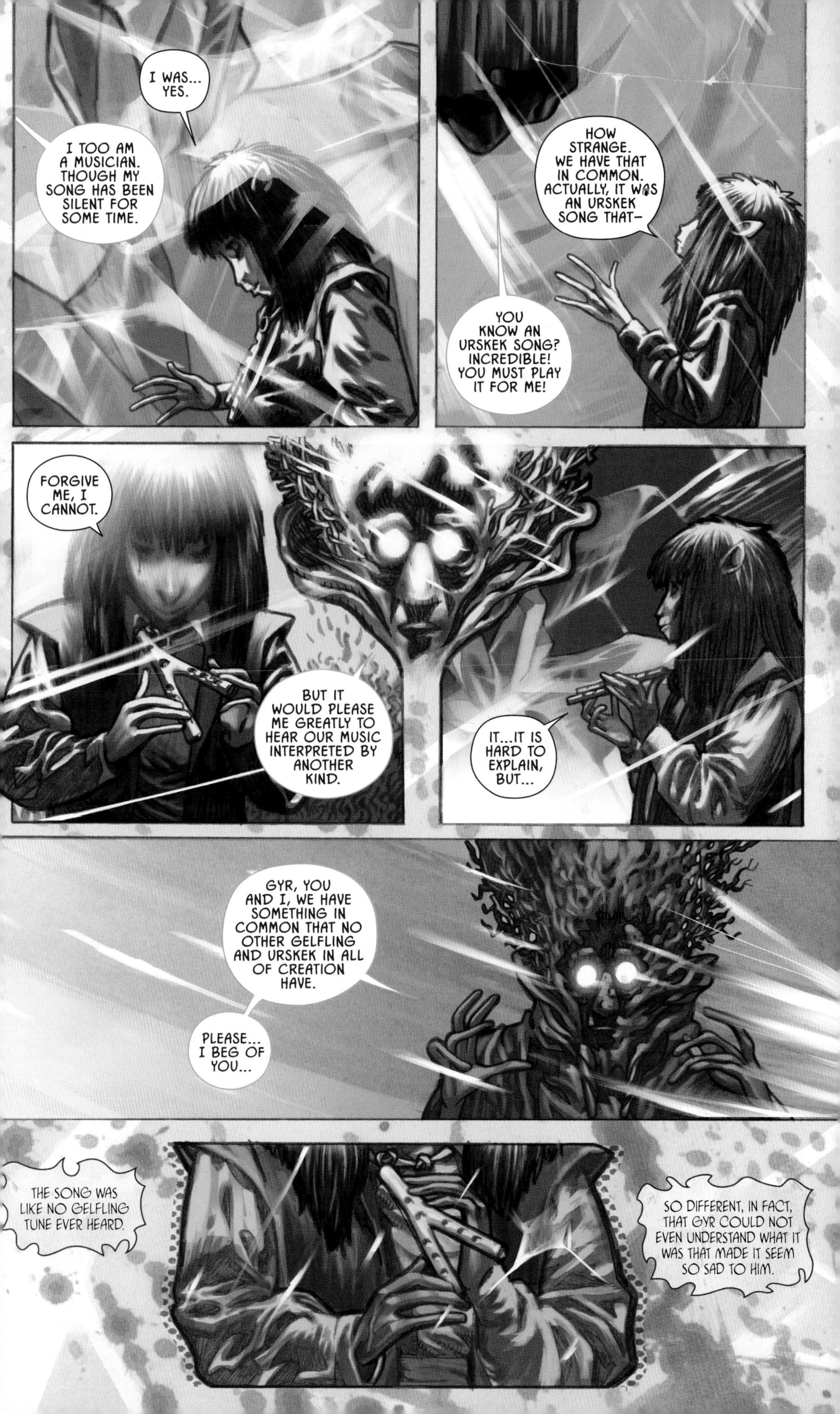
I WAS... YES.
I TOO AM A MUSICIAN. THOUGH MY SONG HAS BEEN SILENT FOR SOME TIME.
HOW STRANGE. WE HAVE THAT IN COMMON. ACTUALLY, IT WAS AN URSKEK SONG THAT–
YOU KNOW AN URSKEK SONG? INCREDIBLE! YOU MUST PLAY IT FOR ME!
FORGIVE ME, I CANNOT.
BUT IT WOULD PLEASE ME GREATLY TO HEAR OUR MUSIC INTERPRETED BY ANOTHER KIND.
IT...IT IS HARD TO EXPLAIN, BUT...
GYR, YOU AND I, WE HAVE SOMETHING IN COMMON THAT NO OTHER GELFLING AND URSKEK IN ALL OF CREATION HAVE.
PLEASE... I BEG OF YOU...
THE SONG WAS LIKE NO GELFLING TUNE EVER HEARD.
SO DIFFERENT, IN FACT, THAT GYR COULD NOT EVEN UNDERSTAND WHAT IT WAS THAT MADE IT SEEM SO SAD TO HIM.

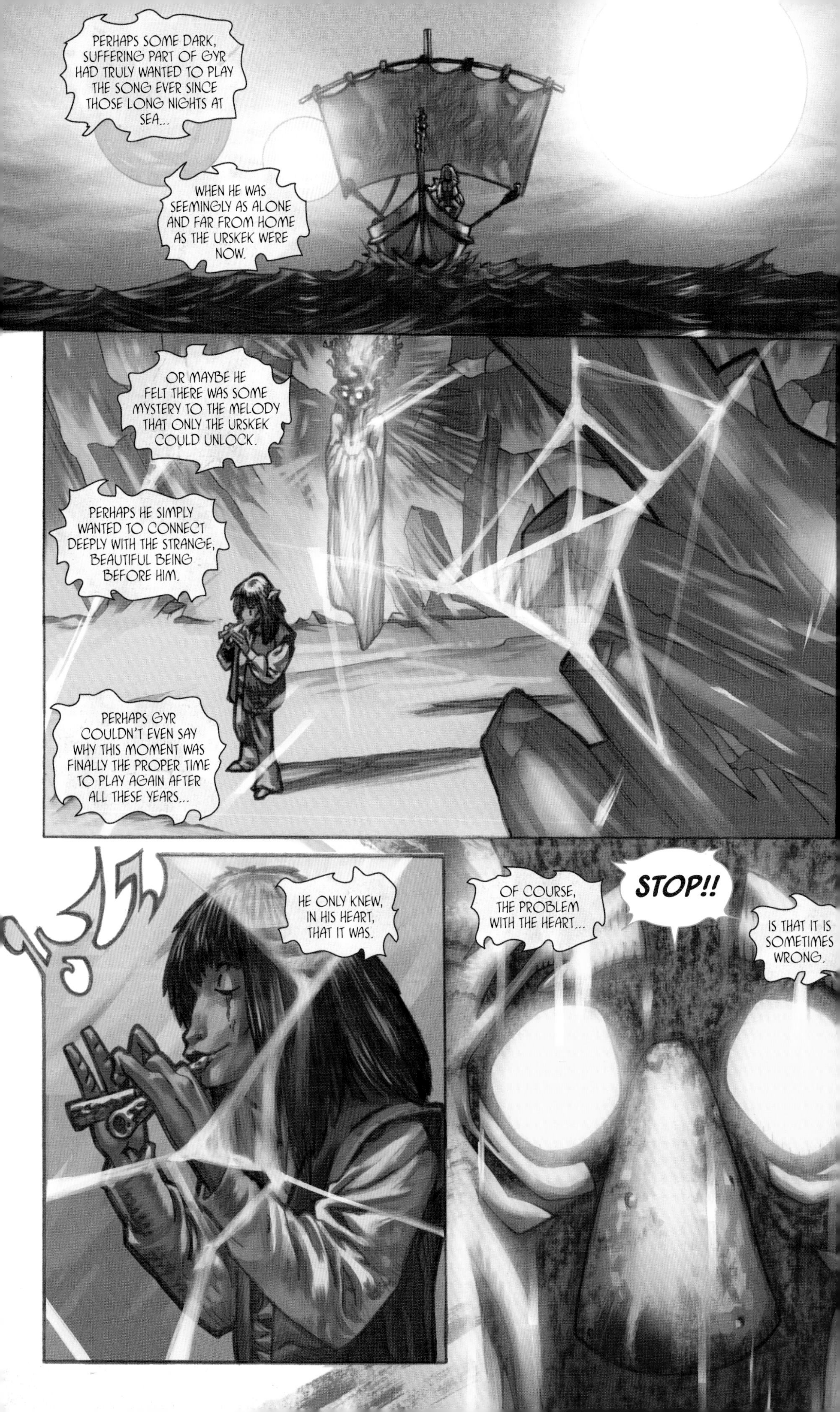
PERHAPS SOME DARK, SUFFERING PART OF GYR HAD TRULY WANTED TO PLAY THE SONG EVER SINCE THOSE LONG NIGHTS AT SEA...
WHEN HE WAS SEEMINGLY AS ALONE AND FAR FROM HOME AS THE URSKEK WERE NOW.
OR MAYBE HE FELT THERE WAS SOME MYSTERY TO THE MELODY THAT ONLY THE URSKEK COULD UNLOCK.
PERHAPS HE SIMPLY WANTED TO CONNECT DEEPLY WITH THE STRANGE, BEAUTIFUL BEING BEFORE HIM.
PERHAPS GYR COULDN'T EVEN SAY WHY THIS MOMENT WAS FINALLY THE PROPER TIME TO PLAY AGAIN AFTER ALL THESE YEARS...
HE ONLY KNEW, IN HIS HEART, THAT IT WAS.
OF COURSE, THE PROBLEM WITH THE HEART...
STOP!!
IS THAT IT IS SOMETIMES WRONG.

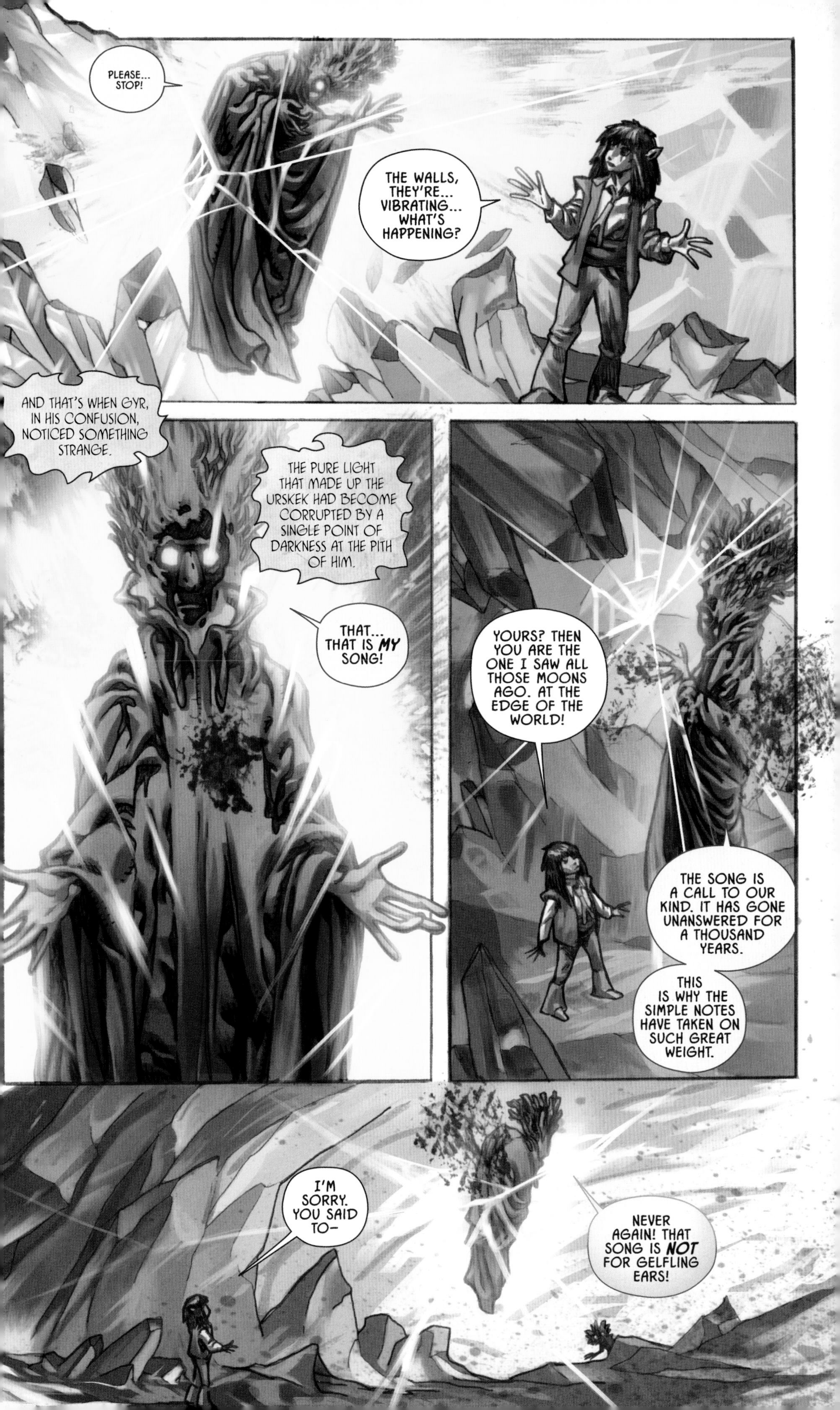
PLEASE... STOP!
THE WALLS, THEY'RE... VIBRATING... WHAT'S HAPPENING?
AND THAT'S WHEN GYR, IN HIS CONFUSION, NOTICED SOMETHING STRANGE.
THE PURE LIGHT THAT MADE UP THE URSKEK HAD BECOME CORRUPTED BY A SINGLE POINT OF DARKNESS AT THE PITH OF HIM.
THAT... THAT IS MY SONG!
YOURS? THEN YOU ARE THE ONE I SAW ALL THOSE MOONS AGO. AT THE EDGE OF THE WORLD!
THE SONG IS A CALL TO OUR KIND. IT HAS GONE UNANSWERED FOR A THOUSAND YEARS.
THIS IS WHY THE SIMPLE NOTES HAVE TAKEN ON SUCH GREAT WEIGHT.
I'M SORRY. YOU SAID TO–
NEVER AGAIN! THAT SONG IS NOT FOR GELFLING EARS!

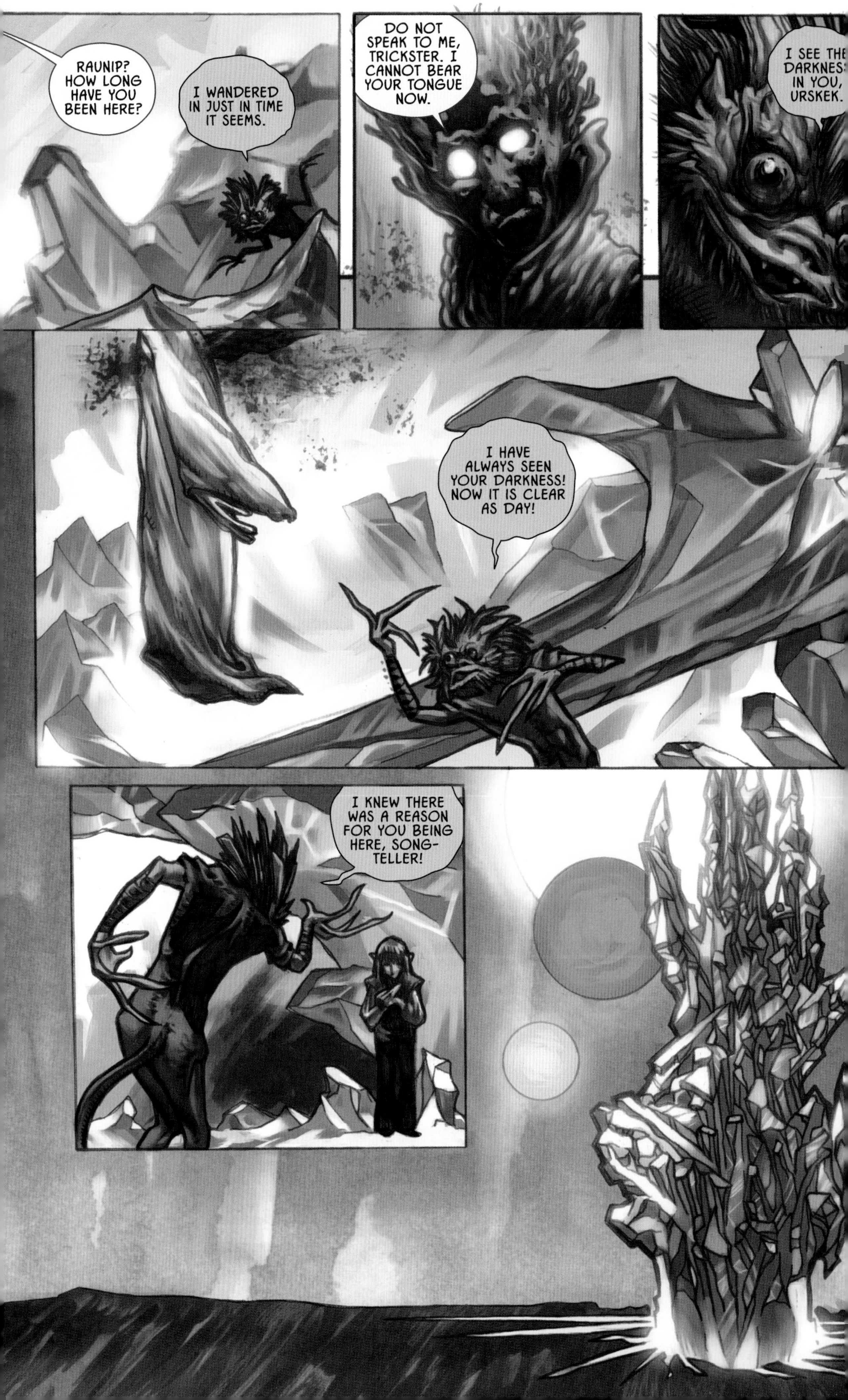
RAUNIP? HOW LONG HAVE YOU BEEN HERE?
I WANDERED IN JUST IN TIME IT SEEMS.
DO NOT SPEAK TO ME, TRICKSTER. I CANNOT BEAR YOUR TONGUE NOW.
I SEE THE DARKNESS IN YOU, URSKEK.
I HAVE ALWAYS SEEN YOUR DARKNESS! NOW IT IS CLEAR AS DAY!
I KNEW THERE WAS A REASON FOR YOU BEING HERE, SONG-TELLER!

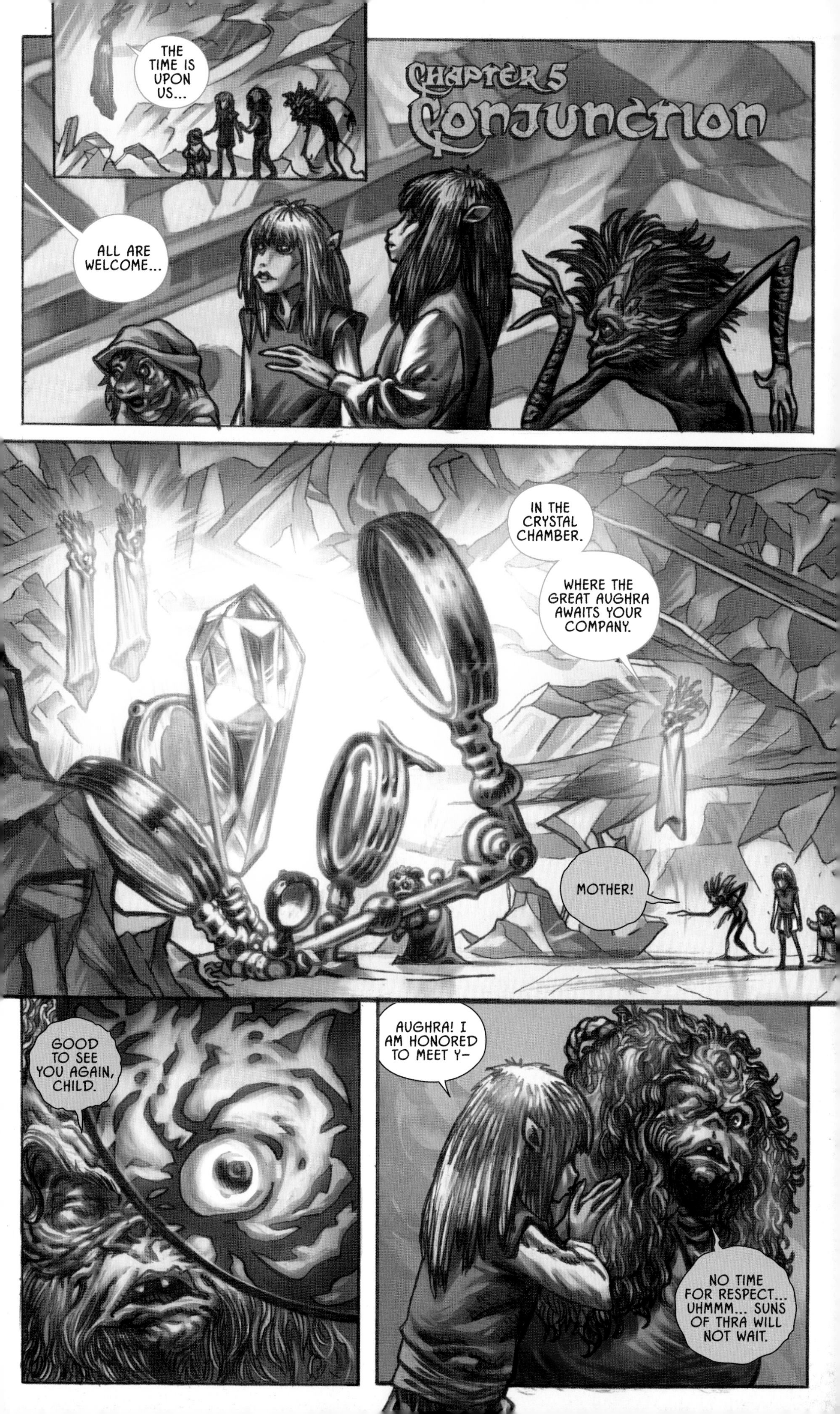

CHAPTER 5
CONJUNCTION
THE TIME IS UPON US...
ALL ARE WELCOME...
IN THE CRYSTAL CHAMBER.
WHERE THE GREAT AUGHRA AWAITS YOUR COMPANY.
MOTHER!
GOOD TO SEE YOU AGAIN, CHILD.
AUGHRA! I AM HONORED TO MEET Y–
NO TIME FOR RESPECT... UHMMM... SUNS OF THRA WILL NOT WAIT.

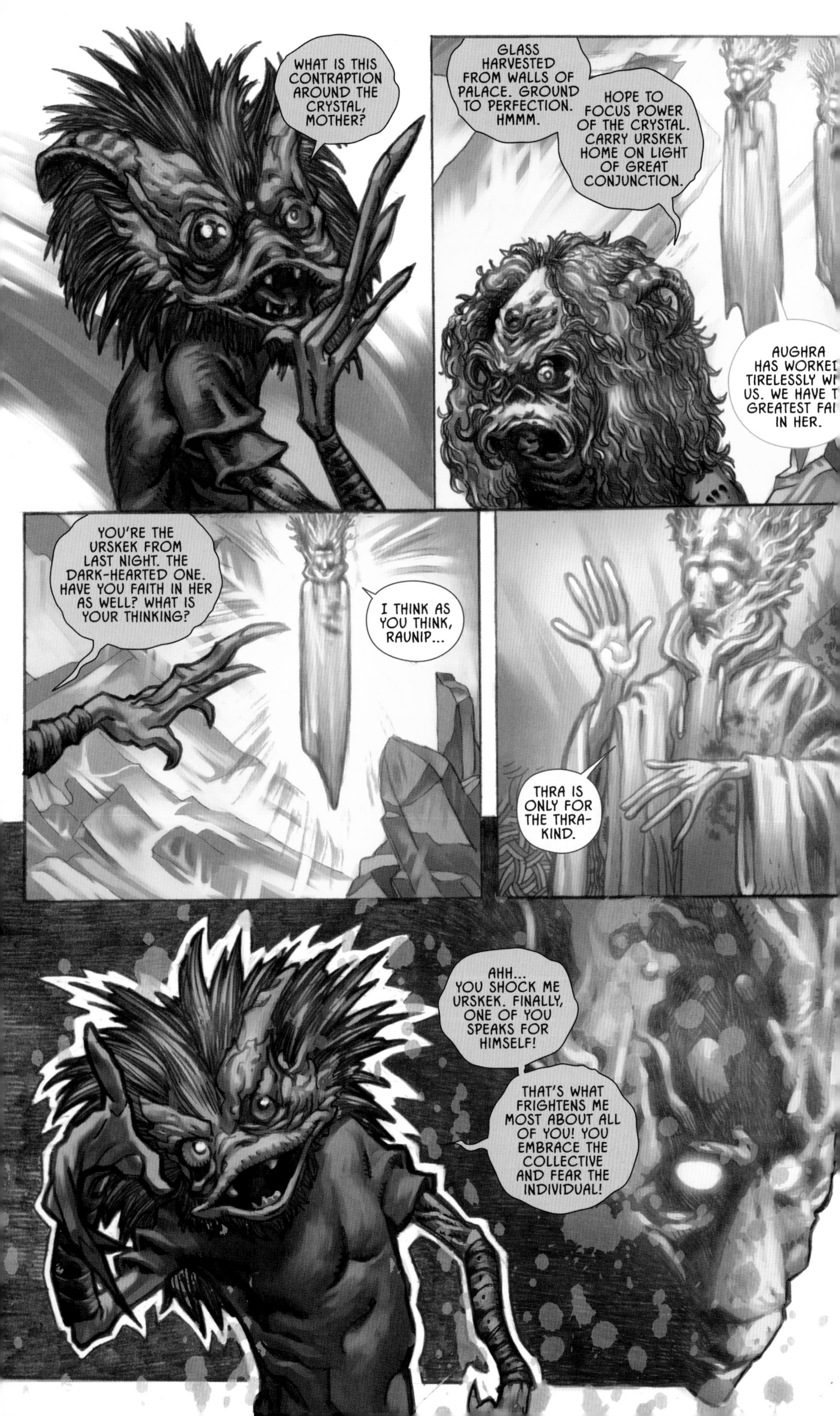
WHAT IS THIS CONTRAPTION AROUND THE CRYSTAL, MOTHER?
GLASS HARVESTED FROM WALLS OF PALACE. GROUND TO PERFECTION. HMMM.
HOPE TO FOCUS POWER OF THE CRYSTAL. CARRY URSKEK HOME ON LIGHT OF GREAT CONJUNCTION.
AUGHRA HAS WORKE TIRELESSLY WI US. WE HAVE T GREATEST FAI IN HER.
YOU'RE THE URSKEK FROM LAST NIGHT. THE DARK-HEARTED ONE. HAVE YOU FAITH IN HER AS WELL? WHAT IS YOUR THINKING?
I THINK AS YOU THINK, RAUNIP...
THRA IS ONLY FOR THE THRA-KIND.
AHH... YOU SHOCK ME URSKEK. FINALLY, ONE OF YOU SPEAKS FOR HIMSELF!
THAT'S WHAT FRIGHTENS ME MOST ABOUT ALL OF YOU! YOU EMBRACE THE COLLECTIVE AND FEAR THE INDIVIDUAL!

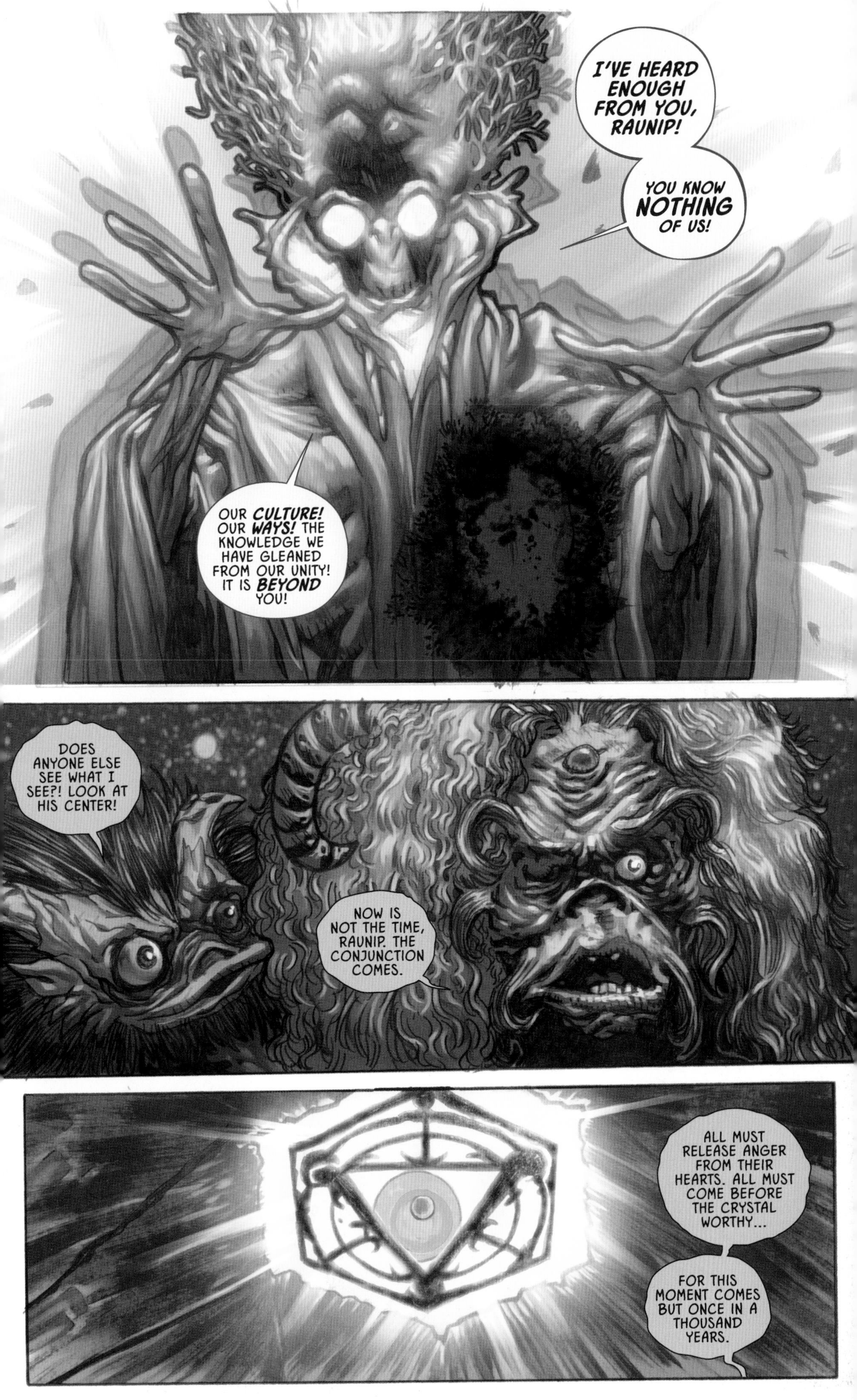
I'VE HEARD ENOUGH FROM YOU, RAUNIP!
YOU KNOW NOTHING OF US!
OUR CULTURE! OUR WAYS! THE KNOWLEDGE WE HAVE GLEANED FROM OUR UNITY! IT IS BEYOND YOU!
DOES ANYONE ELSE SEE WHAT I SEE?! LOOK AT HIS CENTER!
NOW IS NOT THE TIME, RAUNIP. THE CONJUNCTION COMES.
ALL MUST RELEASE ANGER FROM THEIR HEARTS. ALL MUST COME BEFORE THE CRYSTAL WORTHY...
FOR THIS MOMENT COMES BUT ONCE IN A THOUSAND YEARS.

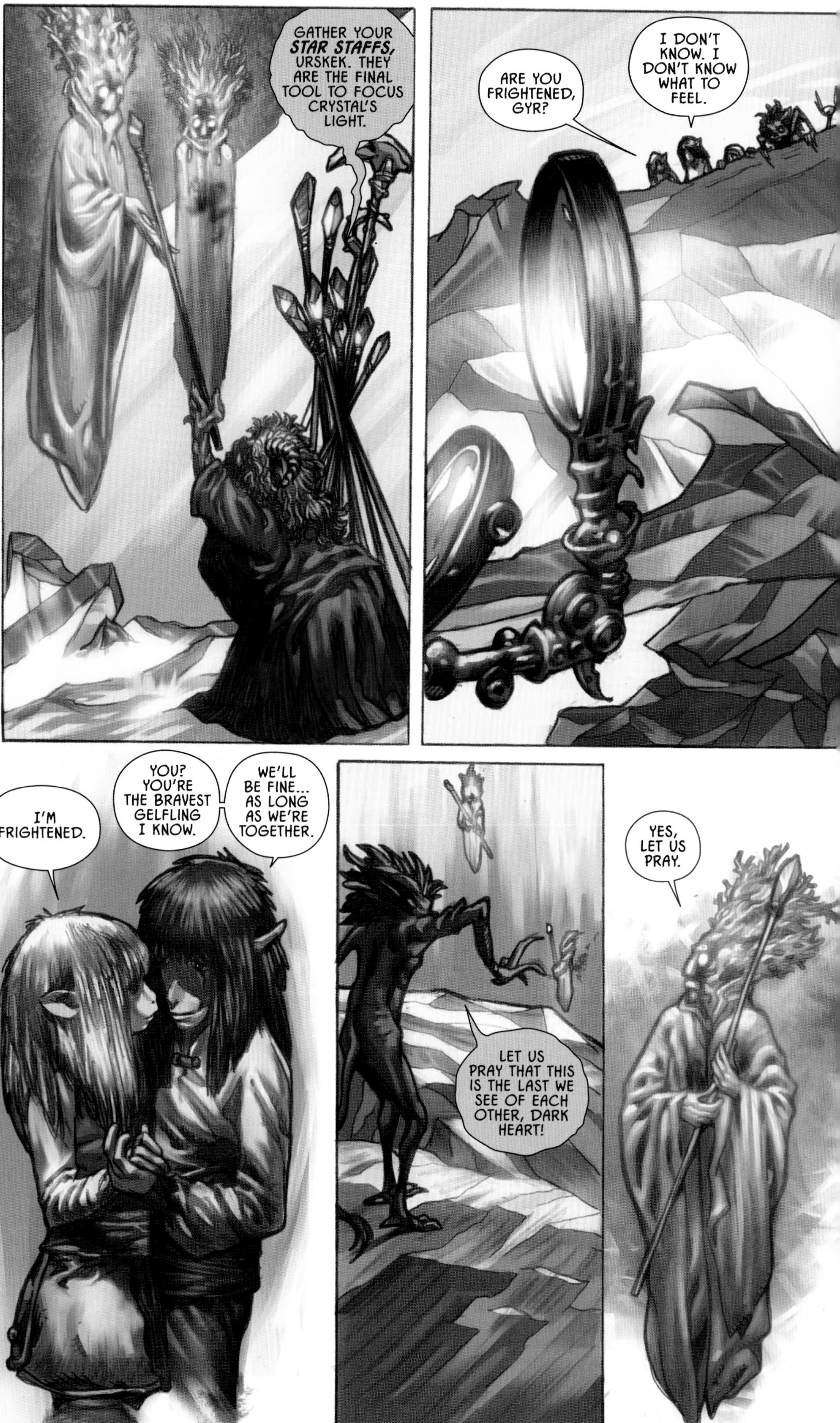

GATHER YOUR STAR STAFFS, URSKEK. THEY ARE THE FINAL TOOL TO FOCUS CRYSTAL'S LIGHT.
ARE YOU FRIGHTENED, GYR?
I DON'T KNOW. I DON'T KNOW WHAT TO FEEL.
I'M FRIGHTENED.
YOU? YOU'RE THE BRAVEST GELFLING I KNOW.
WE'LL BE FINE... AS LONG AS WE'RE TOGETHER.
LET US PRAY THAT THIS IS THE LAST WE SEE OF EACH OTHER, DARK HEART!
YES, LET US PRAY.

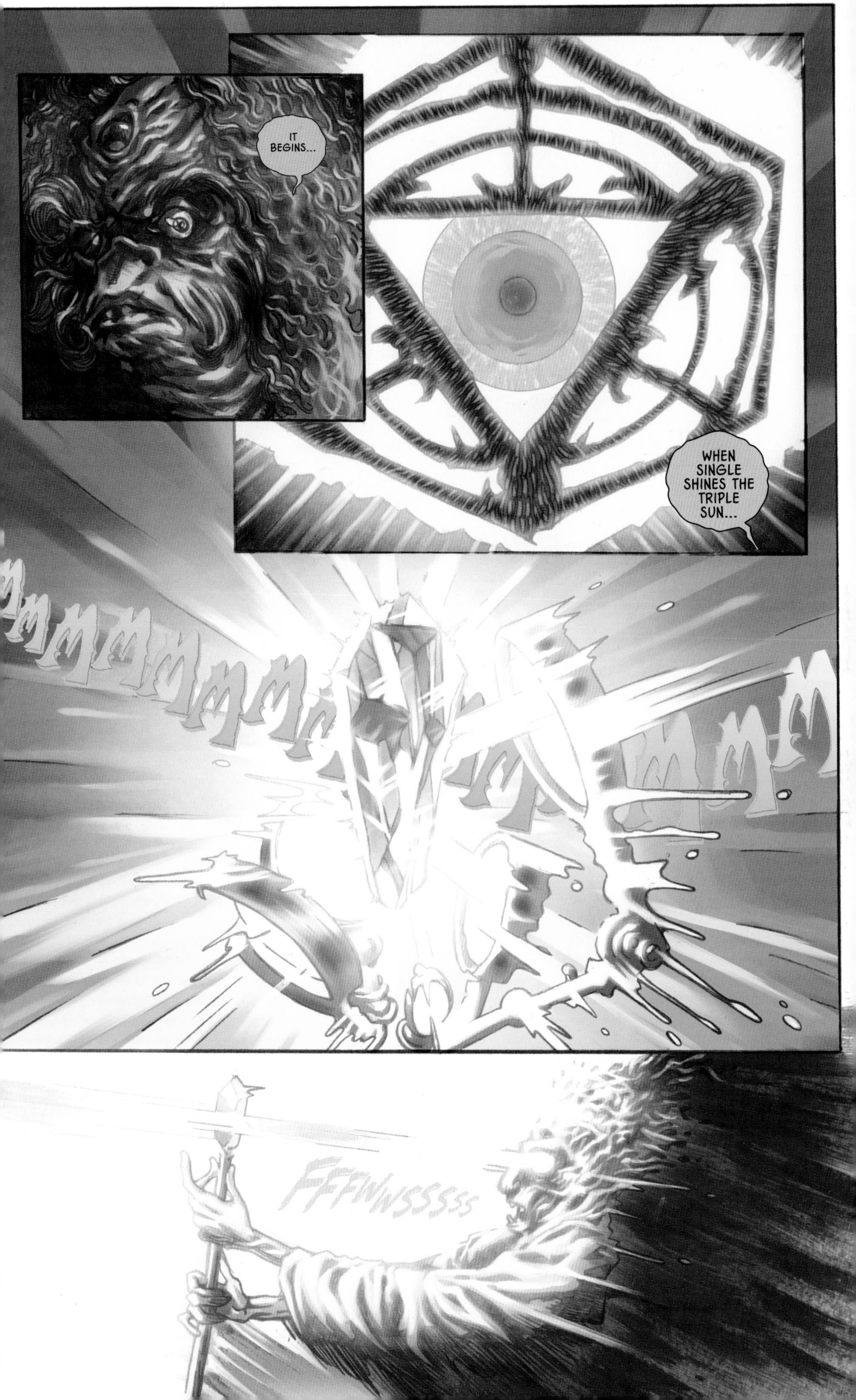

IT BEGINS...
WHEN SINGLE SHINES THE TRIPLE SUN...
MMMMMMMMMMMMMMMMM
FFFWWSSSSS

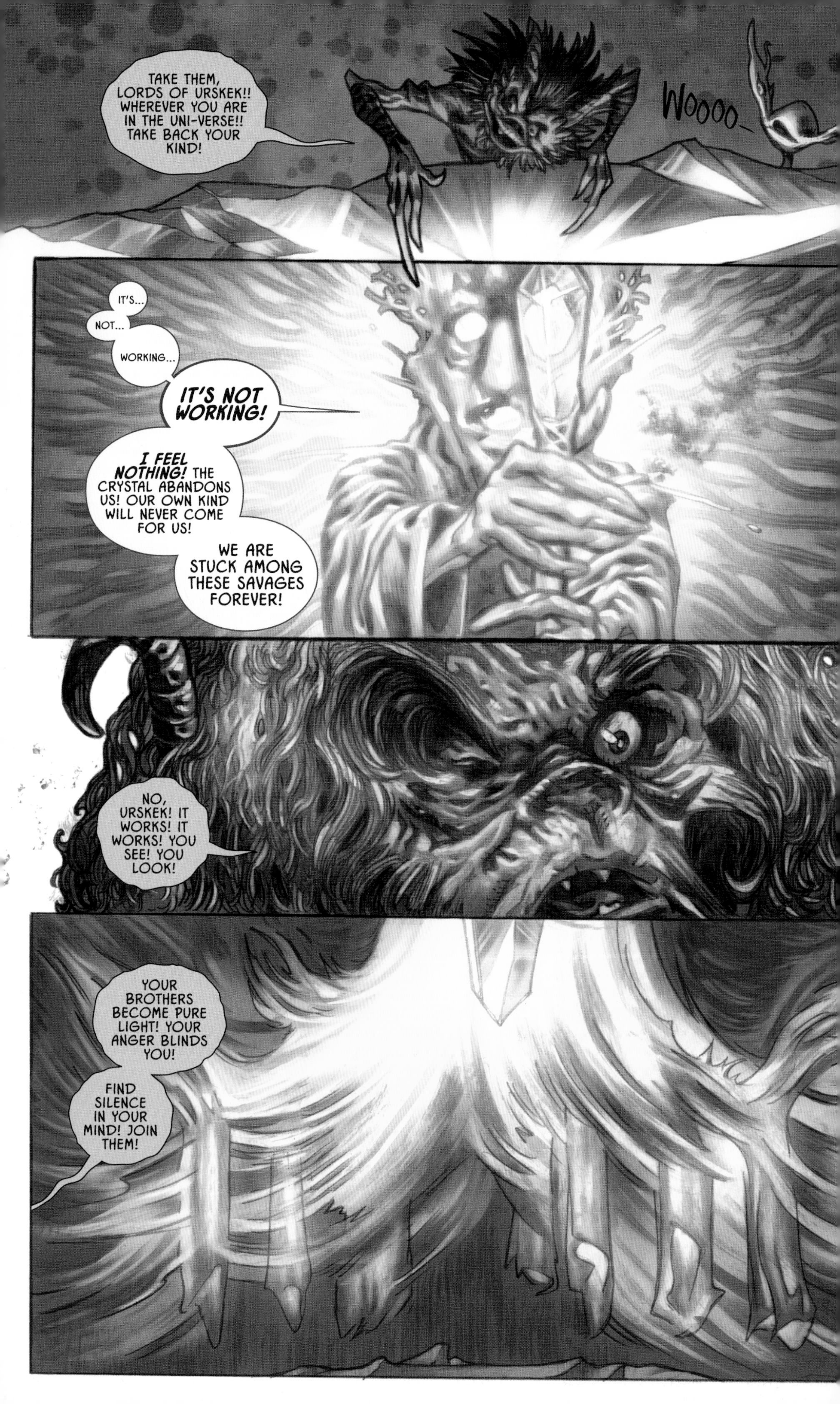
TAKE THEM, LORDS OF URSKEK!! WHEREVER YOU ARE IN THE UNI-VERSE!! TAKE BACK YOUR KIND!
WOOOO-
IT'S...
NOT...
WORKING...
IT'S NOT WORKING!
I FEEL NOTHING! THE CRYSTAL ABANDONS US! OUR OWN KIND WILL NEVER COME FOR US!
WE ARE STUCK AMONG THESE SAVAGES FOREVER!
NO, URSKEK! IT WORKS! IT WORKS! YOU SEE! YOU LOOK!
YOUR BROTHERS BECOME PURE LIGHT! YOUR ANGER BLINDS YOU!
FIND SILENCE IN YOUR MIND! JOIN THEM!

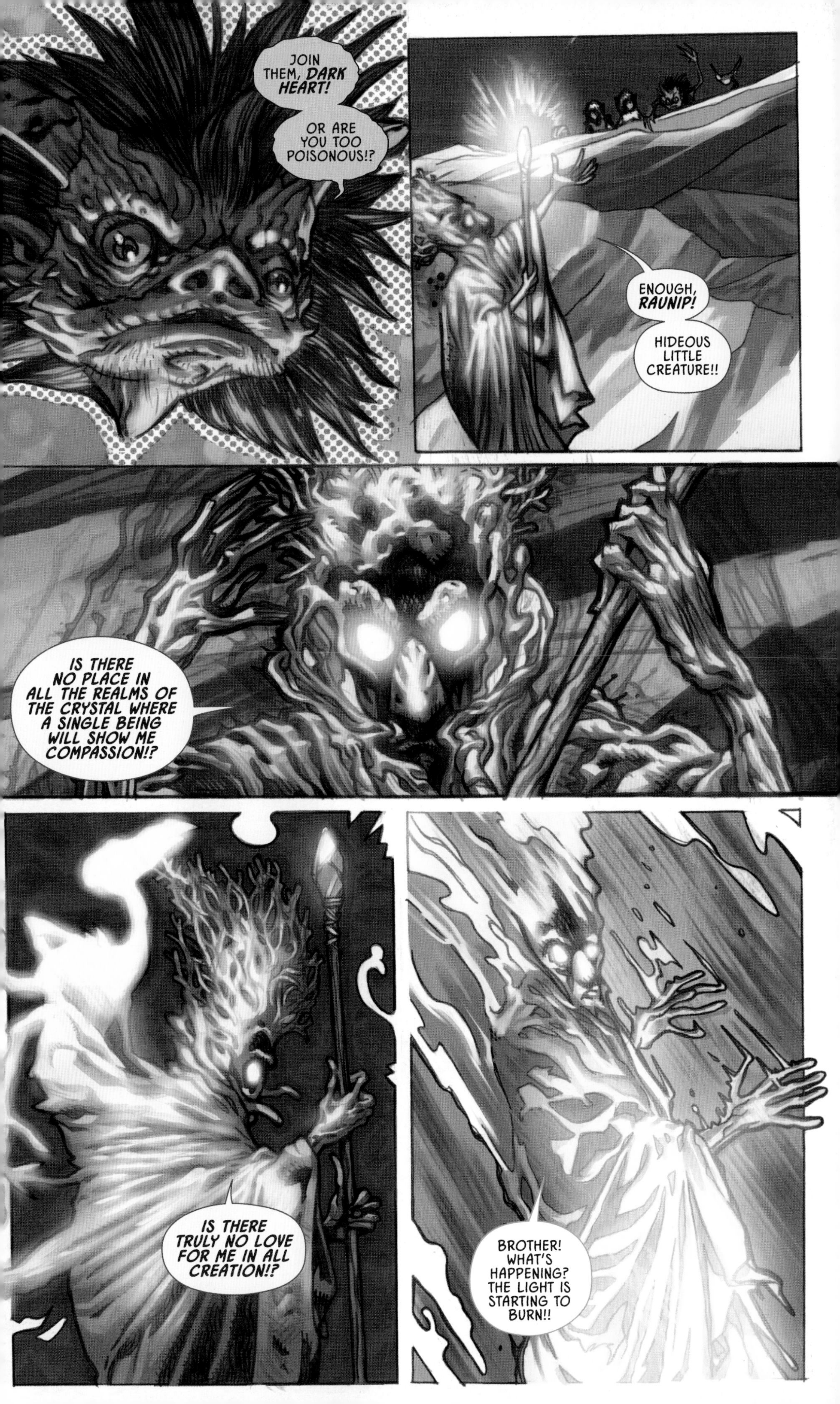
JOIN THEM, DARK HEART!
OR ARE YOU TOO POISONOUS!?
ENOUGH, RAUNIP!
HIDEOUS LITTLE CREATURE!!
IS THERE NO PLACE IN ALL THE REALMS OF THE CRYSTAL WHERE A SINGLE BEING WILL SHOW ME COMPASSION!?
IS THERE TRULY NO LOVE FOR ME IN ALL CREATION!?
BROTHER! WHAT'S HAPPENING? THE LIGHT IS STARTING TO BURN!!

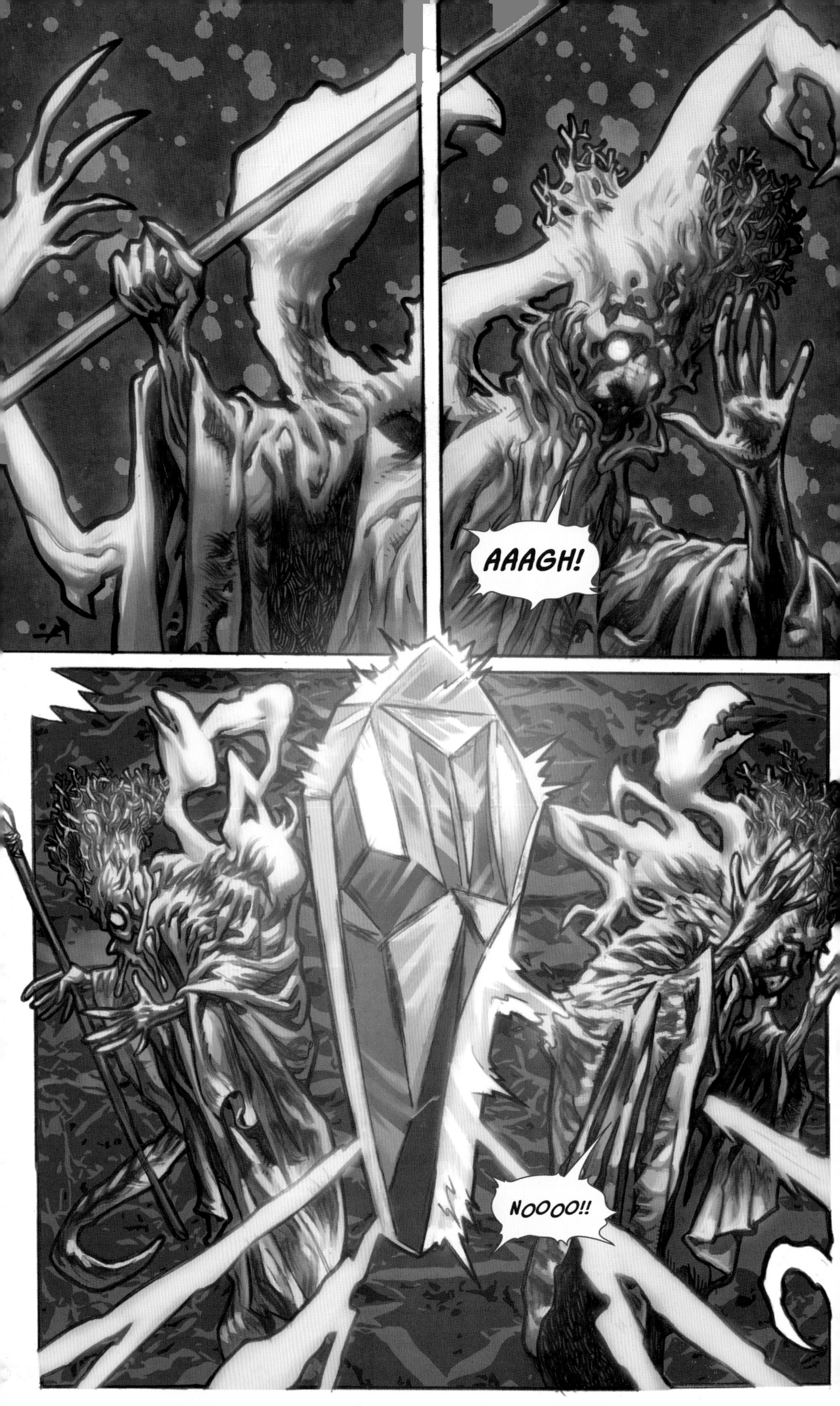
AAAGH!
NOOOO!!

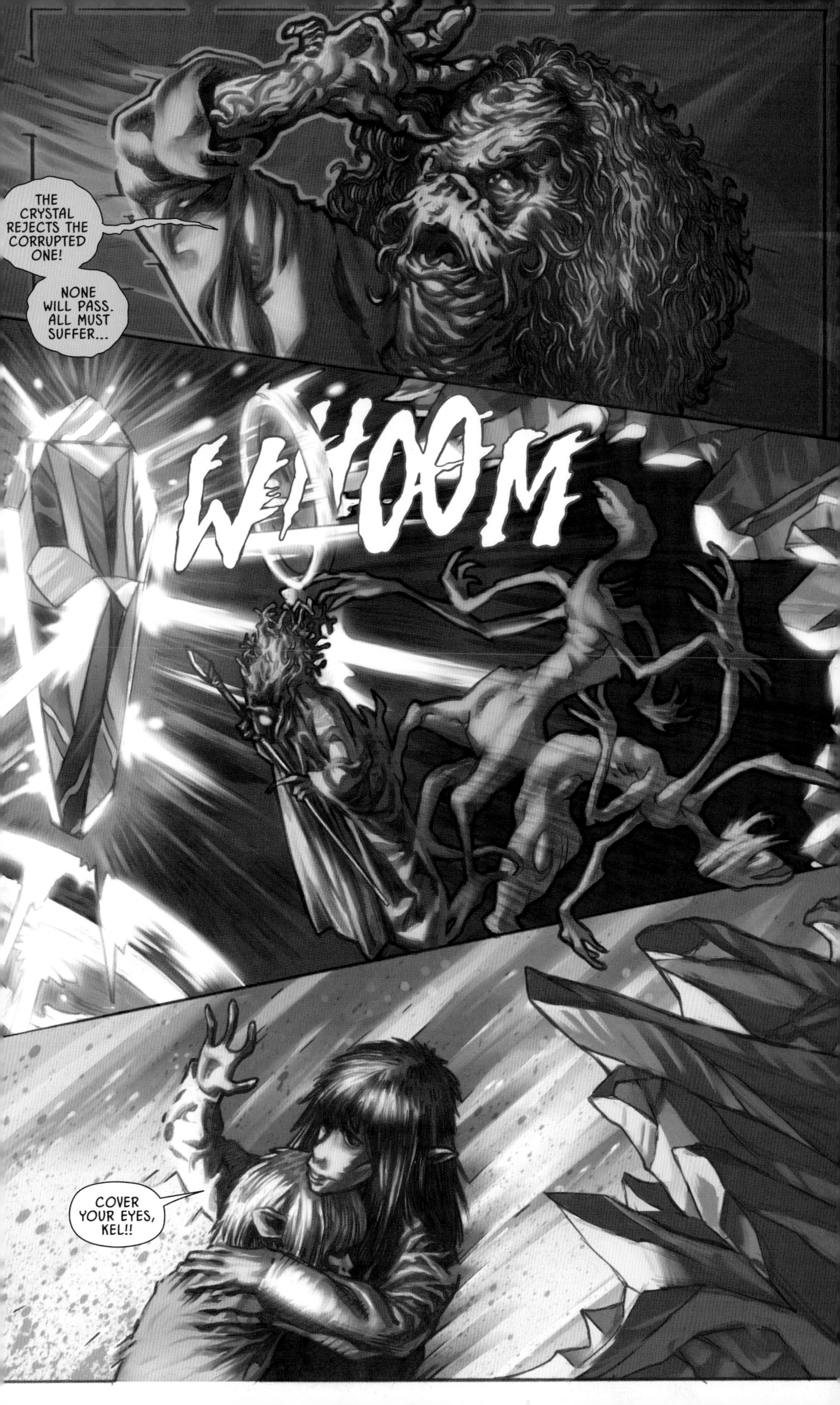
THE CRYSTAL REJECTS THE CORRUPTED ONE!
NONE WILL PASS. ALL MUST SUFFER...
COVER YOUR EYES, KEL!!

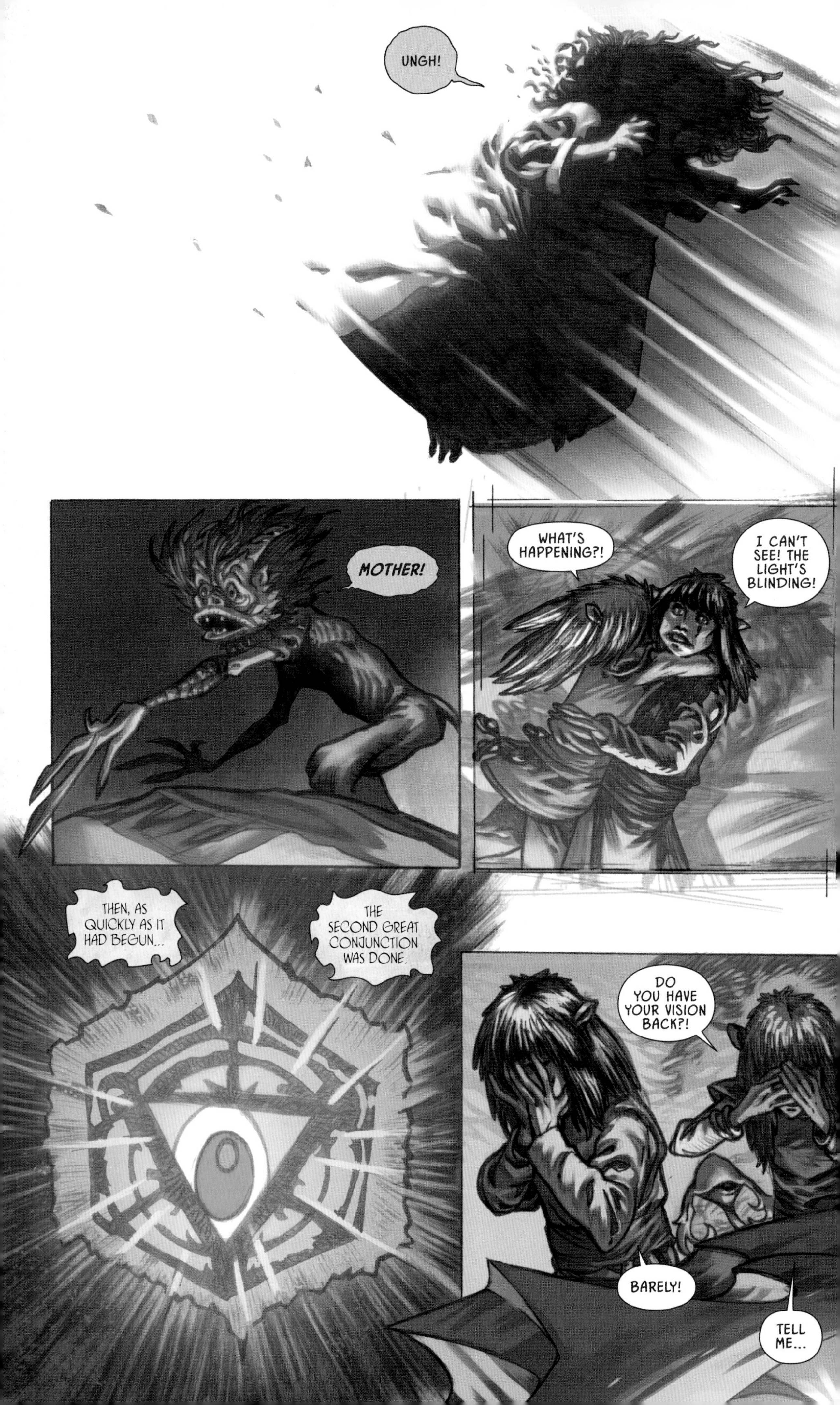
UNGH!
MOTHER!
WHAT'S HAPPENING?!
I CAN'T SEE! THE LIGHT'S BLINDING!
THEN, AS QUICKLY AS IT HAD BEGUN...
THE SECOND GREAT CONJUNCTION WAS DONE.
DO YOU HAVE YOUR VISION BACK?!
BARELY!
TELL ME...

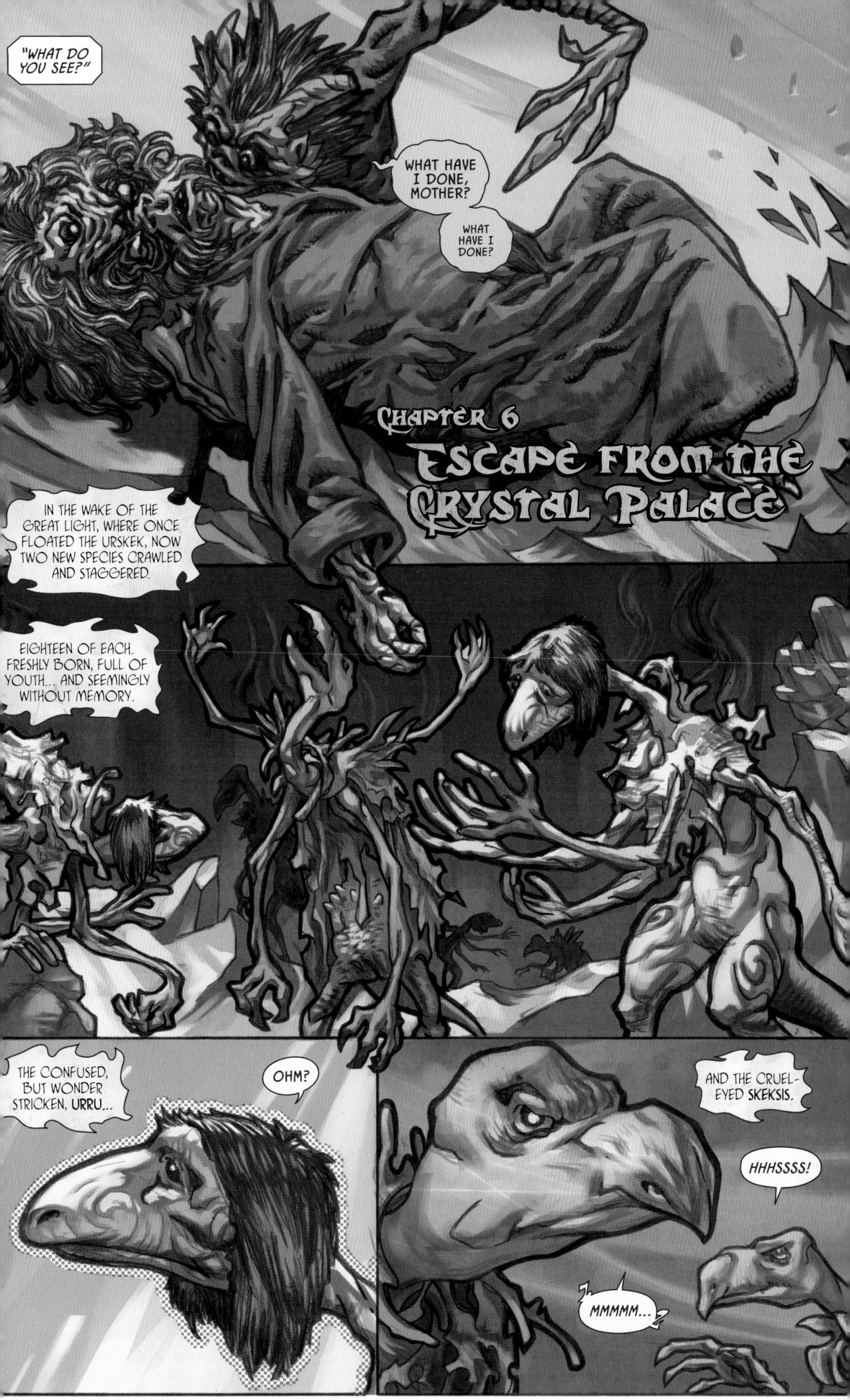
"WHAT DO YOU SEE?"
WHAT HAVE I DONE, MOTHER?
WHAT HAVE I DONE?
CHAPTER 6
ESCAPE FROM THE CRYSTAL PALACE
IN THE WAKE OF THE GREAT LIGHT, WHERE ONCE FLOATED THE URSKEK, NOW TWO NEW SPECIES CRAWLED AND STAGGERED.
EIGHTEEN OF EACH. FRESHLY BORN, FULL OF YOUTH... AND SEEMINGLY WITHOUT MEMORY.
THE CONFUSED, BUT WONDER STRICKEN, URRU...
OHM?
AND THE CRUEL-EYED SKEKSIS.
HHHSSSS!
MMMMM...

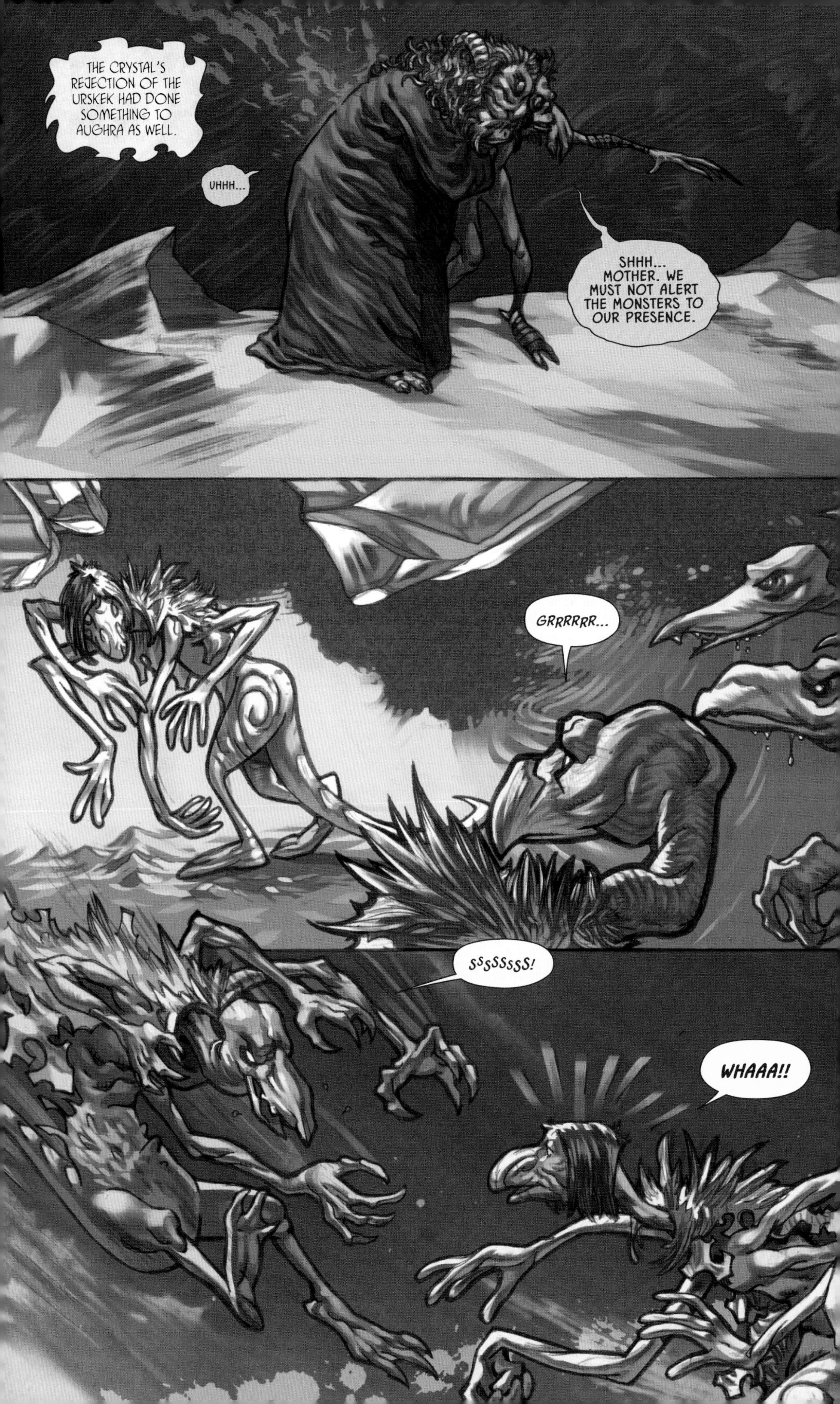
THE CRYSTAL'S REJECTION OF THE URSKEK HAD DONE SOMETHING TO AUGHRA AS WELL.
UHHH...
SHHH... MOTHER. WE MUST NOT ALERT THE MONSTERS TO OUR PRESENCE.
GRRRRRR...
SSSSSSSS!
WHAAA!!

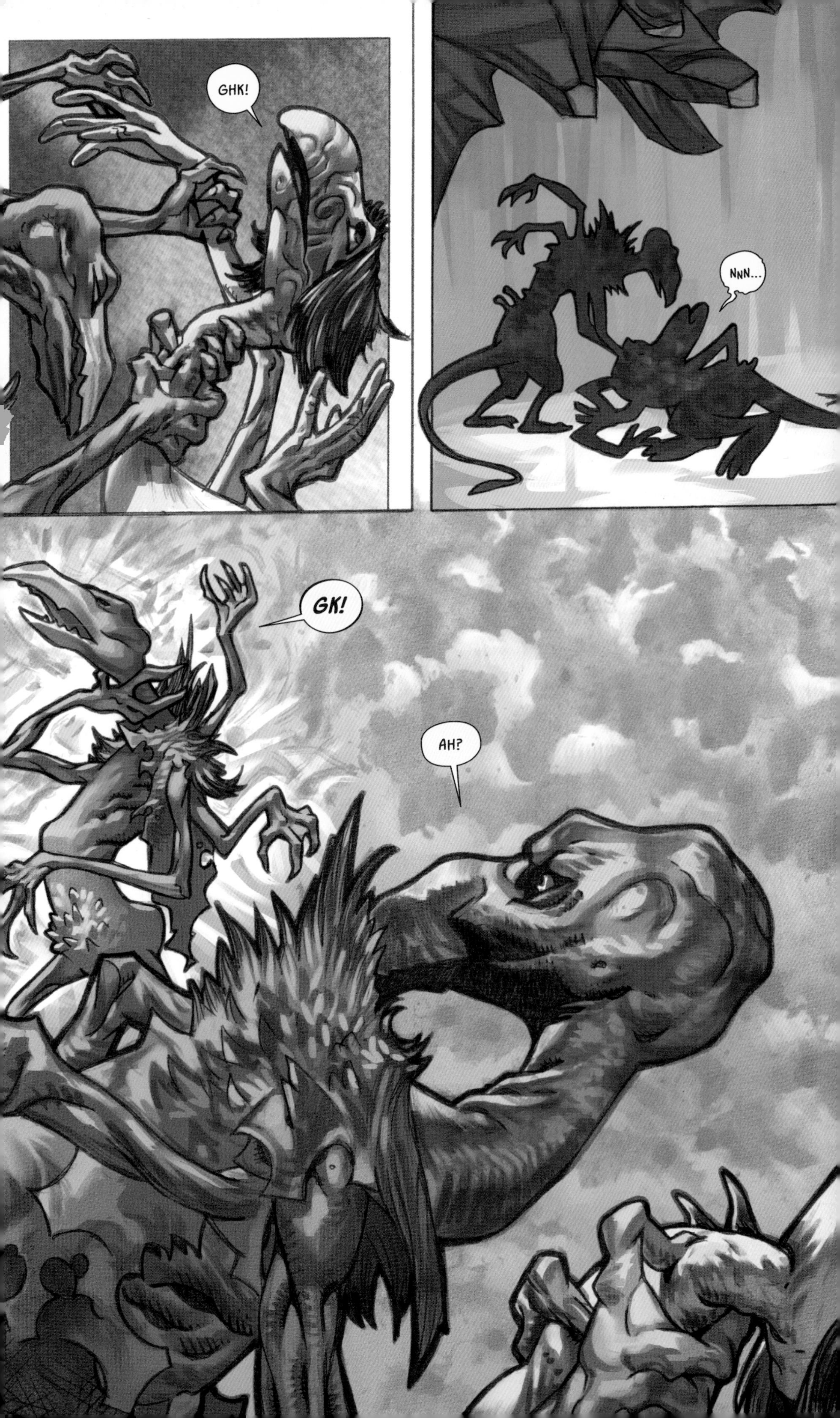
GHK!
NNN...
GK!
AH?

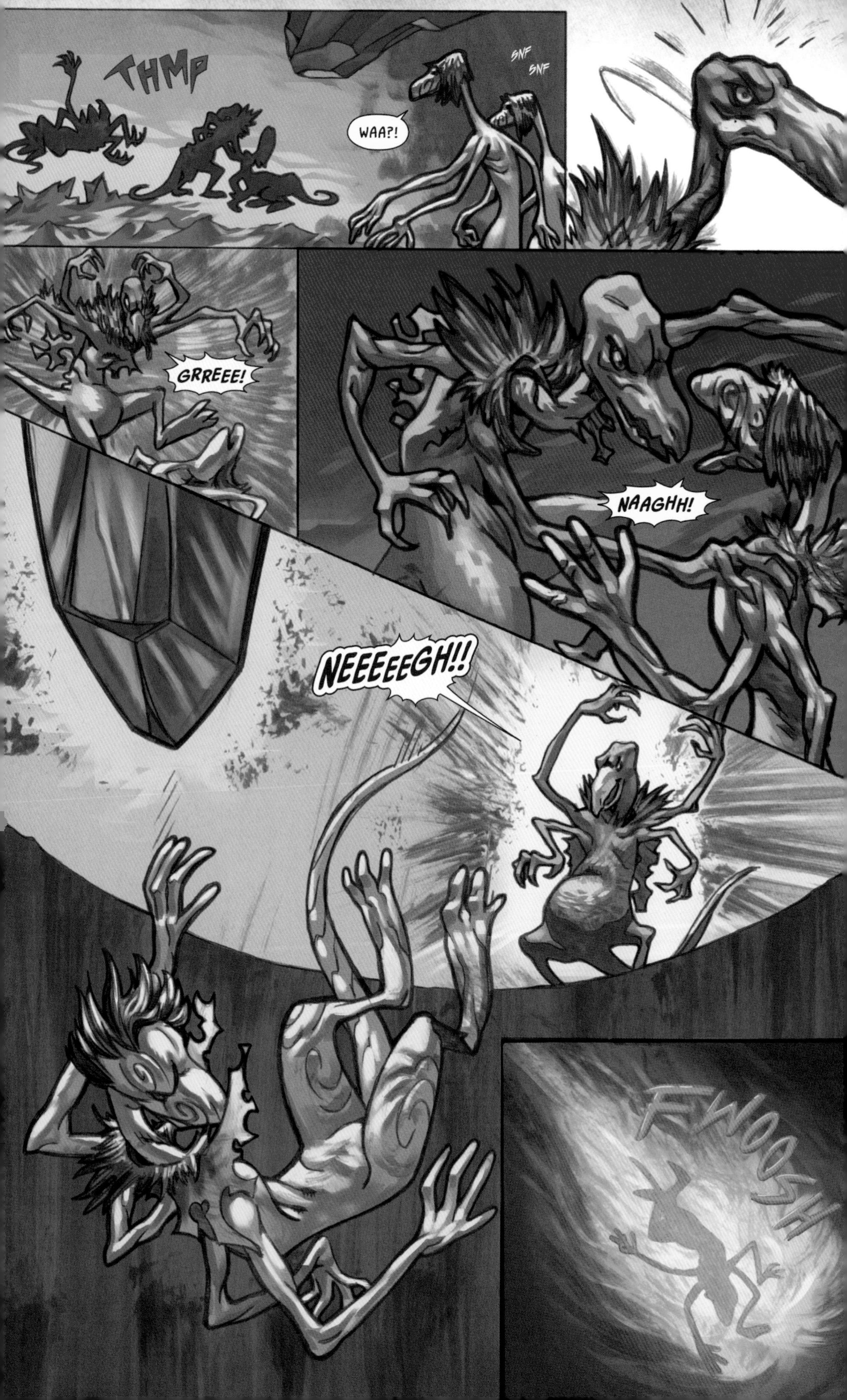
THMP
SNF
SNF
WAA?!
GRREEE!
NAAGHH!
NEEEEEGH!!
FWOOSH

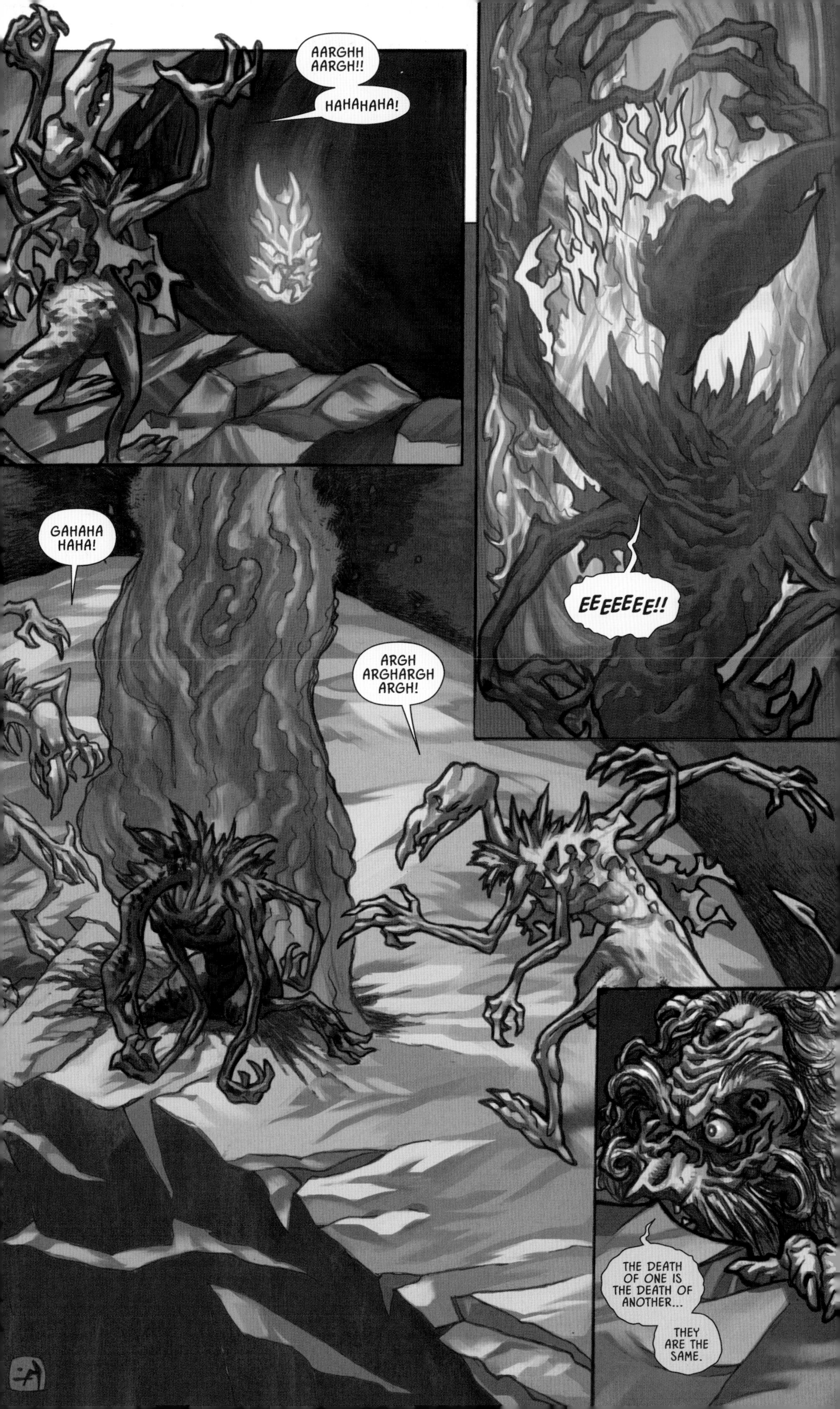
AARGHH AARGH!!
HAHAHAHA!
EEEEEEE!!
GAHAHA HAHA!
ARGH ARGHARGH ARGH!
THE DEATH OF ONE IS THE DEATH OF ANOTHER...
THEY ARE THE SAME.

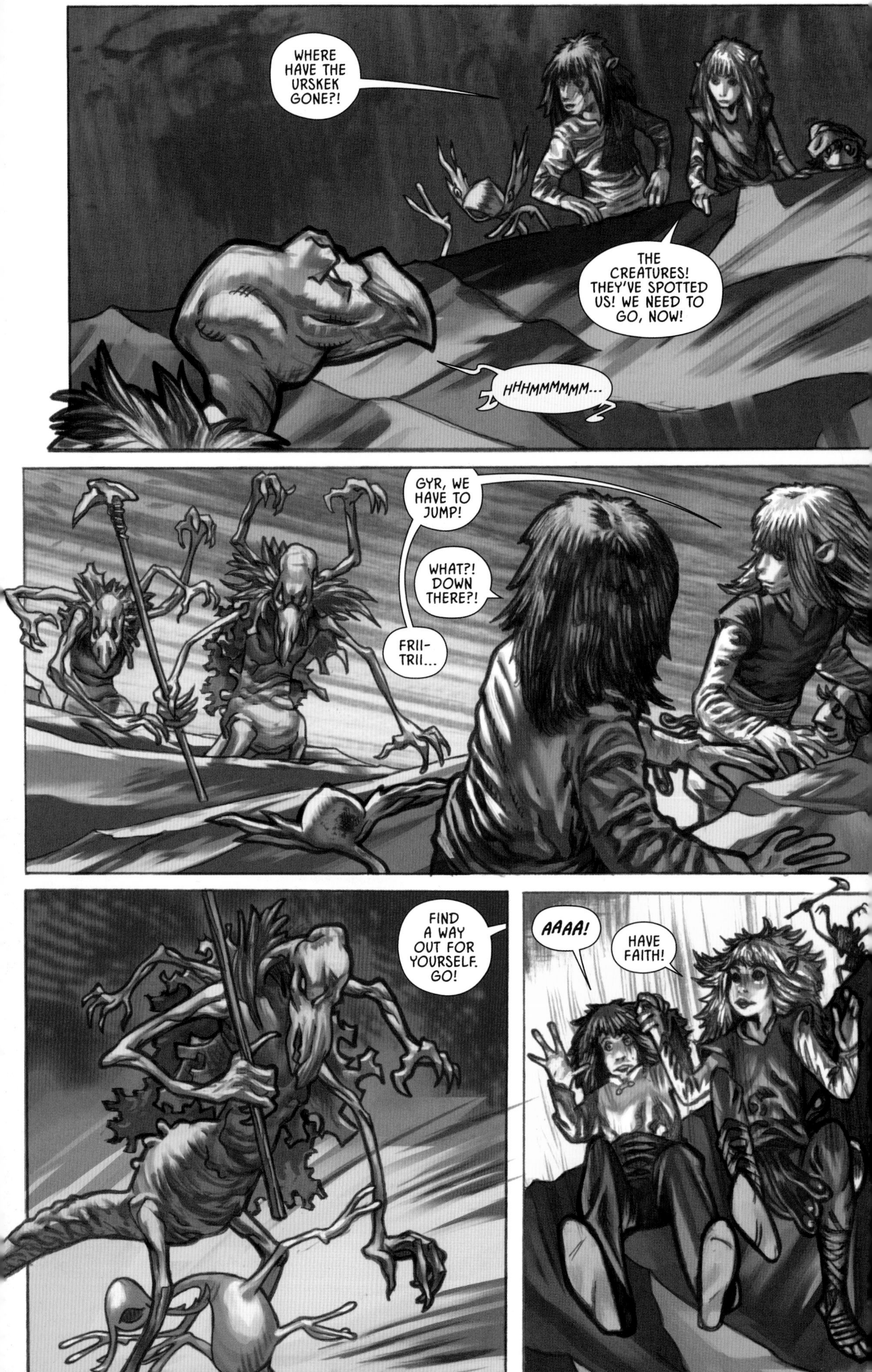
WHERE HAVE THE URSKEK GONE?!
THE CREATURES! THEY'VE SPOTTED US! WE NEED TO GO, NOW!
HHHMMMMMM...
GYR, WE HAVE TO JUMP!
WHAT?! DOWN THERE?!
FRII-TRII...
FIND A WAY OUT FOR YOURSELF. GO!
AAAA!
HAVE FAITH!

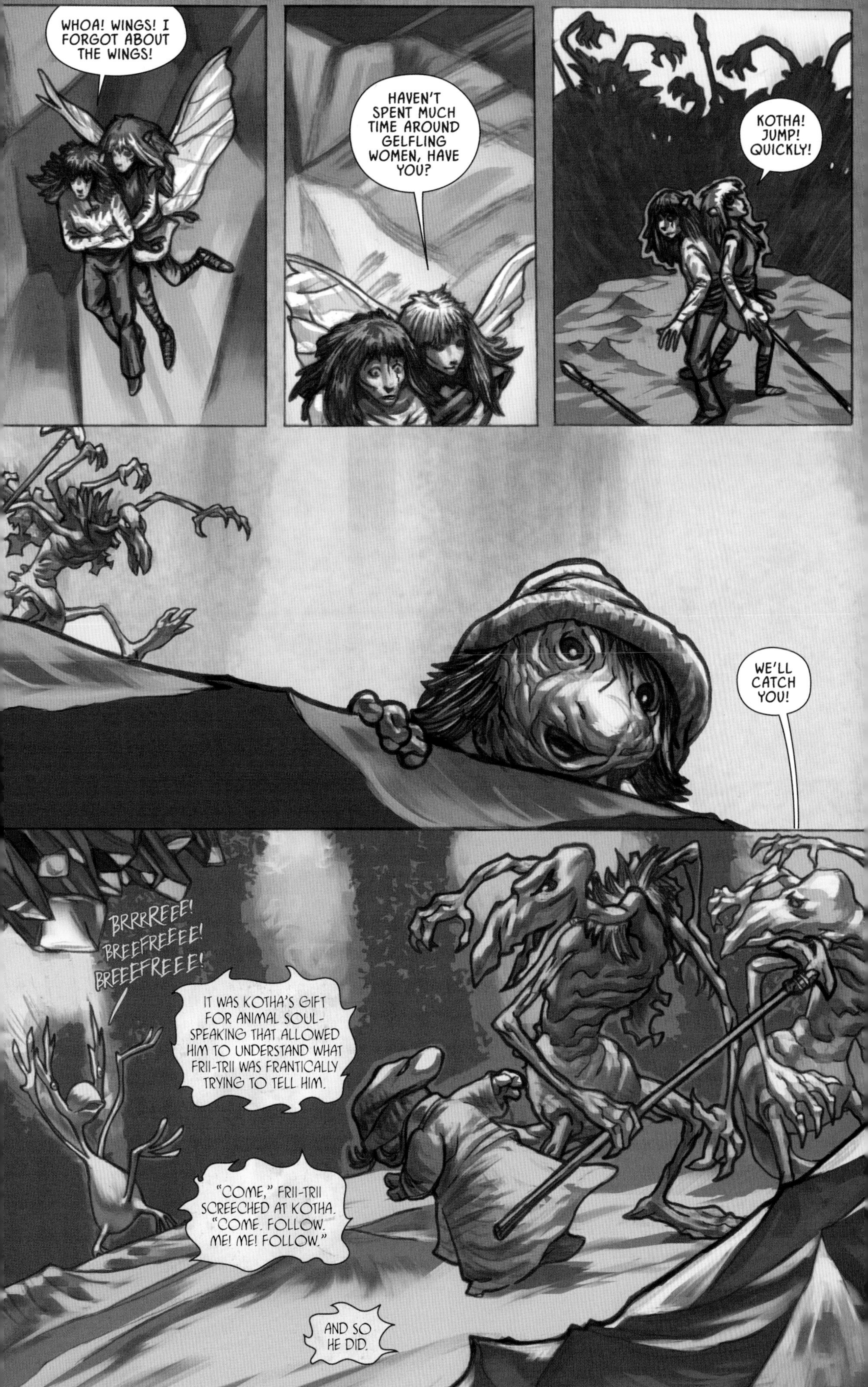

WHOA! WINGS! I FORGOT ABOUT THE WINGS!
HAVEN'T SPENT MUCH TIME AROUND GELFLING WOMEN, HAVE YOU?
KOTHA! JUMP! QUICKLY!
WE'LL CATCH YOU!
BRRRREEE! BREEFREEEE! BREEEFREEE!
IT WAS KOTHA'S GIFT FOR ANIMAL SOUL-SPEAKING THAT ALLOWED HIM TO UNDERSTAND WHAT FRII-TRII WAS FRANTICALLY TRYING TO TELL HIM.
"COME," FRII-TRII SCREECHED AT KOTHA. "COME. FOLLOW. ME! ME! FOLLOW."
AND SO HE DID.

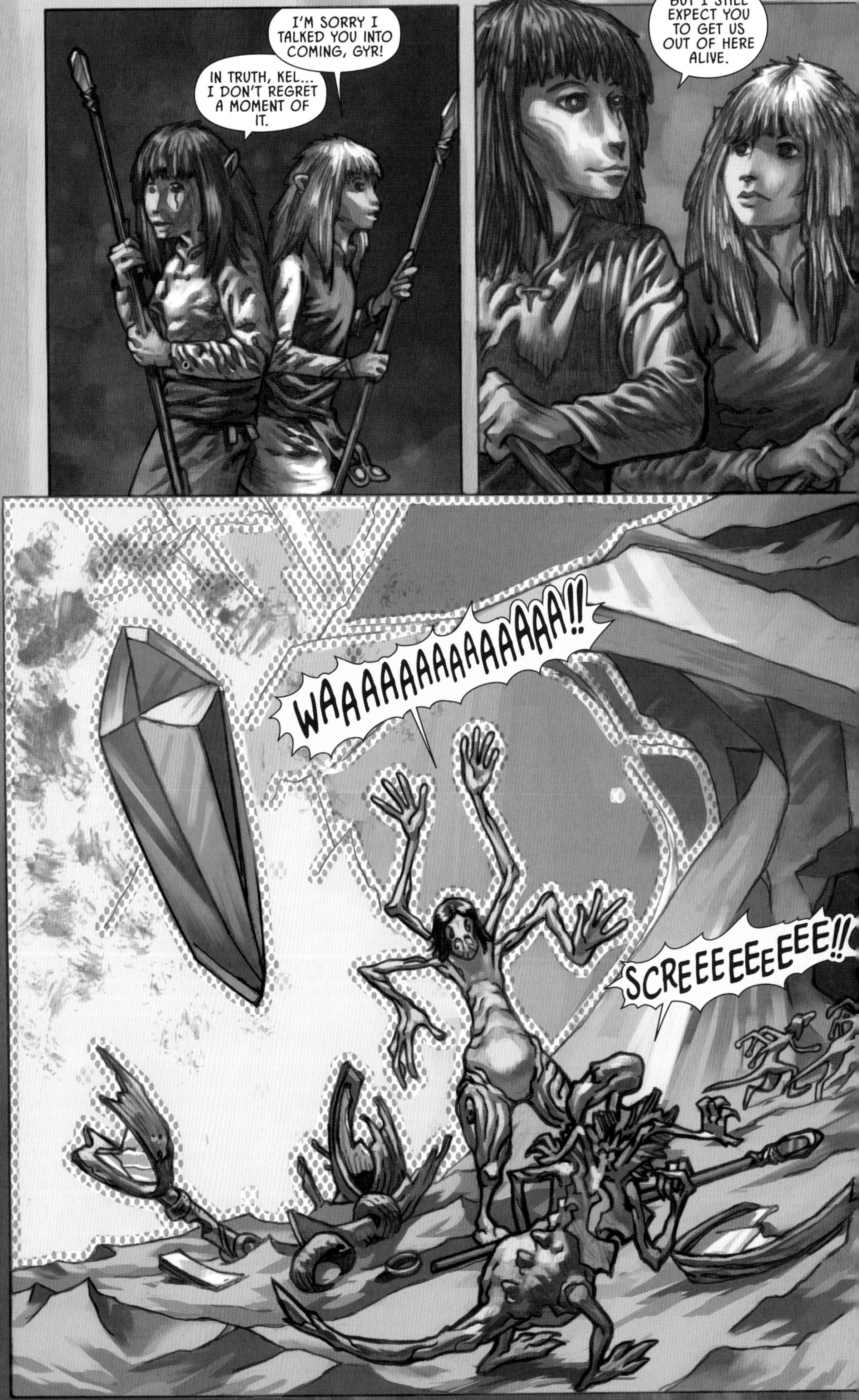
I'M SORRY I TALKED YOU INTO COMING, GYR!
IN TRUTH, KEL... I DON'T REGRET A MOMENT OF IT.
BUT I STILL EXPECT YOU TO GET US OUT OF HERE ALIVE.
WAAAAAAAAAAAAAA!!
SCREEEEEEEEEE!!

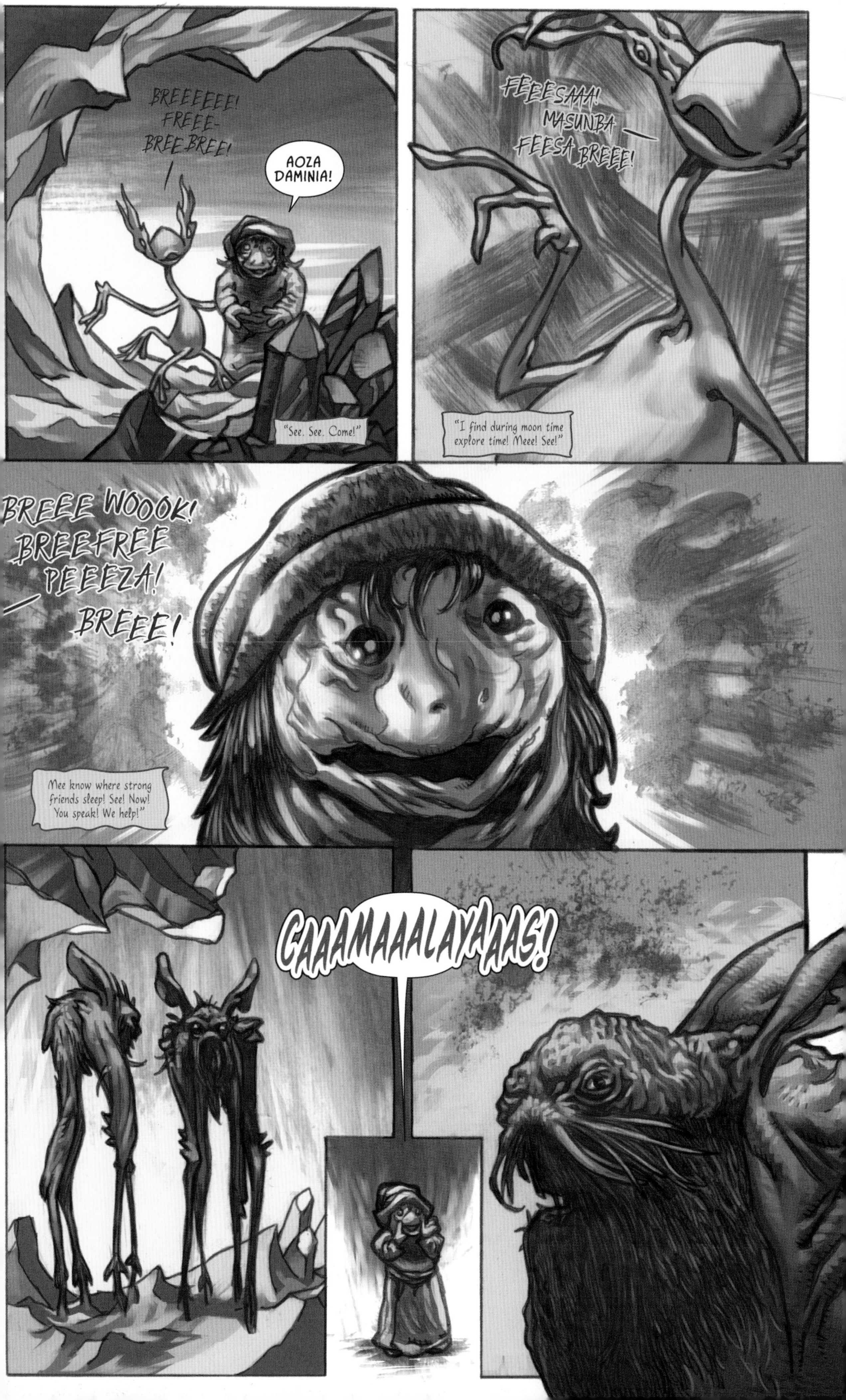
BREEEEEEE! FREEE- BREE BREE!
AOZA DAMINIA!
"See. See. Come!"
FEEESAAA! MASUNBA FEESA BREEE!
"I find during moon time explore time! Meee! See!"
BREEE WOOOK! BREEFREE PEEEZA! BREEE!
Mee know where strong friends sleep! See! Now! You speak! We help!"
CAAAMAAALAYAAAS!

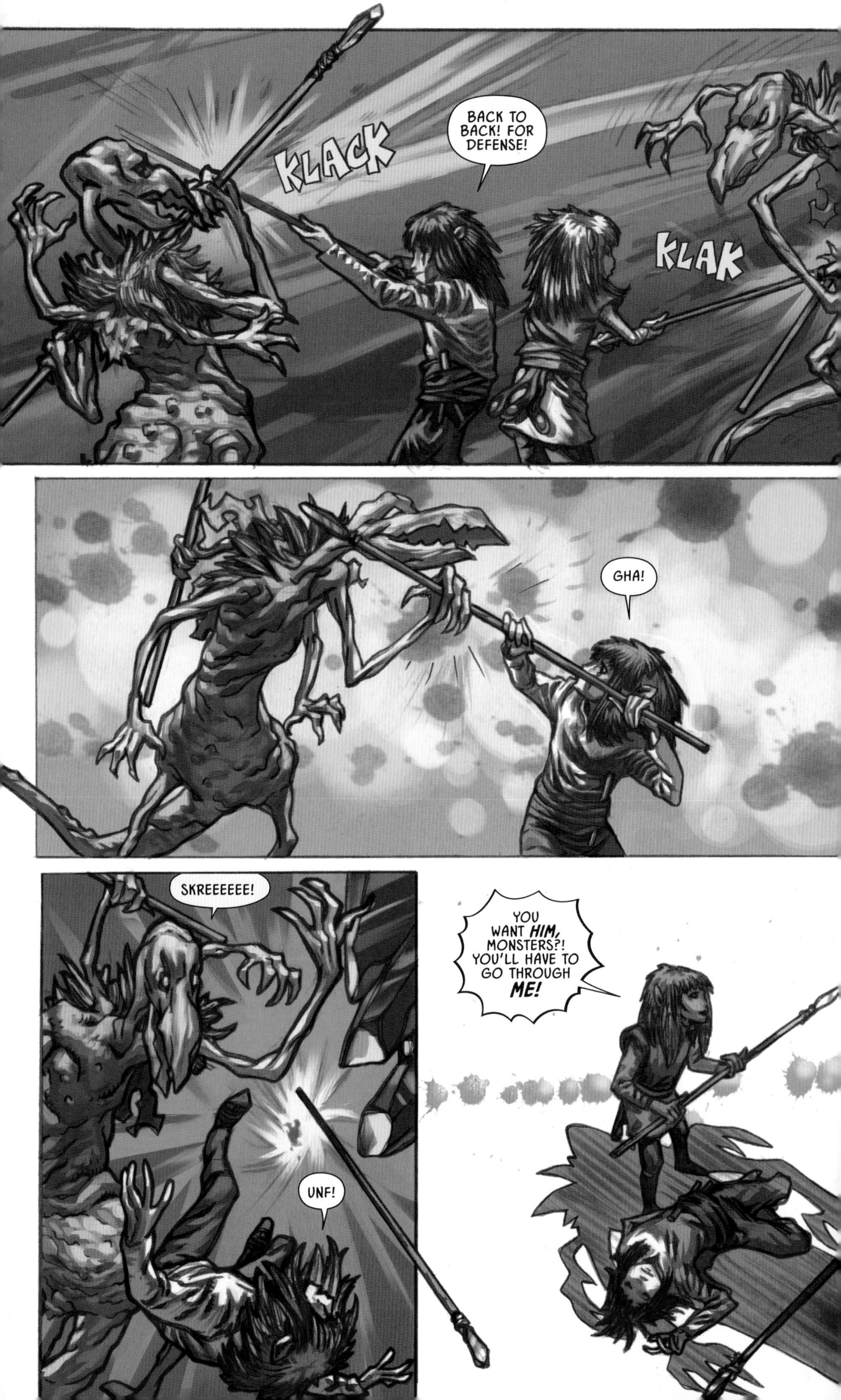
KLACK
BACK TO BACK! FOR DEFENSE!
KLAK
GHA!
SKREEEEEEE!
UNF!
YOU WANT HIM, MONSTERS?! YOU'LL HAVE TO GO THROUGH ME!

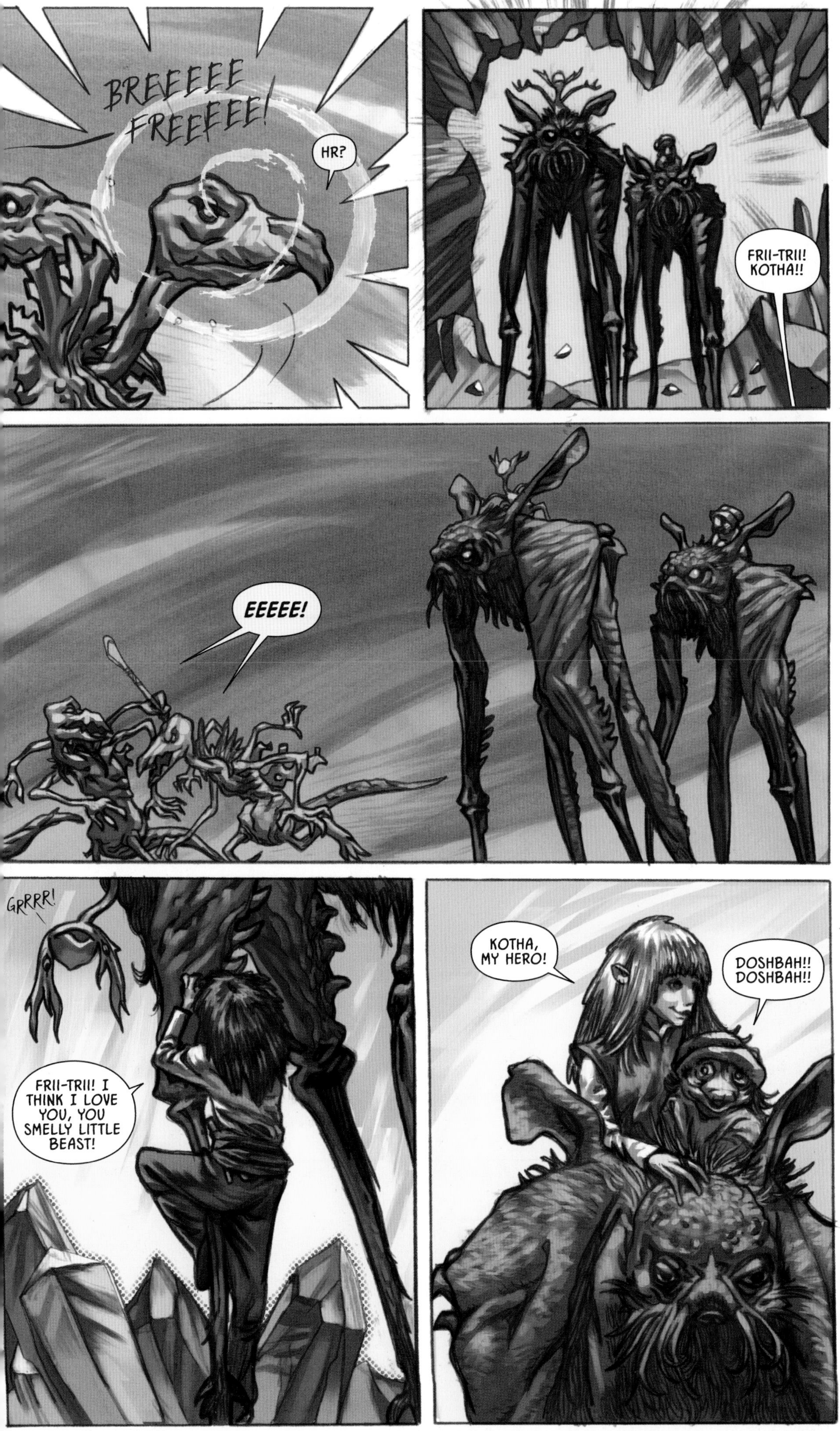
BREEEEE FREEEEE!
HR?
FRII-TRII! KOTHA!!
EEEEE!
GRRRR!
FRII-TRII! I THINK I LOVE YOU, YOU SMELLY LITTLE BEAST!
KOTHA, MY HERO!
DOSHBAH!! DOSHBAH!!

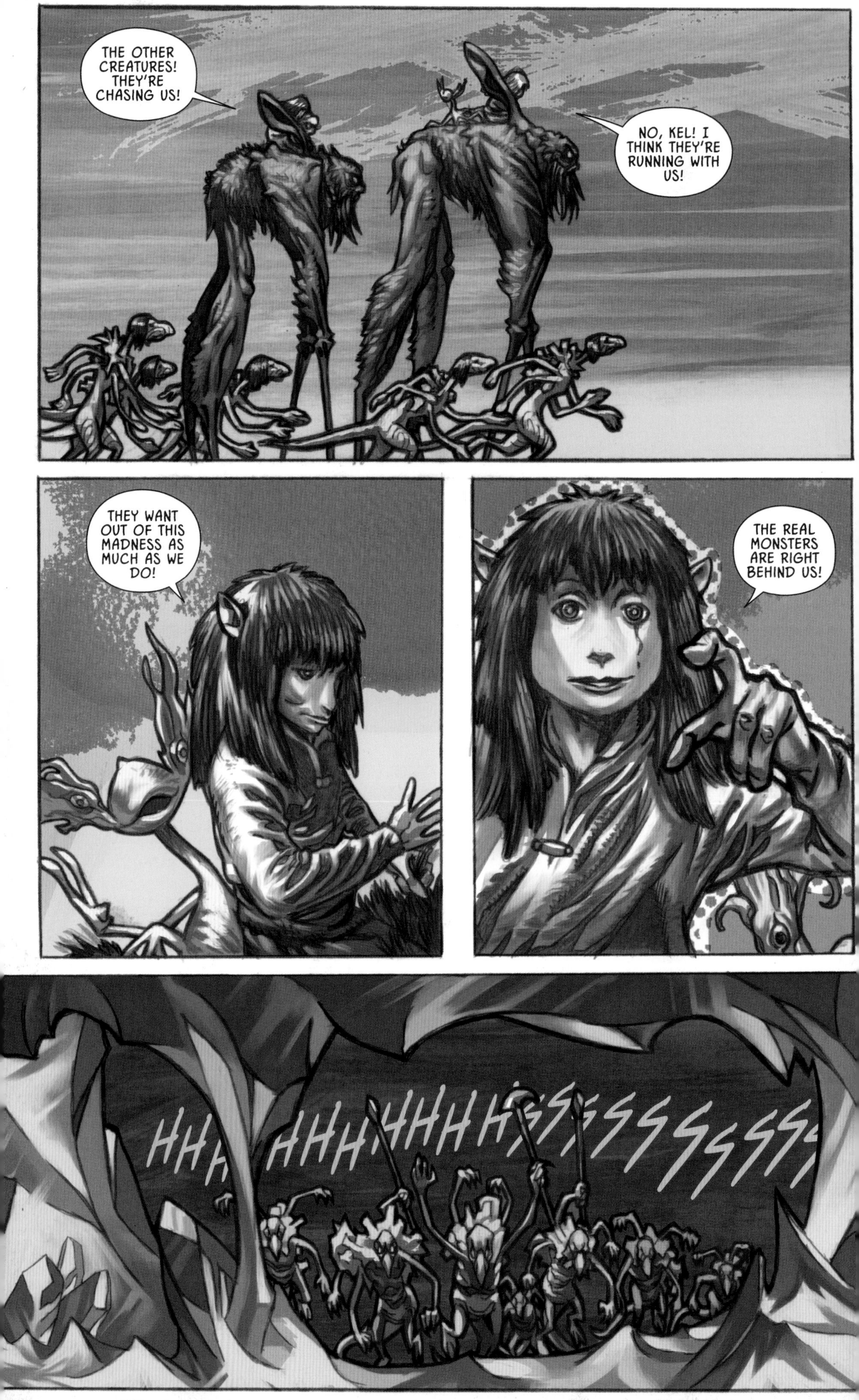
THE OTHER CREATURES! THEY'RE CHASING US!
NO, KEL! I THINK THEY'RE RUNNING WITH US!
THEY WANT OUT OF THIS MADNESS AS MUCH AS WE DO!
THE REAL MONSTERS ARE RIGHT BEHIND US!
HHHHHHHHHHSSSSSSSSSSS

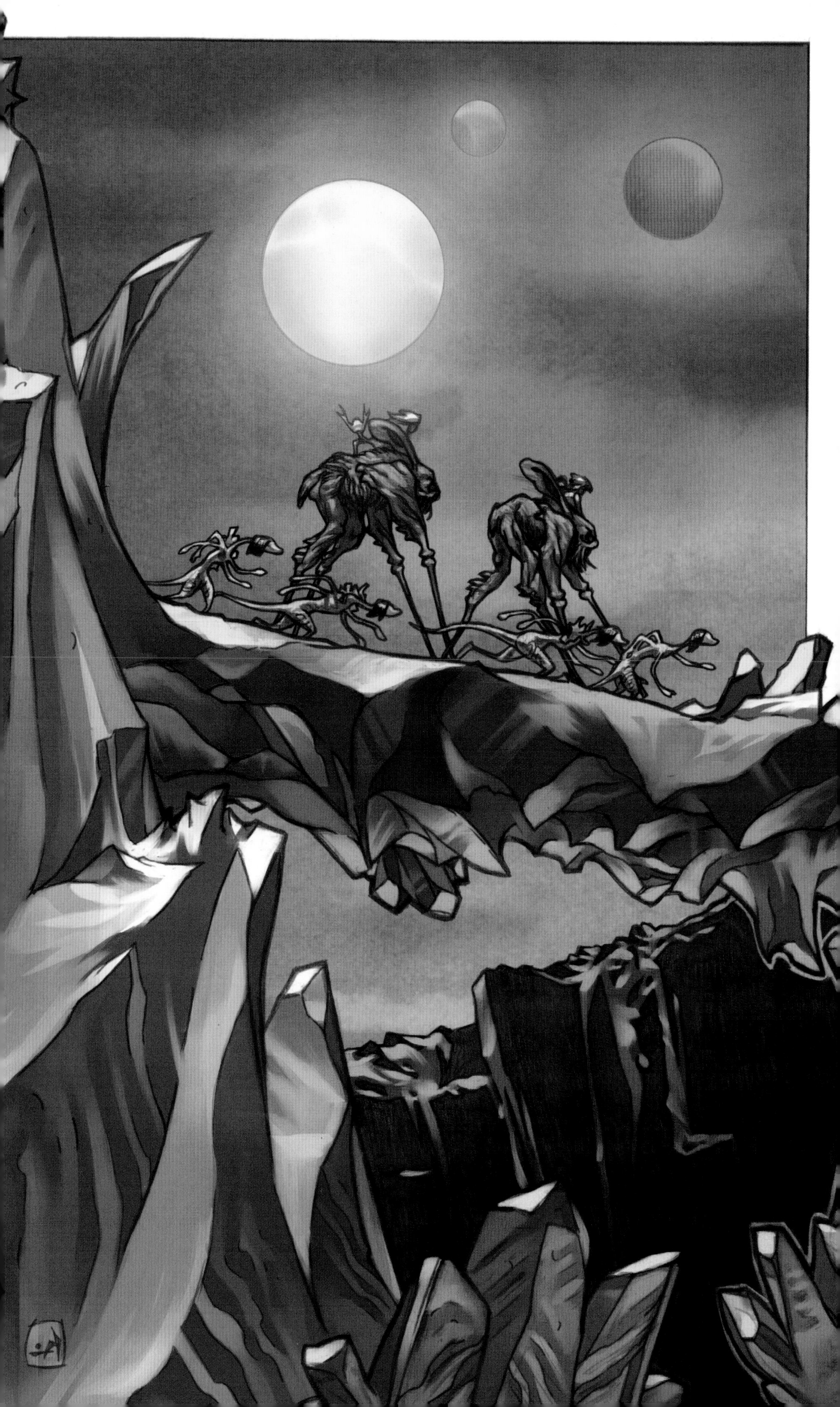

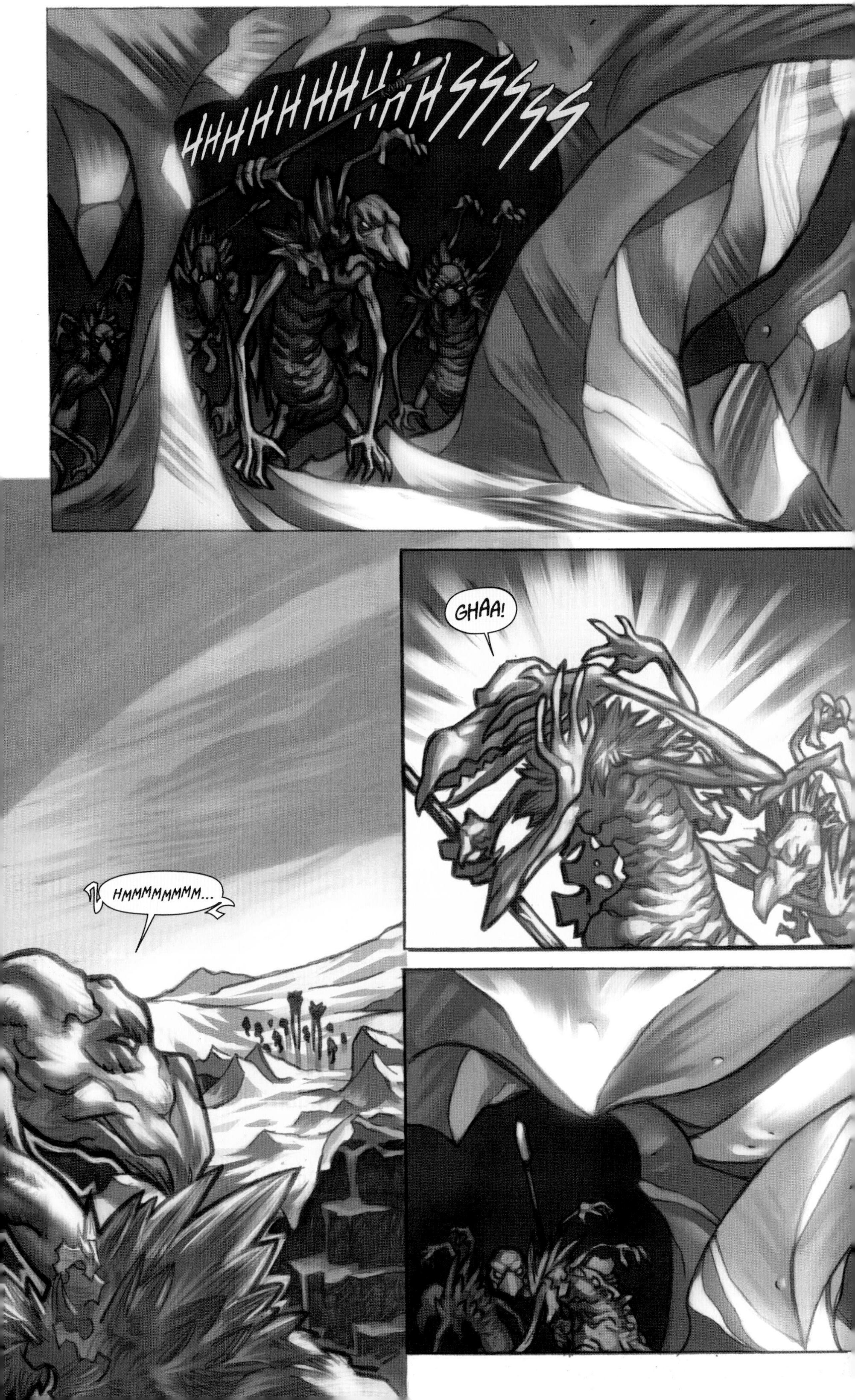
HHHHHHHH...HHHSSSSSS
GHAA!
HMMMMMMMM...

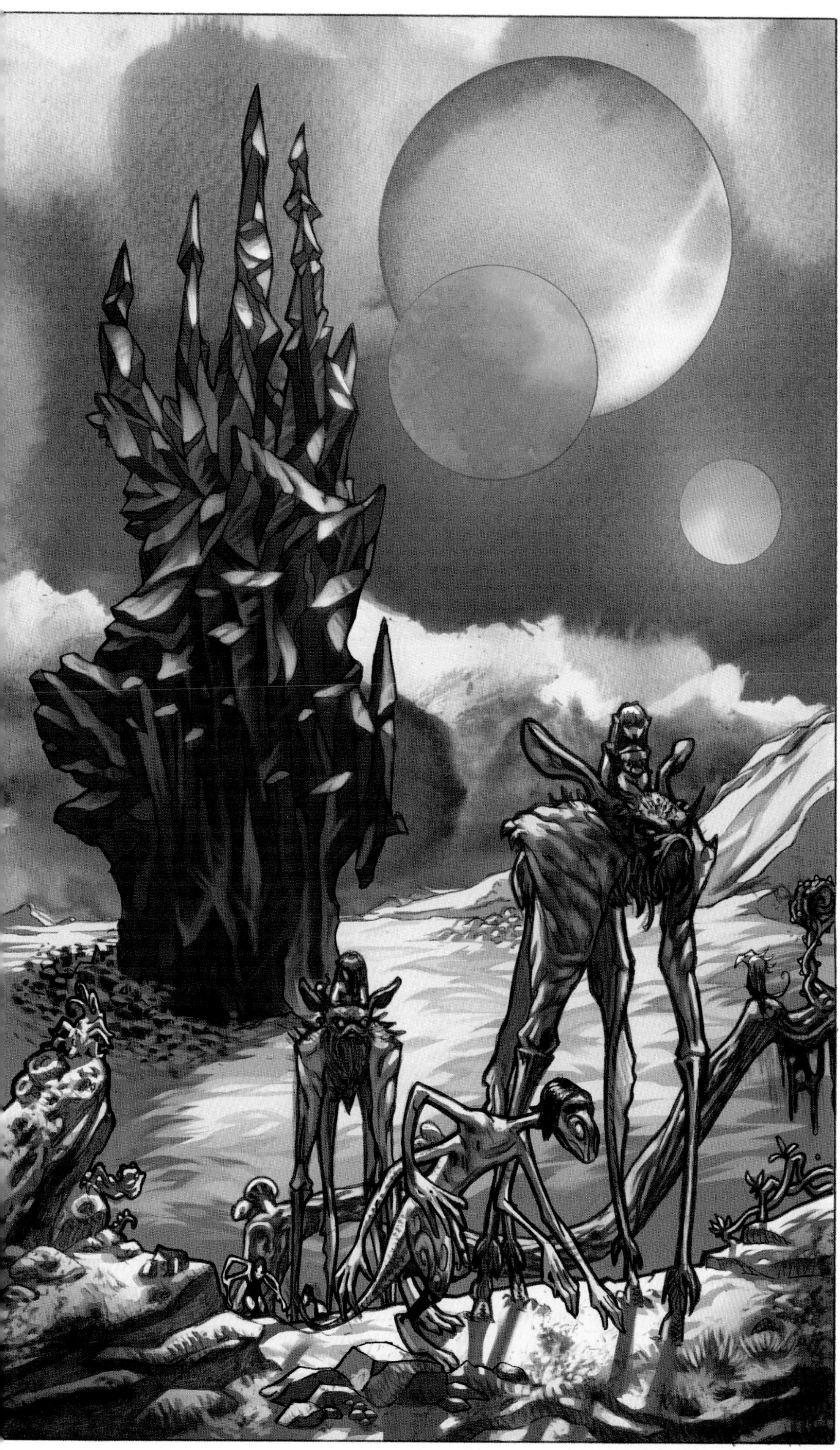

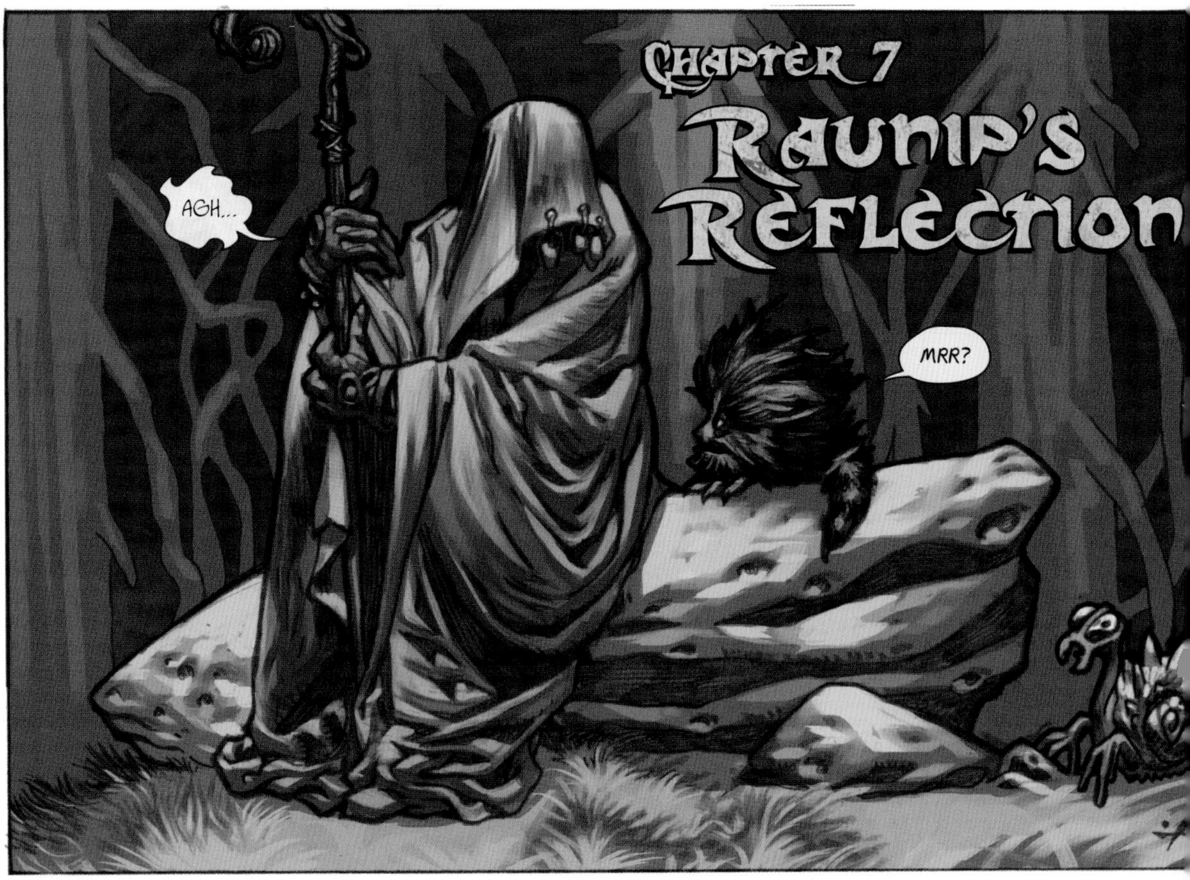
CHAPTER 7
RAUNIP'S REFLECTION
AGH...
MRR?

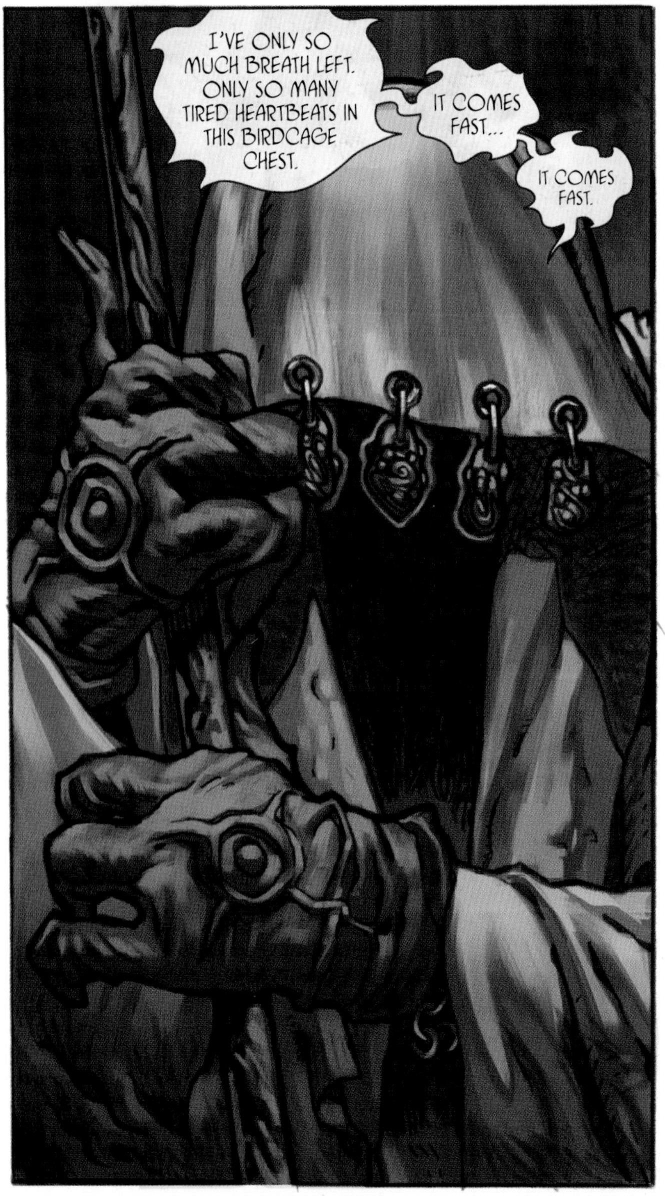
I'VE ONLY SO MUCH BREATH LEFT. ONLY SO MANY TIRED HEARTBEATS IN THIS BIRDCAGE CHEST.
IT COMES FAST...
IT COMES FAST.

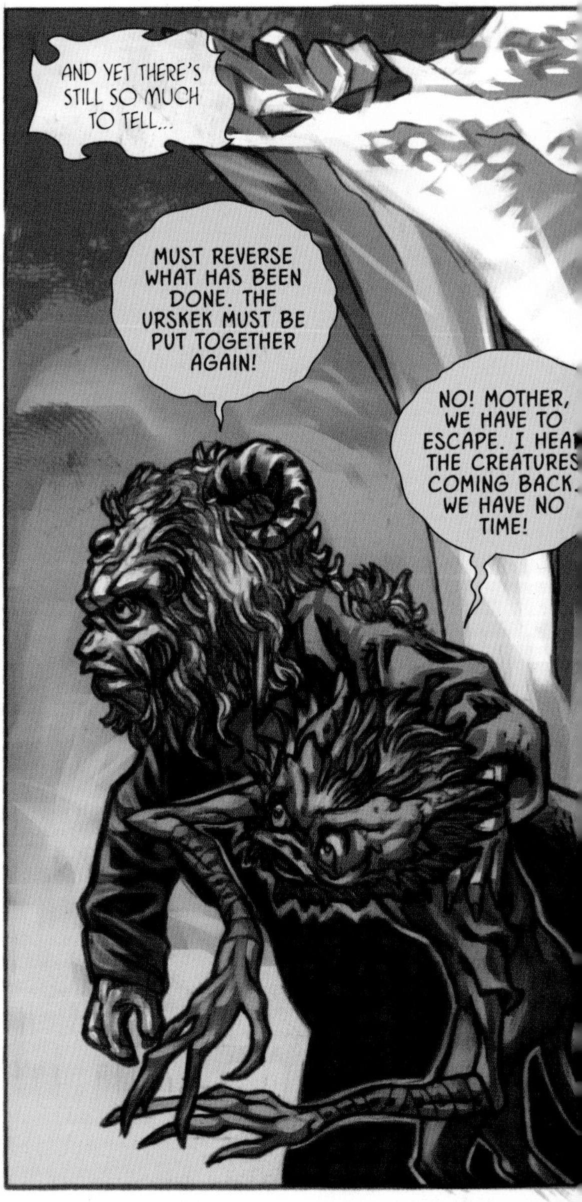
AND YET THERE'S STILL SO MUCH TO TELL...
MUST REVERSE WHAT HAS BEEN DONE. THE URSKEK MUST BE PUT TOGETHER AGAIN!
NO! MOTHER, WE HAVE TO ESCAPE. I HEA THE CREATURES COMING BACK. WE HAVE NO TIME!

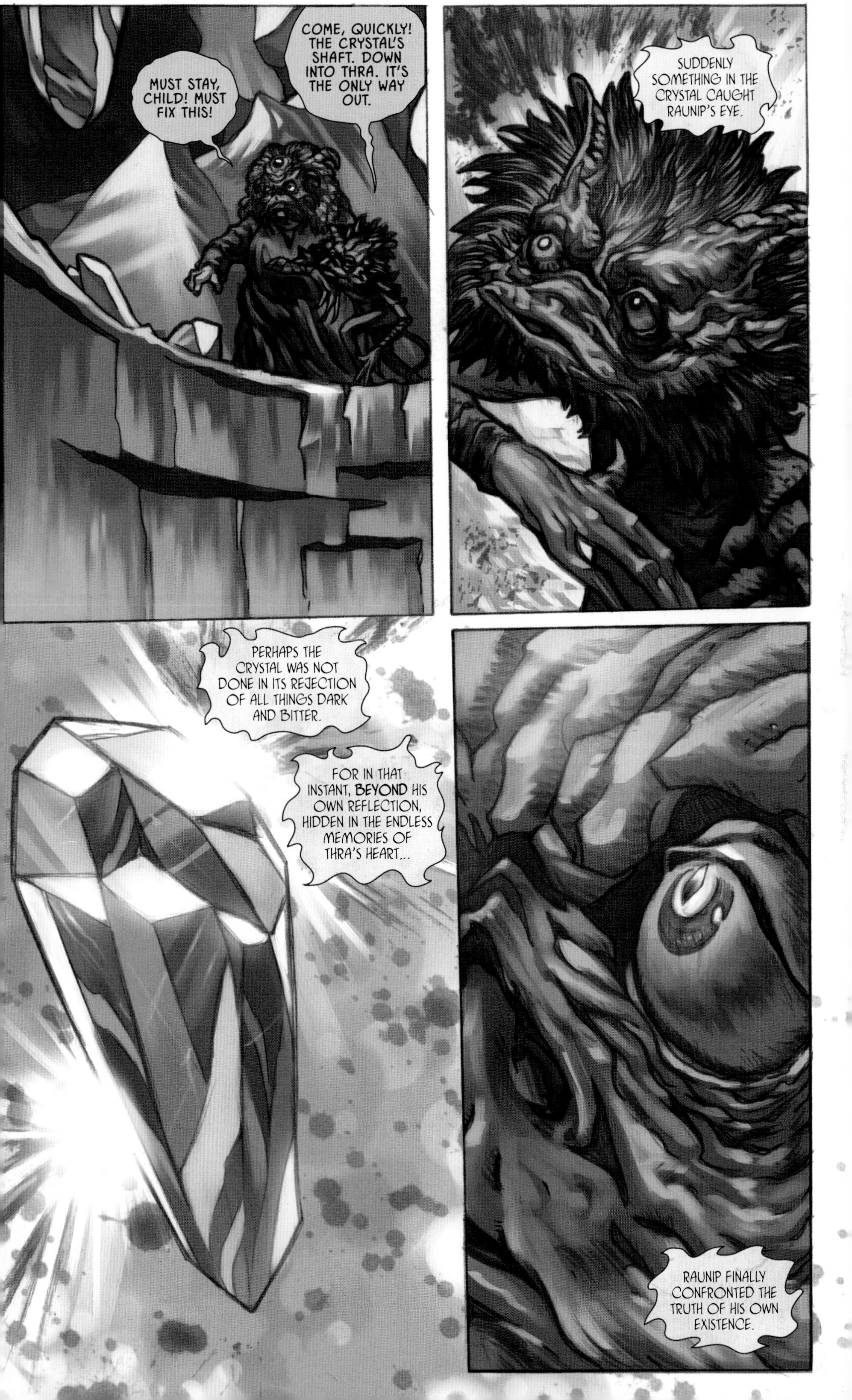
COME, QUICKLY! THE CRYSTAL'S SHAFT. DOWN INTO THRA. IT'S THE ONLY WAY OUT.
MUST STAY, CHILD! MUST FIX THIS!
SUDDENLY SOMETHING IN THE CRYSTAL CAUGHT RAUNIP'S EYE.
PERHAPS THE CRYSTAL WAS NOT DONE IN ITS REJECTION OF ALL THINGS DARK AND BITTER.
FOR IN THAT INSTANT, BEYOND HIS OWN REFLECTION, HIDDEN IN THE ENDLESS MEMORIES OF THRA'S HEART...
RAUNIP FINALLY CONFRONTED THE TRUTH OF HIS OWN EXISTENCE.

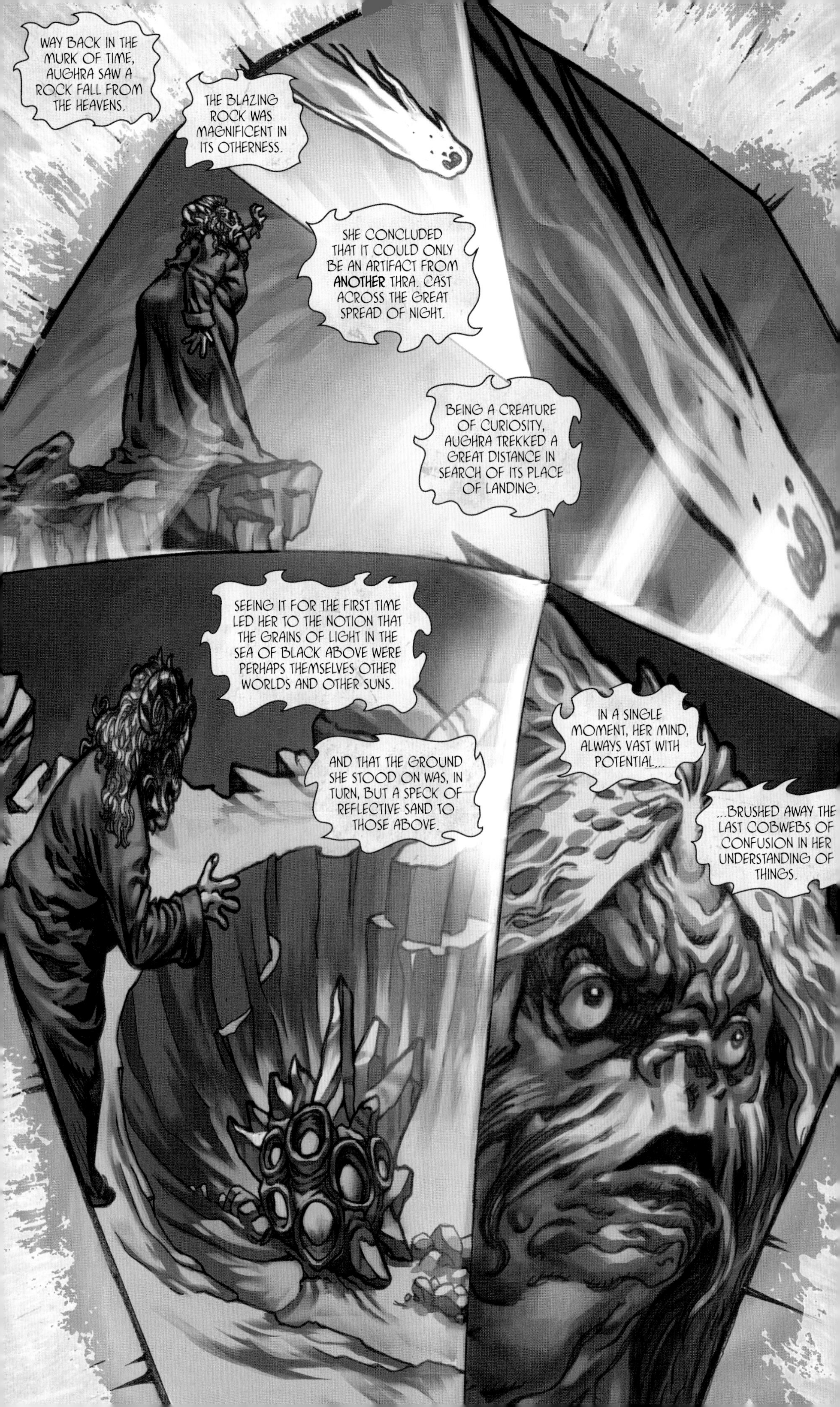

WAY BACK IN THE MURK OF TIME, AUGHRA SAW A ROCK FALL FROM THE HEAVENS.
THE BLAZING ROCK WAS MAGNIFICENT IN ITS OTHERNESS.
SHE CONCLUDED THAT IT COULD ONLY BE AN ARTIFACT FROM ANOTHER THRA. CAST ACROSS THE GREAT SPREAD OF NIGHT.
BEING A CREATURE OF CURIOSITY, AUGHRA TREKKED A GREAT DISTANCE IN SEARCH OF ITS PLACE OF LANDING.
SEEING IT FOR THE FIRST TIME LED HER TO THE NOTION THAT THE GRAINS OF LIGHT IN THE SEA OF BLACK ABOVE WERE PERHAPS THEMSELVES OTHER WORLDS AND OTHER SUNS.
AND THAT THE GROUND SHE STOOD ON WAS, IN TURN, BUT A SPECK OF REFLECTIVE SAND TO THOSE ABOVE.
IN A SINGLE MOMENT, HER MIND, ALWAYS VAST WITH POTENTIAL...
...BRUSHED AWAY THE LAST COBWEBS OF CONFUSION IN HER UNDERSTANDING OF THINGS.

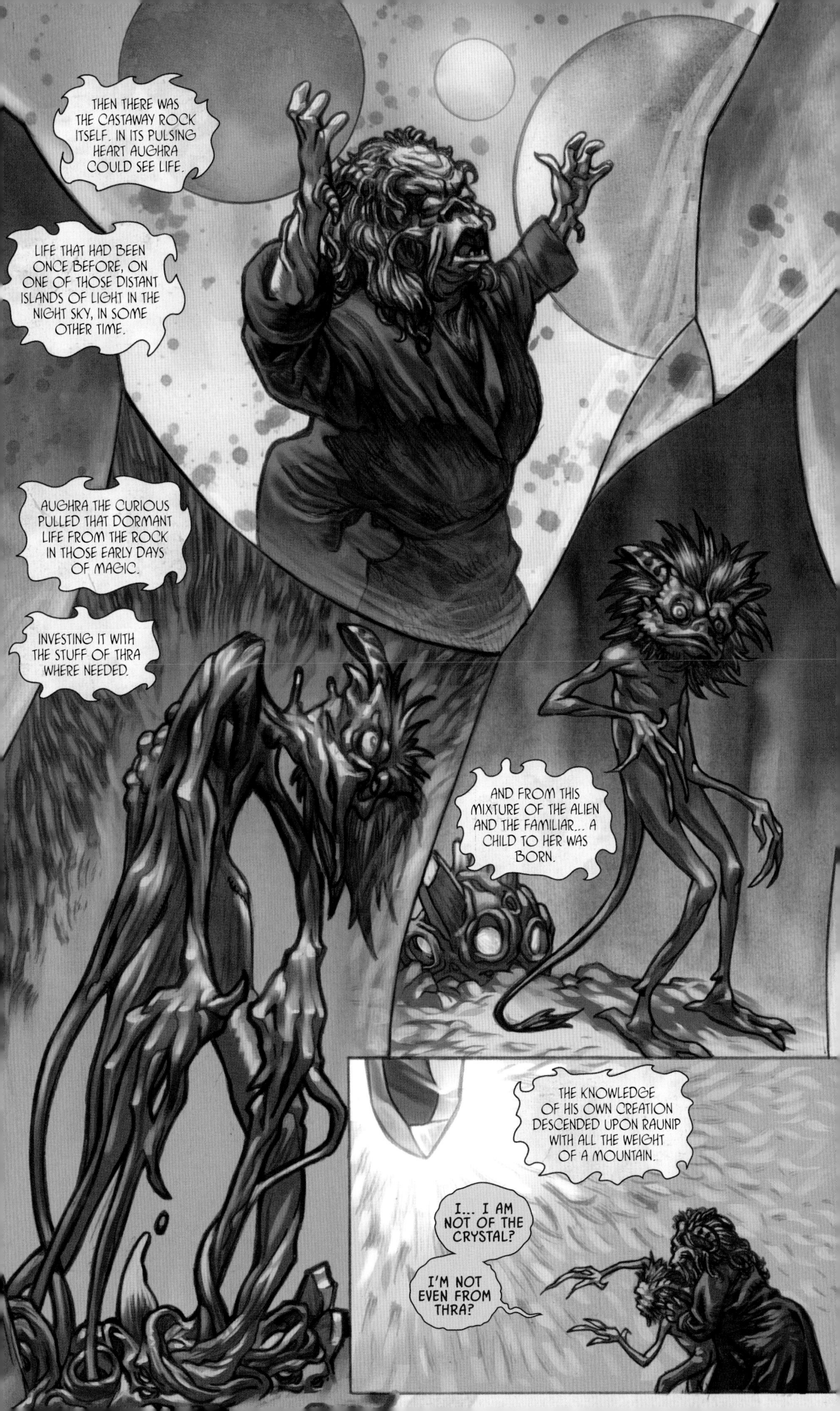
THEN THERE WAS THE CASTAWAY ROCK ITSELF. IN ITS PULSING HEART AUGHRA COULD SEE LIFE.
LIFE THAT HAD BEEN ONCE BEFORE, ON ONE OF THOSE DISTANT ISLANDS OF LIGHT IN THE NIGHT SKY, IN SOME OTHER TIME.
AUGHRA THE CURIOUS PULLED THAT DORMANT LIFE FROM THE ROCK IN THOSE EARLY DAYS OF MAGIC.
INVESTING IT WITH THE STUFF OF THRA WHERE NEEDED.
AND FROM THIS MIXTURE OF THE ALIEN AND THE FAMILIAR... A CHILD TO HER WAS BORN.
THE KNOWLEDGE OF HIS OWN CREATION DESCENDED UPON RAUNIP WITH ALL THE WEIGHT OF A MOUNTAIN.
I... I AM NOT OF THE CRYSTAL?
I'M NOT EVEN FROM THRA?

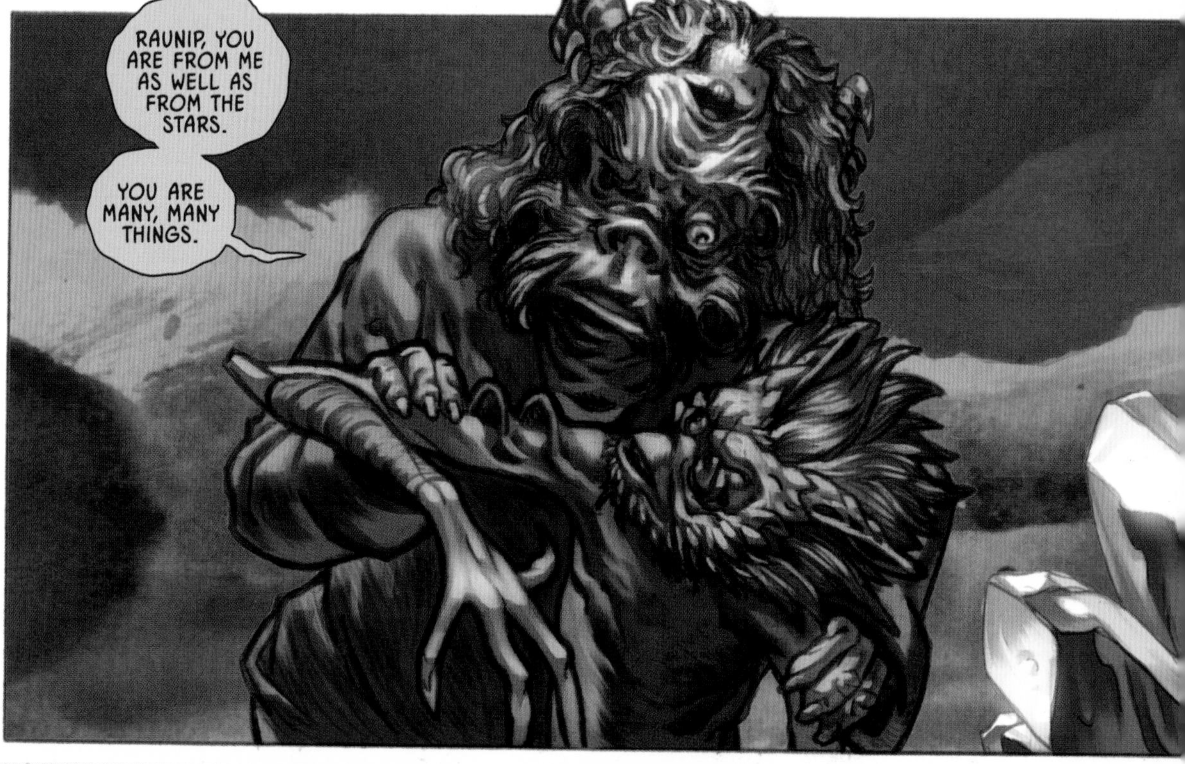
RAUNIP, YOU ARE FROM ME AS WELL AS FROM THE STARS.
YOU ARE MANY, MANY THINGS.

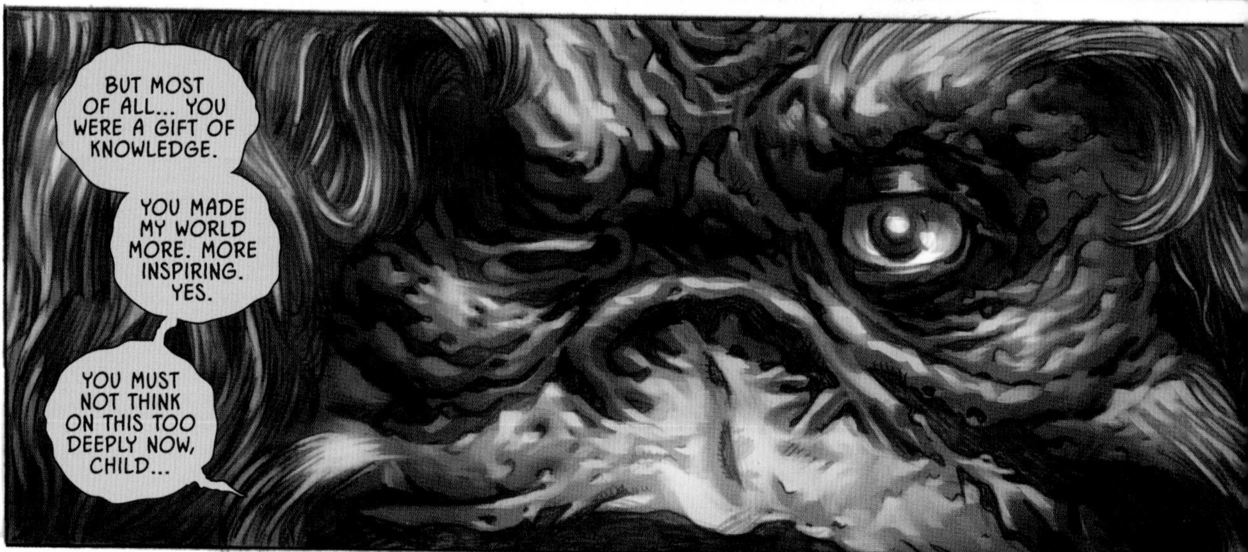
BUT MOST OF ALL... YOU WERE A GIFT OF KNOWLEDGE.
YOU MADE MY WORLD MORE. MORE INSPIRING. YES.
YOU MUST NOT THINK ON THIS TOO DEEPLY NOW, CHILD...

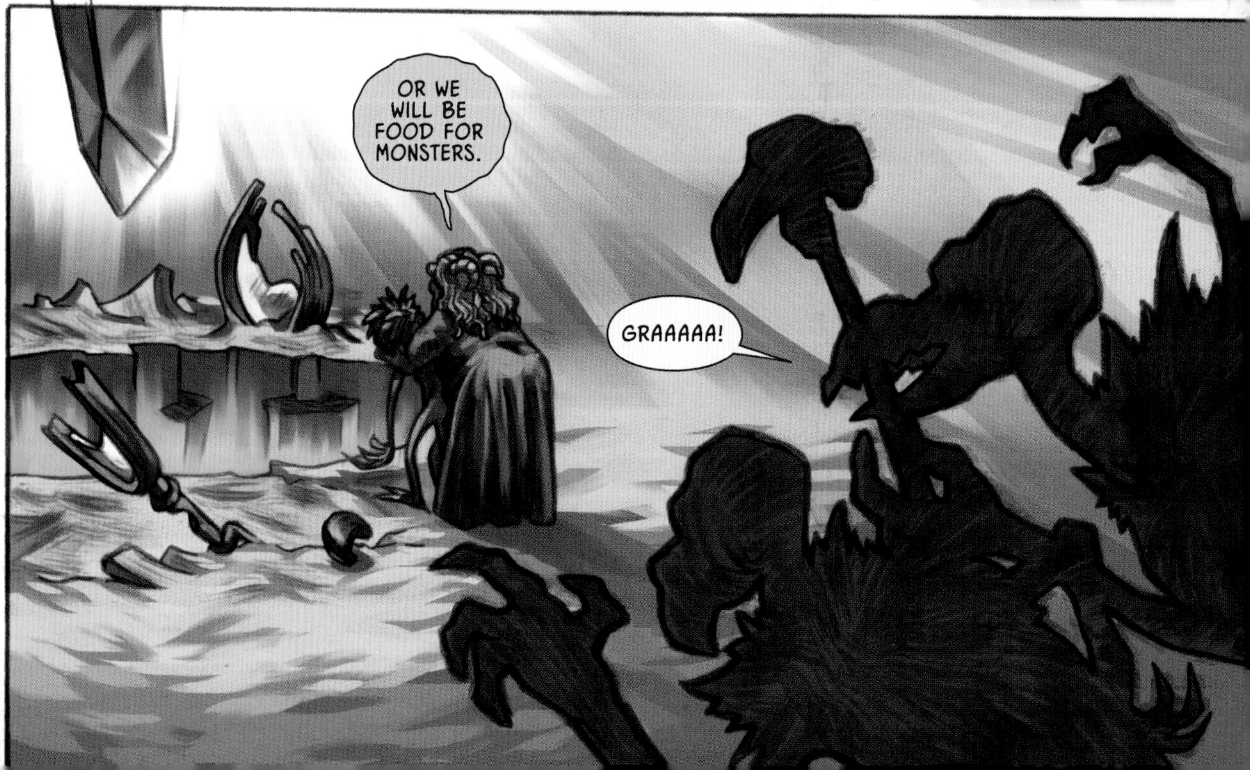
OR WE WILL BE FOOD FOR MONSTERS.
GRAAAAA!

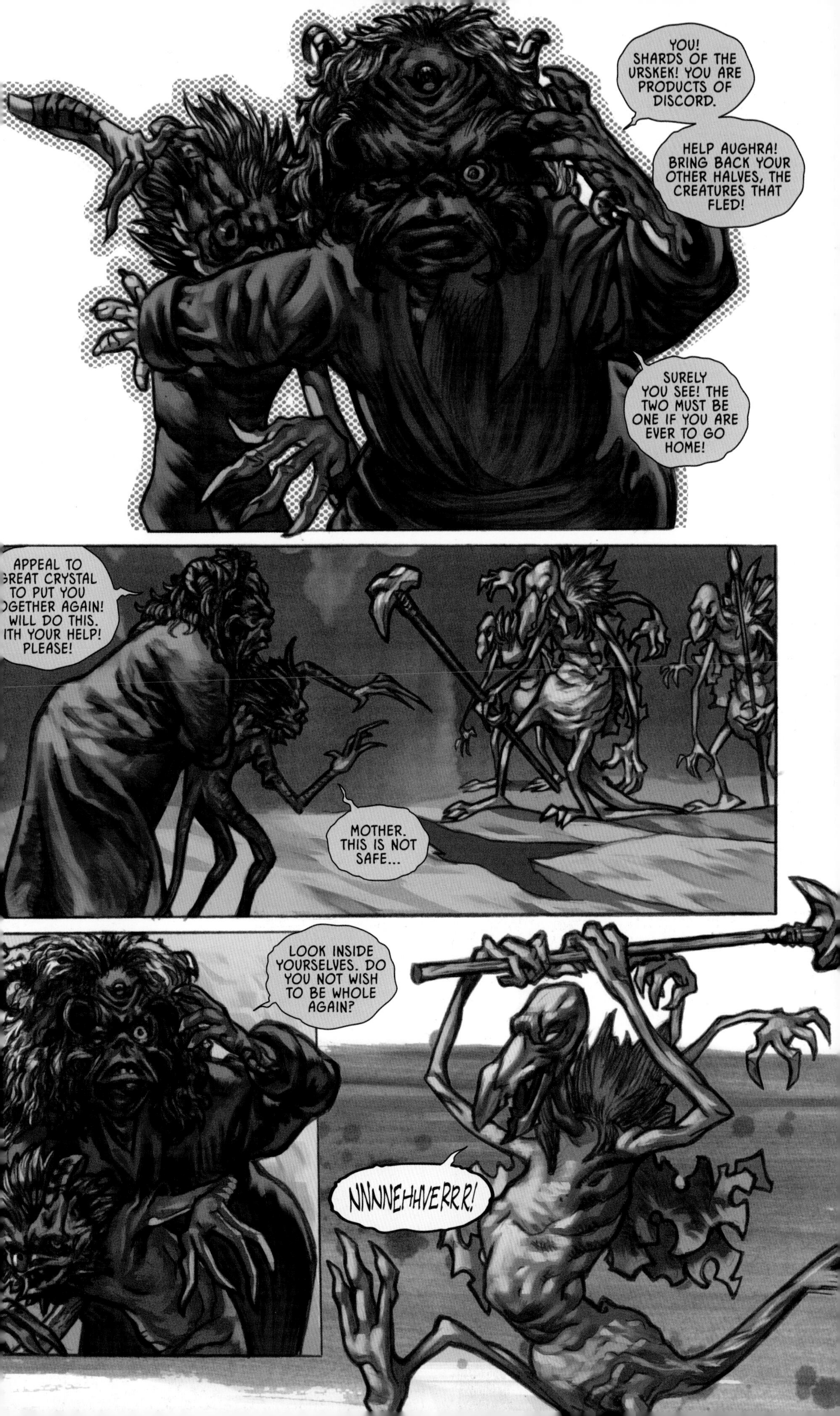
YOU! SHARDS OF THE URSKEK! YOU ARE PRODUCTS OF DISCORD.
HELP AUGHRA! BRING BACK YOUR OTHER HALVES, THE CREATURES THAT FLED!
SURELY YOU SEE! THE TWO MUST BE ONE IF YOU ARE EVER TO GO HOME!
APPEAL TO GREAT CRYSTAL TO PUT YOU OGETHER AGAIN! WILL DO THIS. ITH YOUR HELP! PLEASE!
MOTHER. THIS IS NOT SAFE...
LOOK INSIDE YOURSELVES. DO YOU NOT WISH TO BE WHOLE AGAIN?
NNNNEHHVERRR!

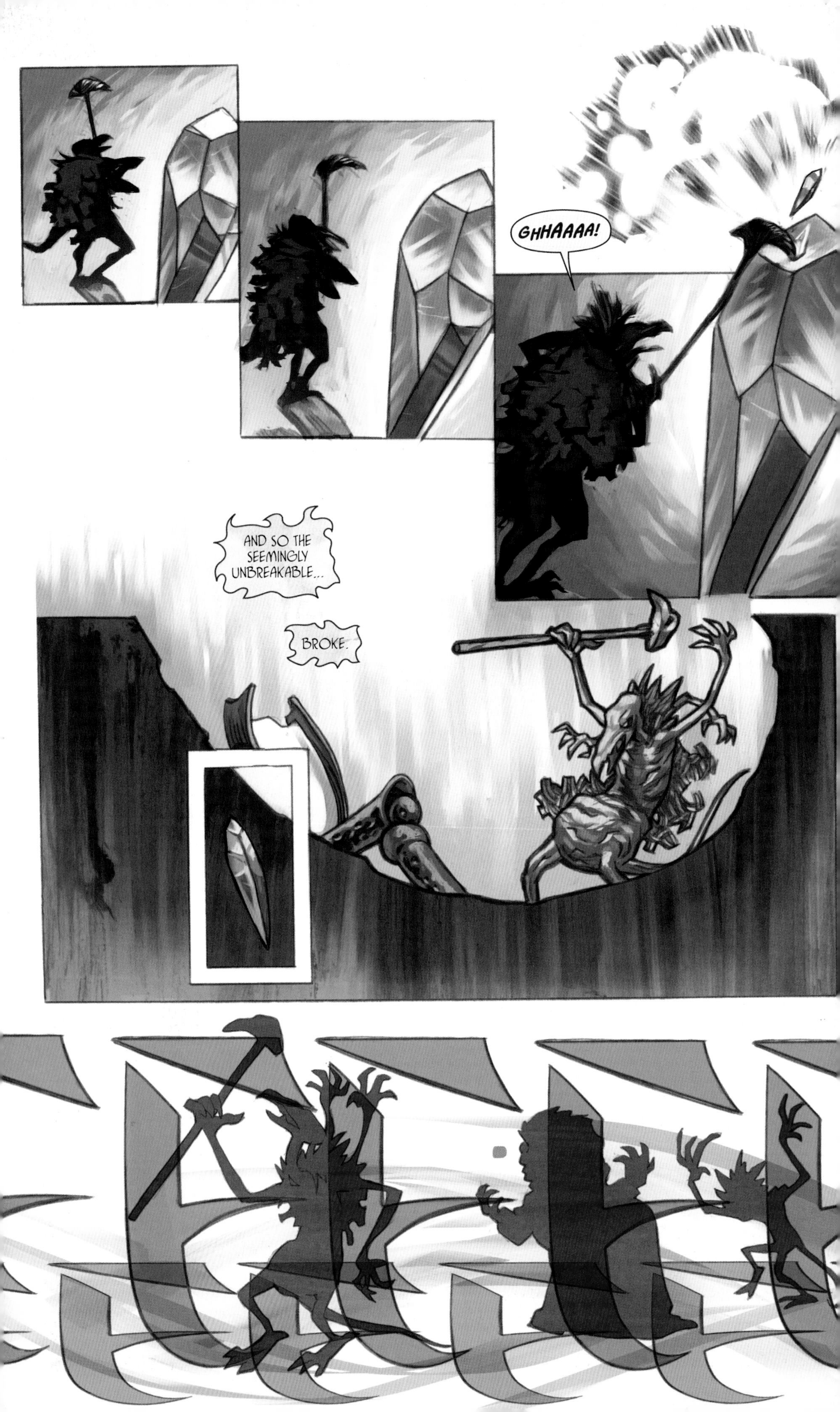
GHHAAAA!
AND SO THE SEEMINGLY UNBREAKABLE...
BROKE.

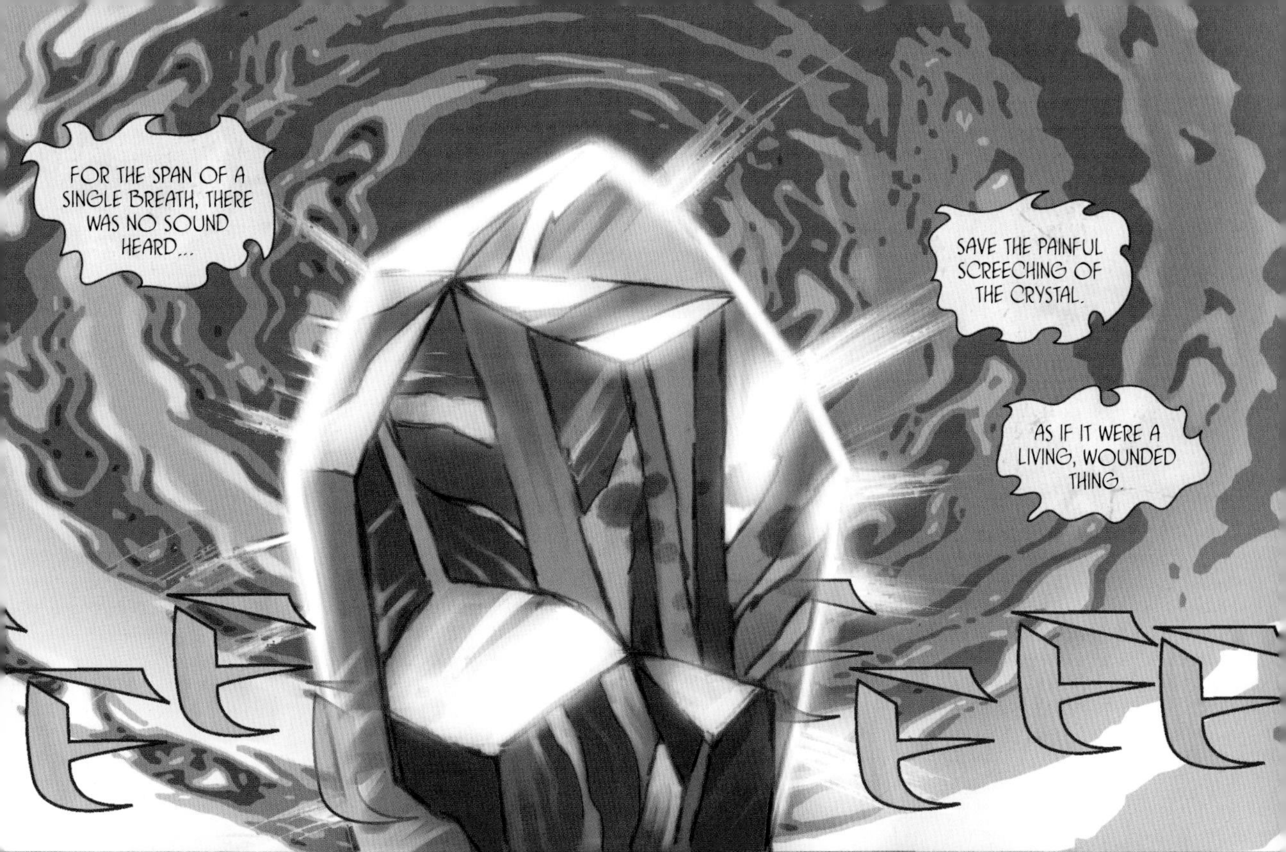
FOR THE SPAN OF A SINGLE BREATH, THERE WAS NO SOUND HEARD...
SAVE THE PAINFUL SCREECHING OF THE CRYSTAL.
AS IF IT WERE A LIVING, WOUNDED THING.

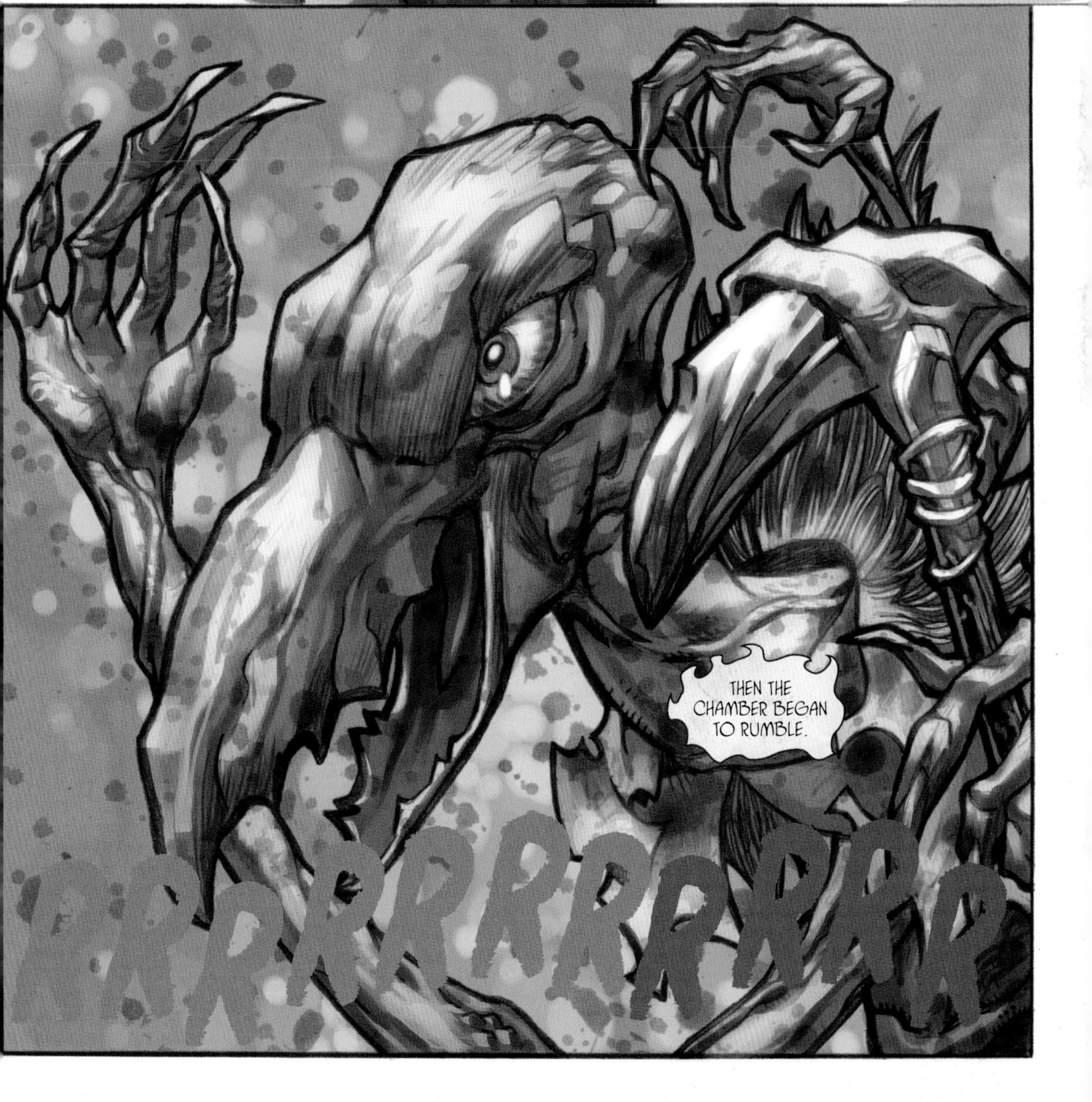
THEN THE CHAMBER BEGAN TO RUMBLE.
RRRRRRRRRRR

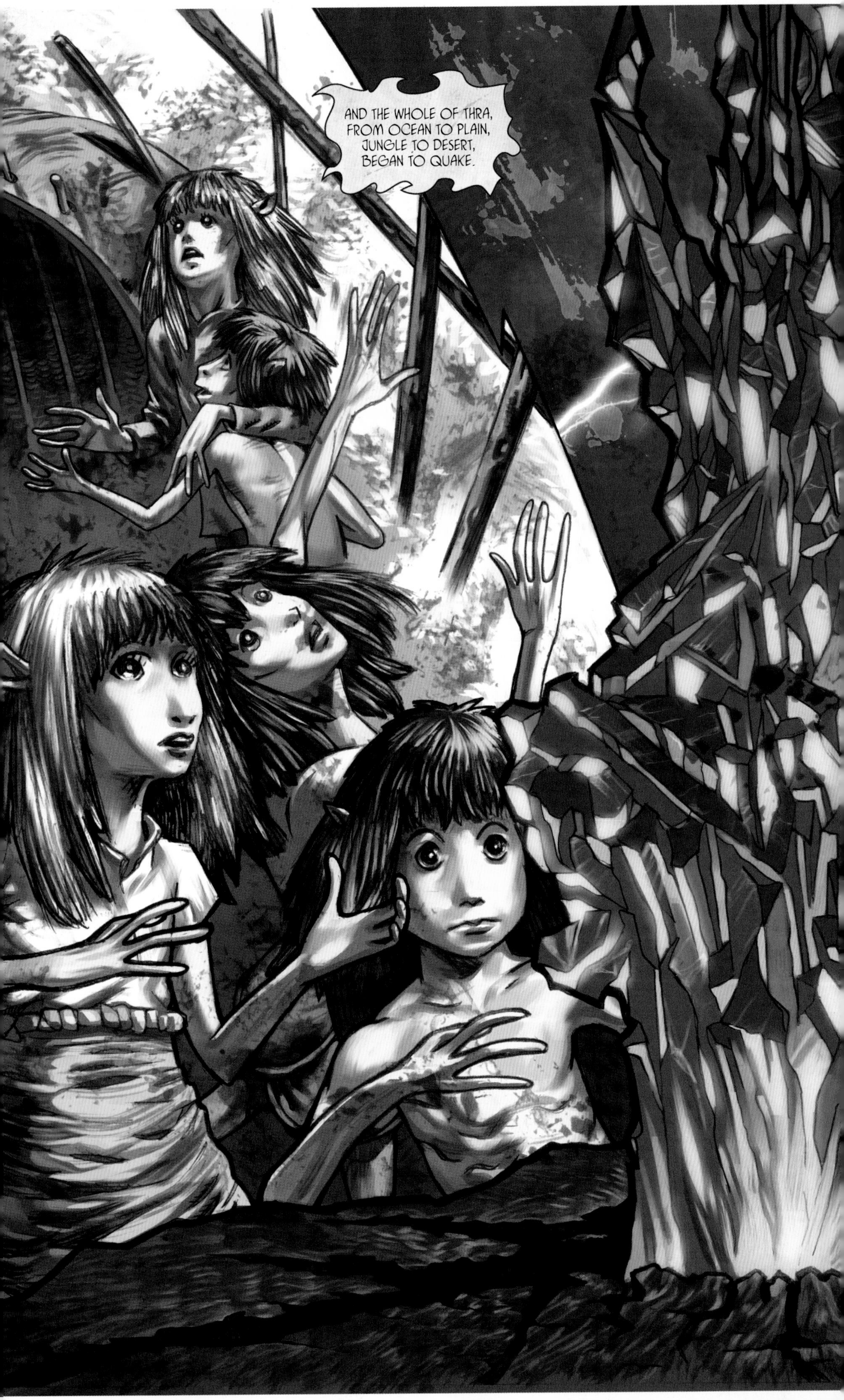
AND THE WHOLE OF THRA, FROM OCEAN TO PLAIN, JUNGLE TO DESERT, BEGAN TO QUAKE.

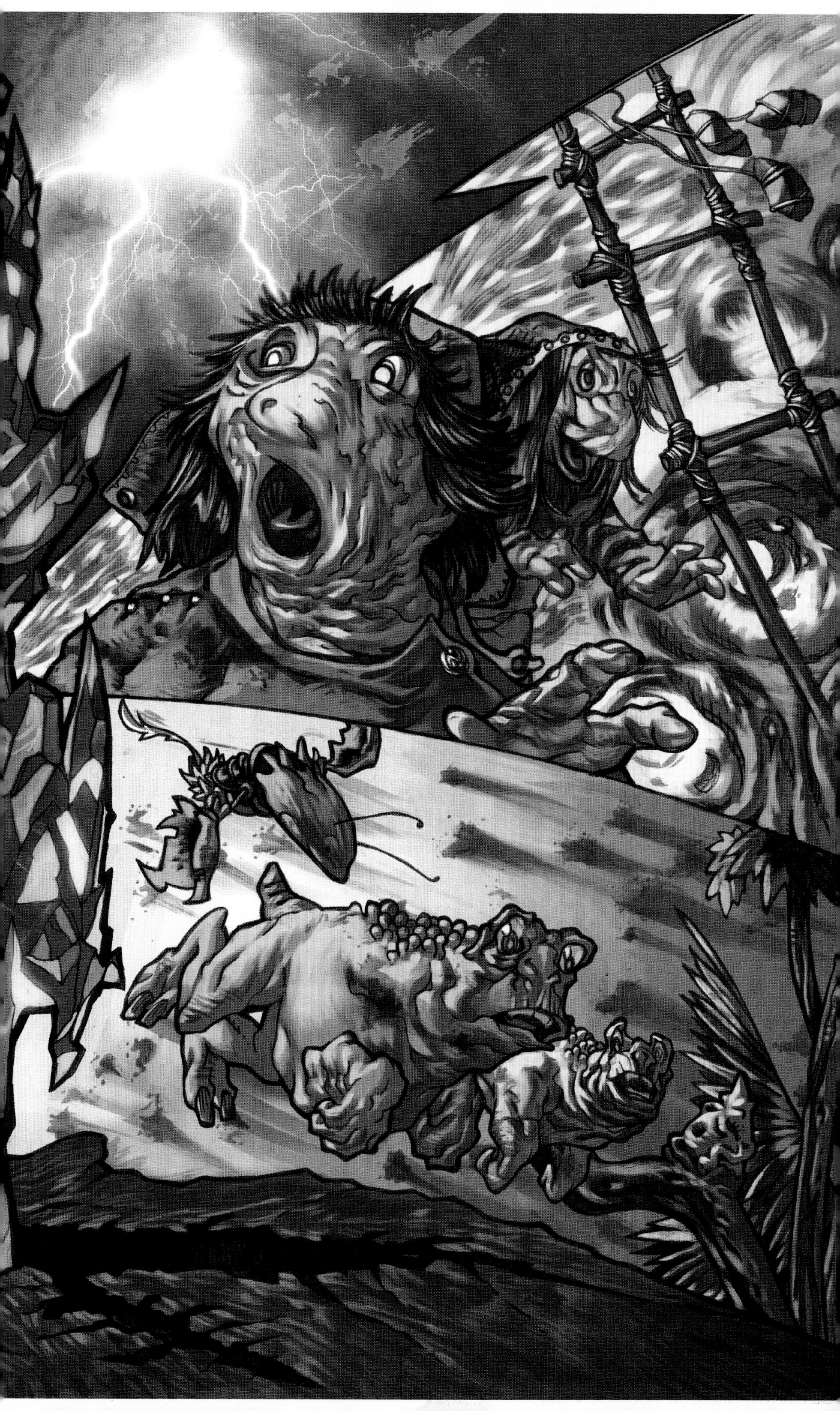

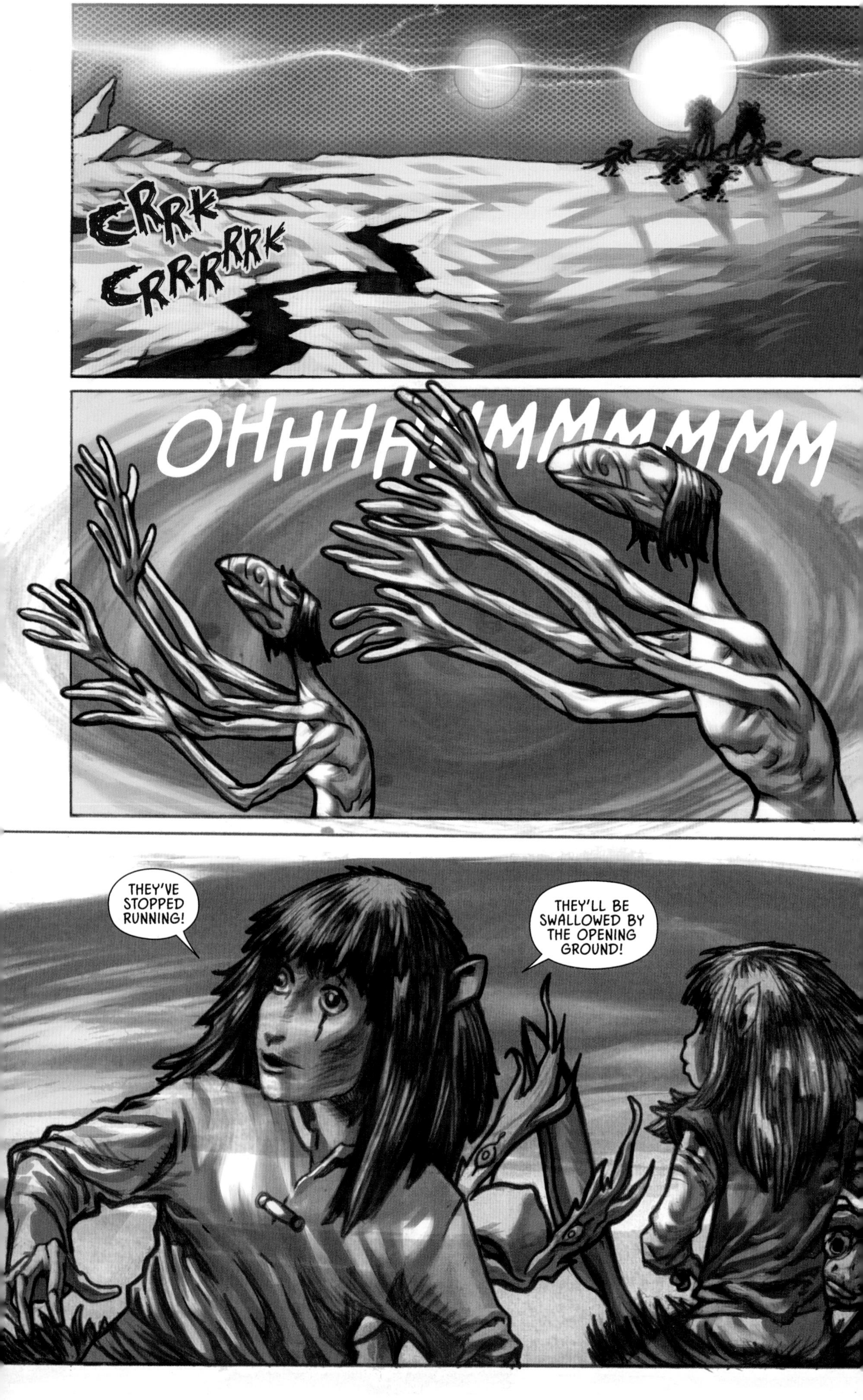
CRRK
CRRRRRK
OHHHHMMMMMMM
THEY'VE STOPPED RUNNING!
THEY'LL BE SWALLOWED BY THE OPENING GROUND!

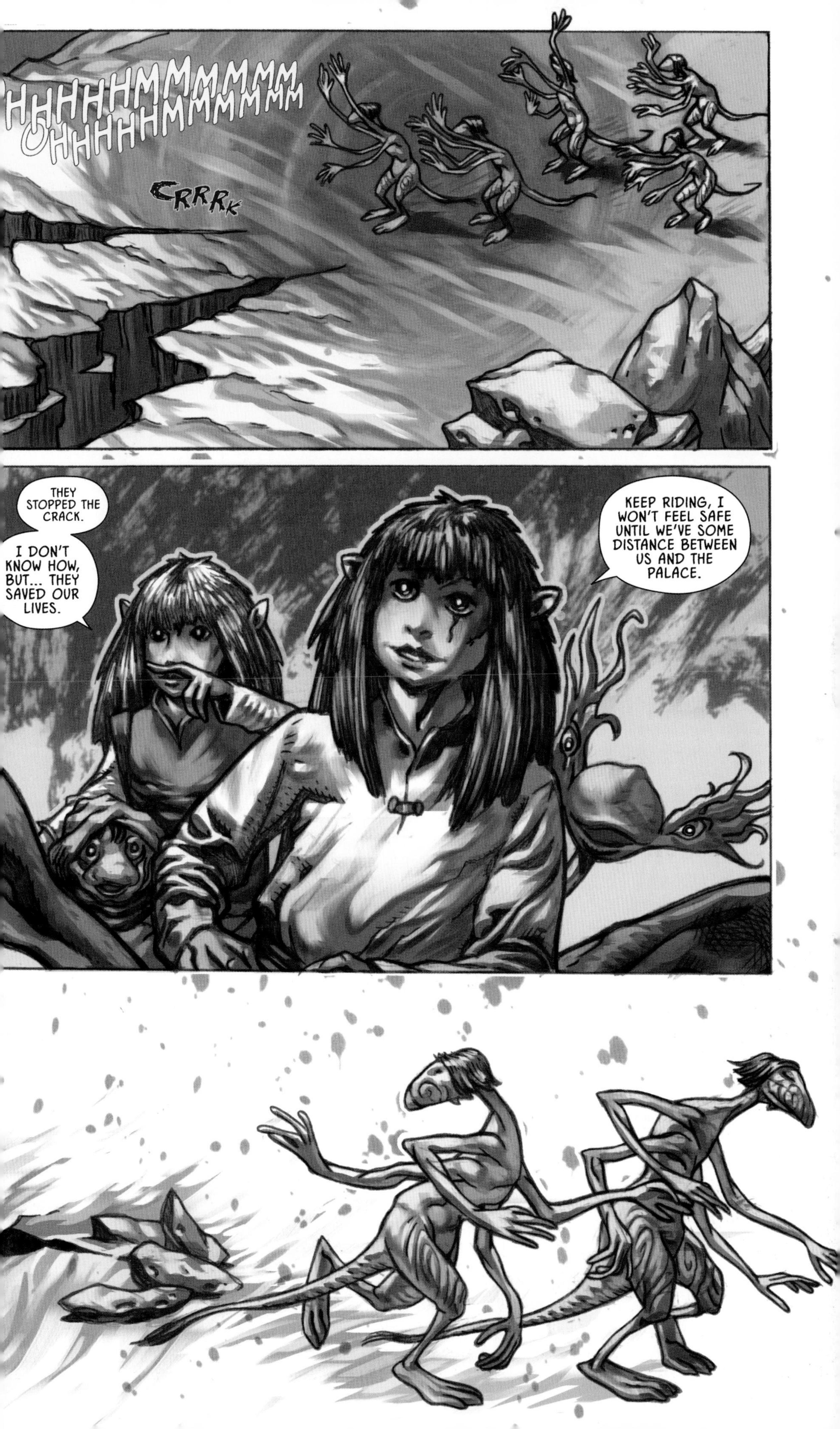
HHHHHMMMMMM
OHHHHHMMMMMM
CRRRK
THEY STOPPED THE CRACK.
I DON'T KNOW HOW, BUT... THEY SAVED OUR LIVES.
KEEP RIDING, I WON'T FEEL SAFE UNTIL WE'VE SOME DISTANCE BETWEEN US AND THE PALACE.

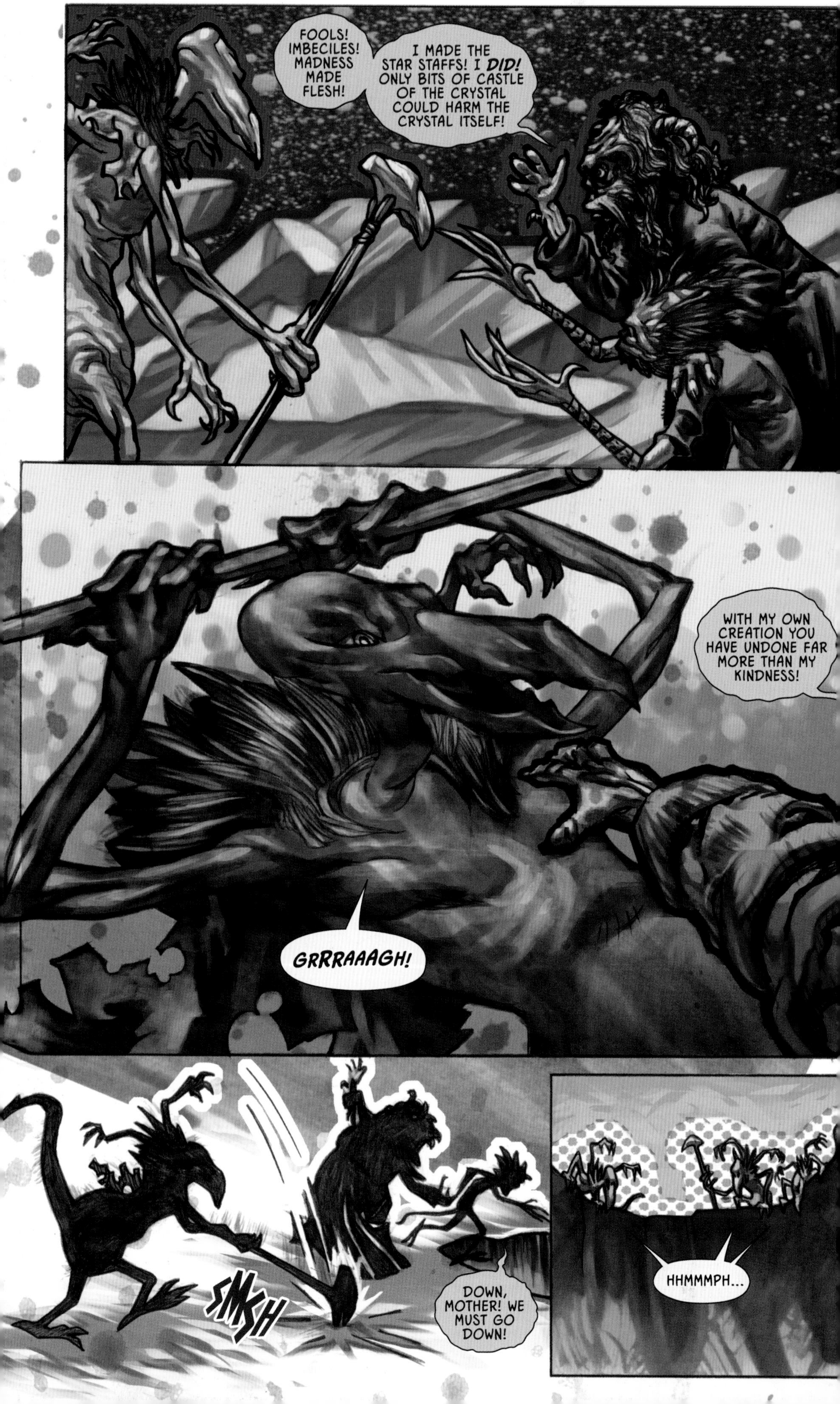
FOOLS! IMBECILES! MADNESS MADE FLESH!
I MADE THE STAR STAFFS! I *DID!* ONLY BITS OF CASTLE OF THE CRYSTAL COULD HARM THE CRYSTAL ITSELF!
WITH MY OWN CREATION YOU HAVE UNDONE FAR MORE THAN MY KINDNESS!
GRRRAAAGH!
SMSH
DOWN, MOTHER! WE MUST GO DOWN!
HHMMMPH...

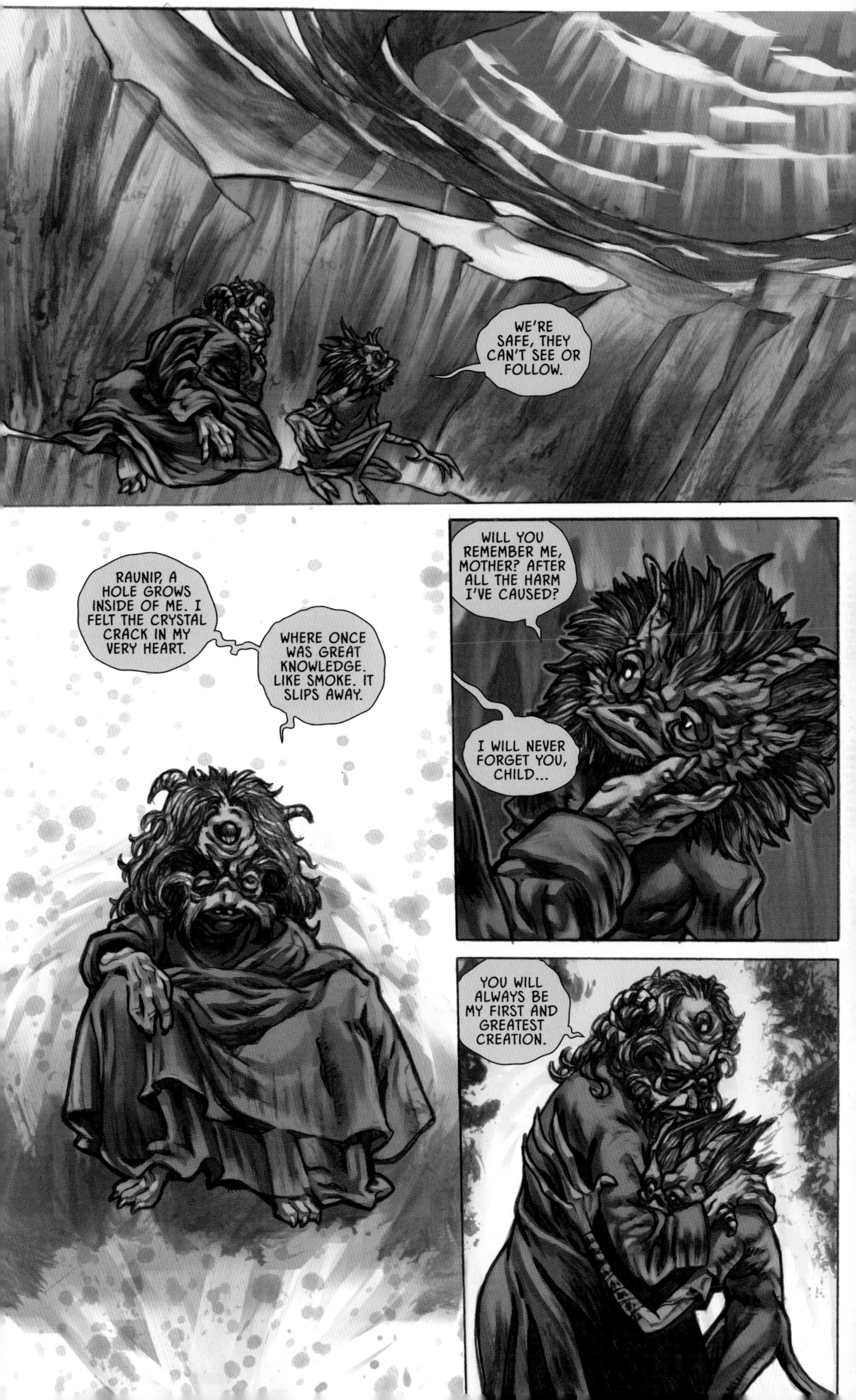
WE'RE SAFE, THEY CAN'T SEE OR FOLLOW.
RAUNIP, A HOLE GROWS INSIDE OF ME. I FELT THE CRYSTAL CRACK IN MY VERY HEART.
WHERE ONCE WAS GREAT KNOWLEDGE. LIKE SMOKE. IT SLIPS AWAY.
WILL YOU REMEMBER ME, MOTHER? AFTER ALL THE HARM I'VE CAUSED?
I WILL NEVER FORGET YOU, CHILD...
YOU WILL ALWAYS BE MY FIRST AND GREATEST CREATION.

Chapter 8
Dark Times

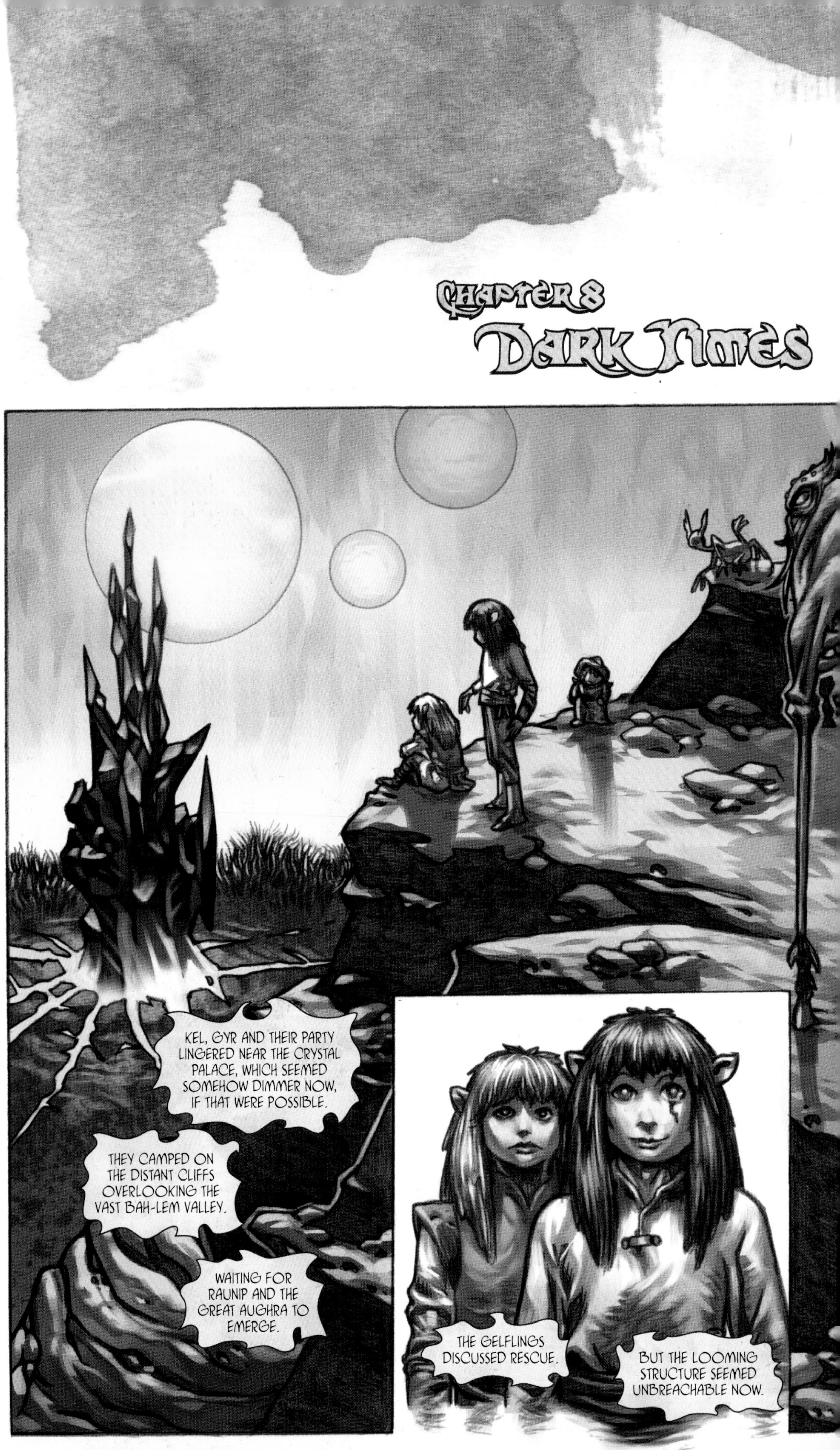
KEL, GYR AND THEIR PARTY LINGERED NEAR THE CRYSTAL PALACE, WHICH SEEMED SOMEHOW DIMMER NOW, IF THAT WERE POSSIBLE.
THEY CAMPED ON THE DISTANT CLIFFS OVERLOOKING THE VAST BAH-LEM VALLEY.
WAITING FOR RAUNIP AND THE GREAT AUGHRA TO EMERGE.
THE GELFLINGS DISCUSSED RESCUE.
BUT THE LOOMING STRUCTURE SEEMED UNBREACHABLE NOW.

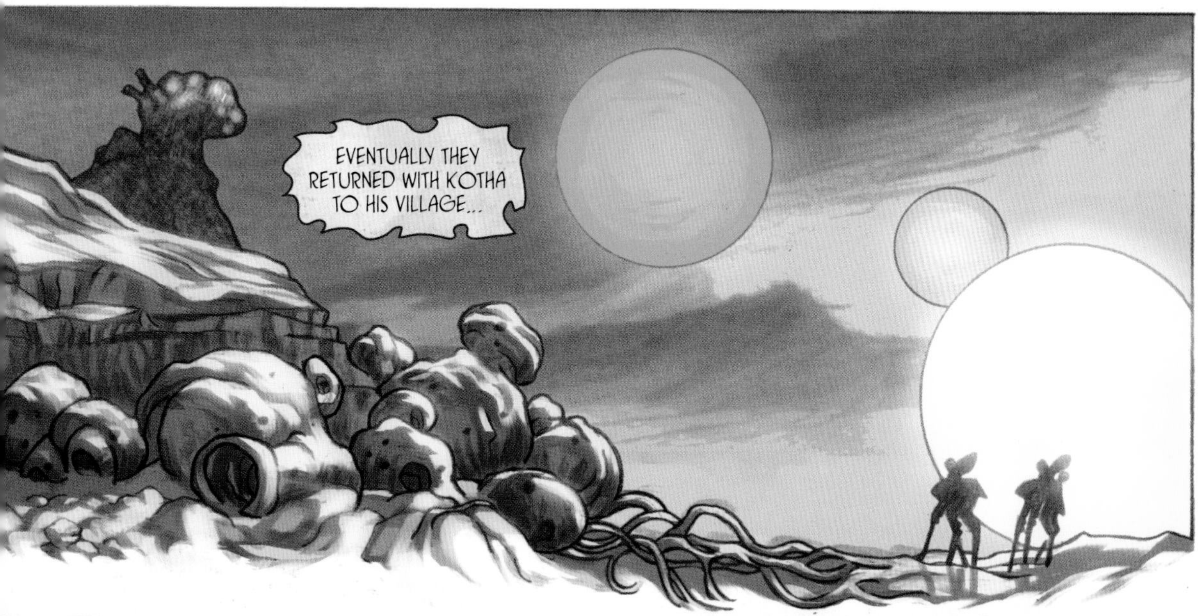
EVENTUALLY THEY RETURNED WITH KOTHA TO HIS VILLAGE...

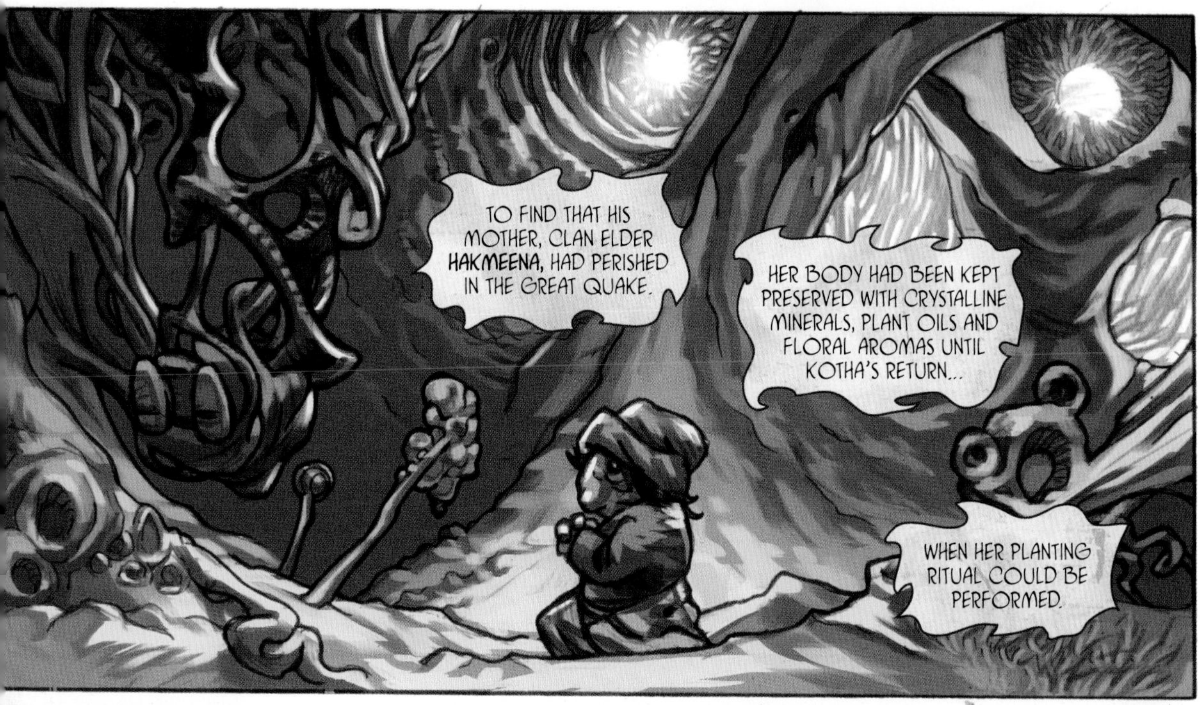
TO FIND THAT HIS MOTHER, CLAN ELDER HAKMEENA, HAD PERISHED IN THE GREAT QUAKE.
HER BODY HAD BEEN KEPT PRESERVED WITH CRYSTALLINE MINERALS, PLANT OILS AND FLORAL AROMAS UNTIL KOTHA'S RETURN...
WHEN HER PLANTING RITUAL COULD BE PERFORMED.

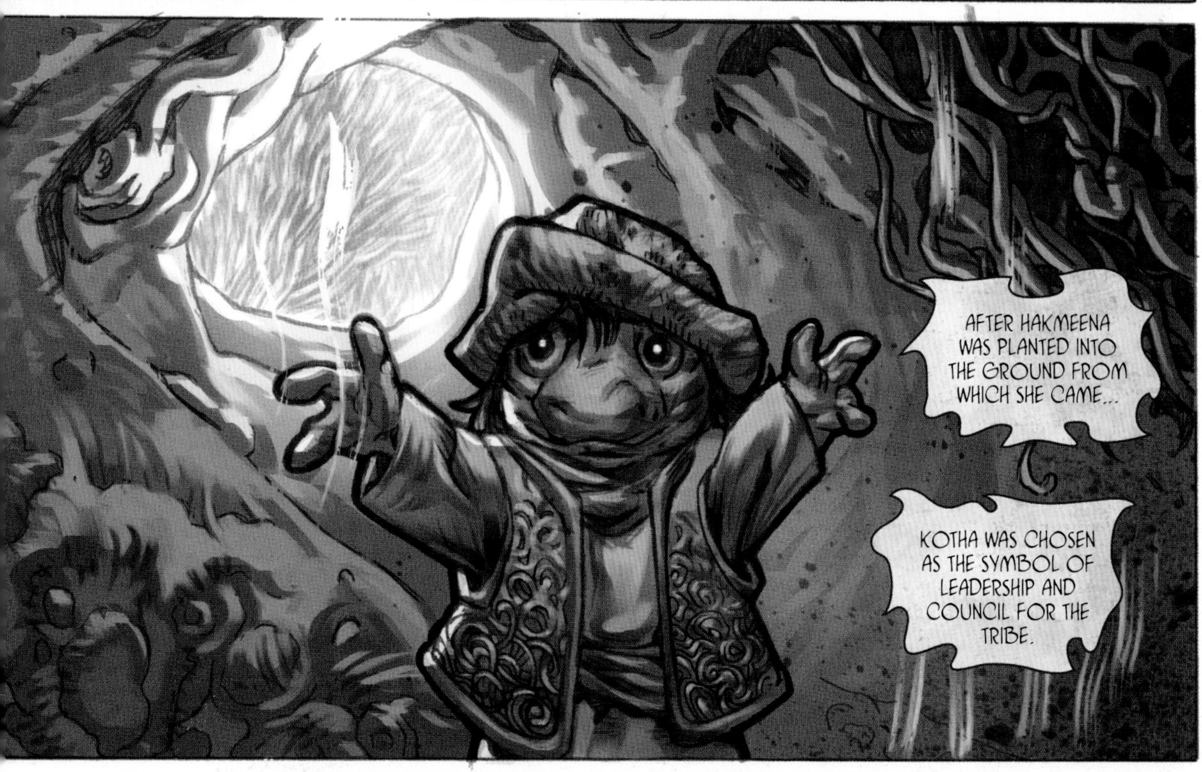
AFTER HAKMEENA WAS PLANTED INTO THE GROUND FROM WHICH SHE CAME...
KOTHA WAS CHOSEN AS THE SYMBOL OF LEADERSHIP AND COUNCIL FOR THE TRIBE.

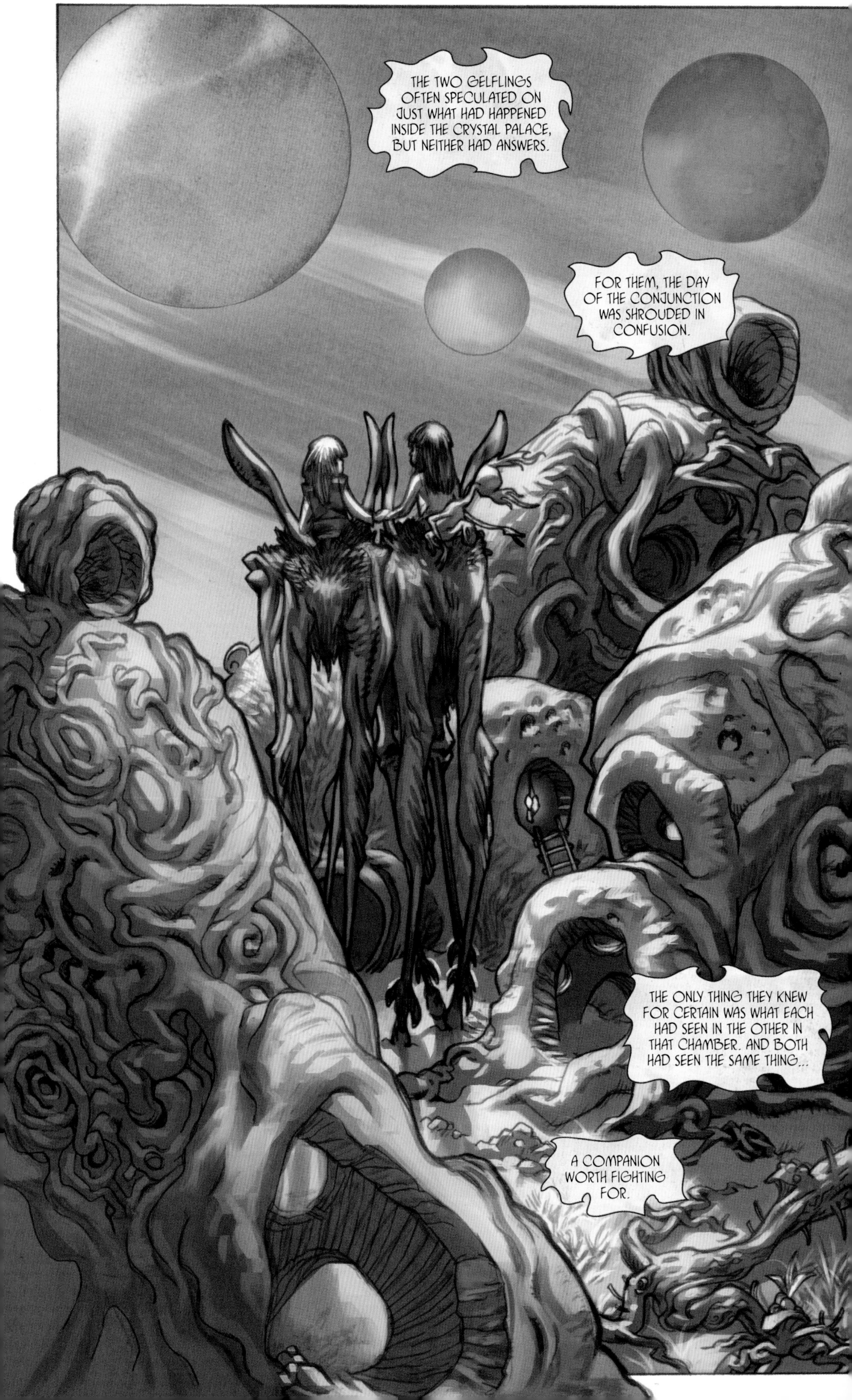
THE TWO GELFLINGS OFTEN SPECULATED ON JUST WHAT HAD HAPPENED INSIDE THE CRYSTAL PALACE, BUT NEITHER HAD ANSWERS.
FOR THEM, THE DAY OF THE CONJUNCTION WAS SHROUDED IN CONFUSION.
THE ONLY THING THEY KNEW FOR CERTAIN WAS WHAT EACH HAD SEEN IN THE OTHER IN THAT CHAMBER. AND BOTH HAD SEEN THE SAME THING...
A COMPANION WORTH FIGHTING FOR.

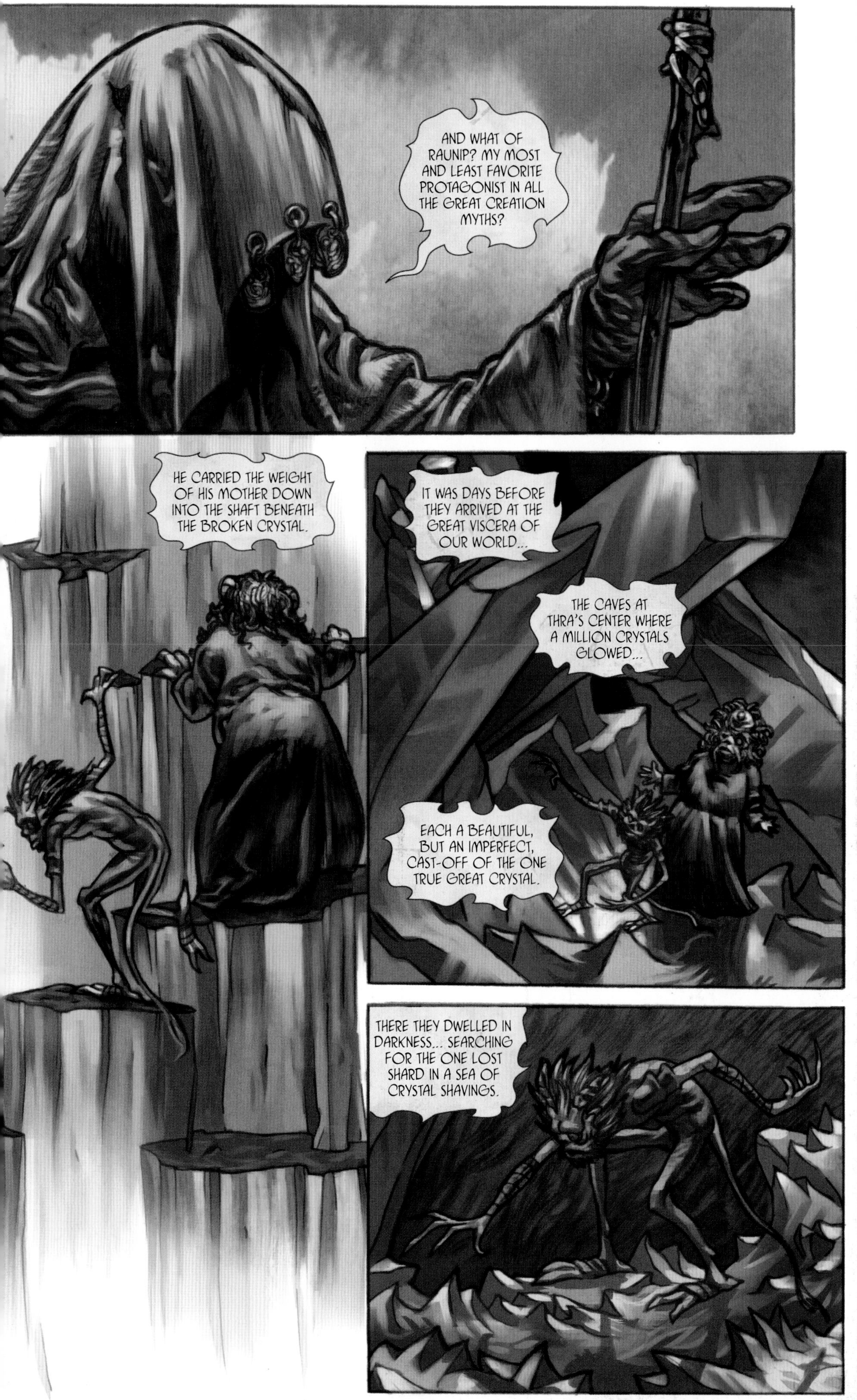
AND WHAT OF RAUNIP? MY MOST AND LEAST FAVORITE PROTAGONIST IN ALL THE GREAT CREATION MYTHS?
HE CARRIED THE WEIGHT OF HIS MOTHER DOWN INTO THE SHAFT BENEATH THE BROKEN CRYSTAL.
IT WAS DAYS BEFORE THEY ARRIVED AT THE GREAT VISCERA OF OUR WORLD...
THE CAVES AT THRA'S CENTER WHERE A MILLION CRYSTALS GLOWED...
EACH A BEAUTIFUL, BUT AN IMPERFECT, CAST-OFF OF THE ONE TRUE GREAT CRYSTAL.
THERE THEY DWELLED IN DARKNESS... SEARCHING FOR THE ONE LOST SHARD IN A SEA OF CRYSTAL SHAVINGS.

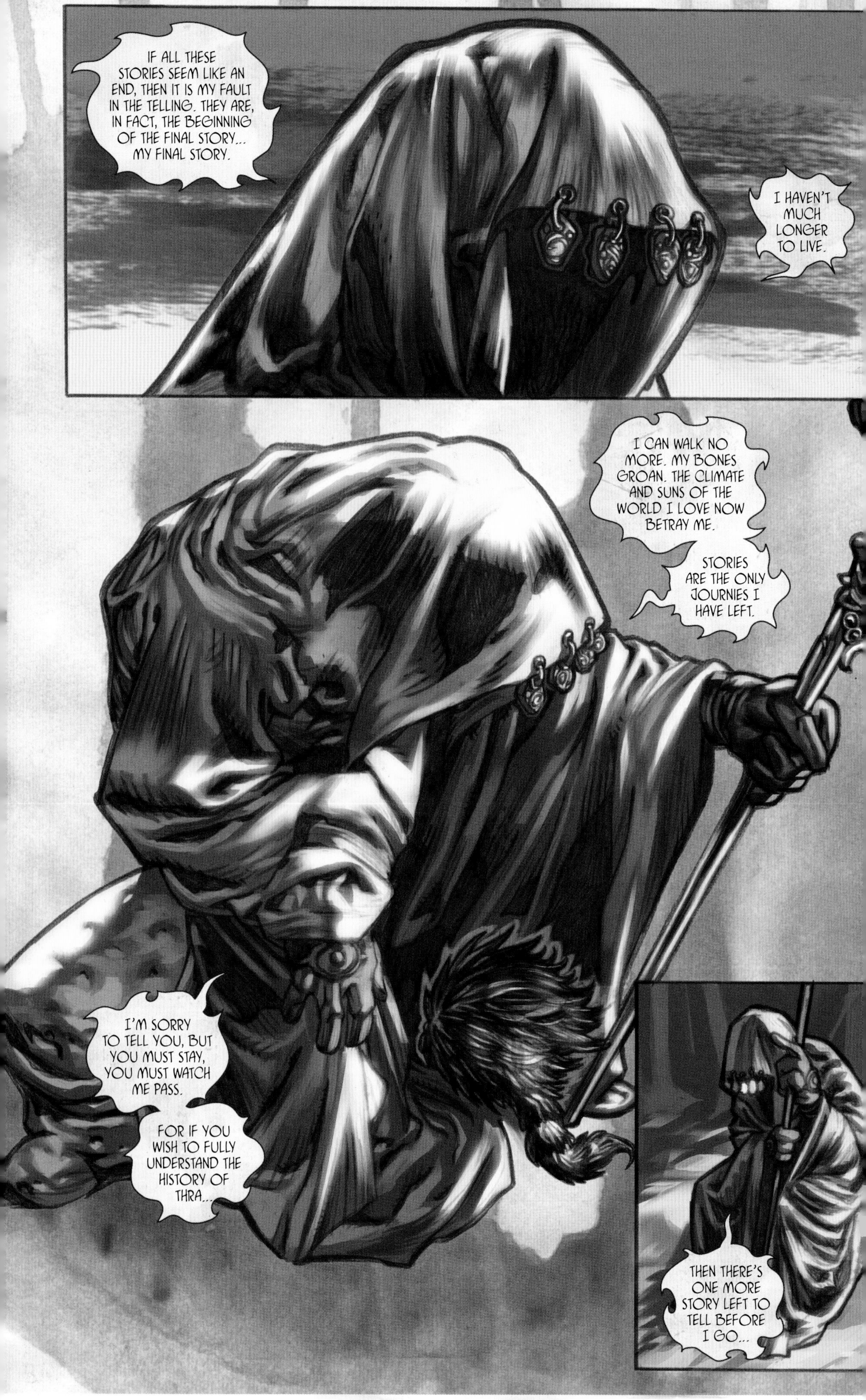
IF ALL THESE STORIES SEEM LIKE AN END, THEN IT IS MY FAULT IN THE TELLING. THEY ARE, IN FACT, THE BEGINNING OF THE FINAL STORY... MY FINAL STORY.
I HAVEN'T MUCH LONGER TO LIVE.
I CAN WALK NO MORE. MY BONES GROAN. THE CLIMATE AND SUNS OF THE WORLD I LOVE NOW BETRAY ME.
STORIES ARE THE ONLY JOURNIES I HAVE LEFT.
I'M SORRY TO TELL YOU, BUT YOU MUST STAY, YOU MUST WATCH ME PASS.
FOR IF YOU WISH TO FULLY UNDERSTAND THE HISTORY OF THRA...
THEN THERE'S ONE MORE STORY LEFT TO TELL BEFORE I GO...

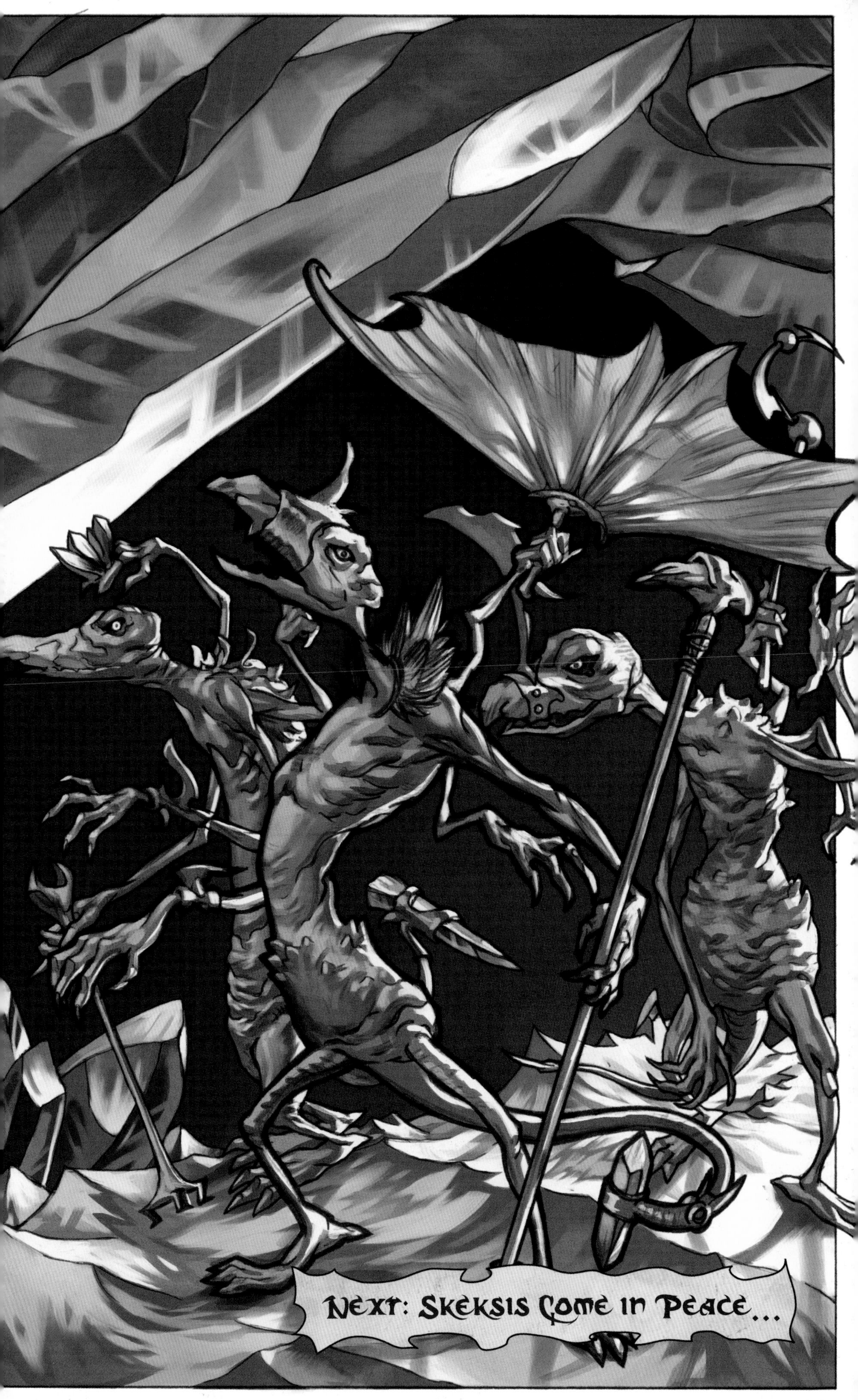
Next: Skeksis Come in Peace...

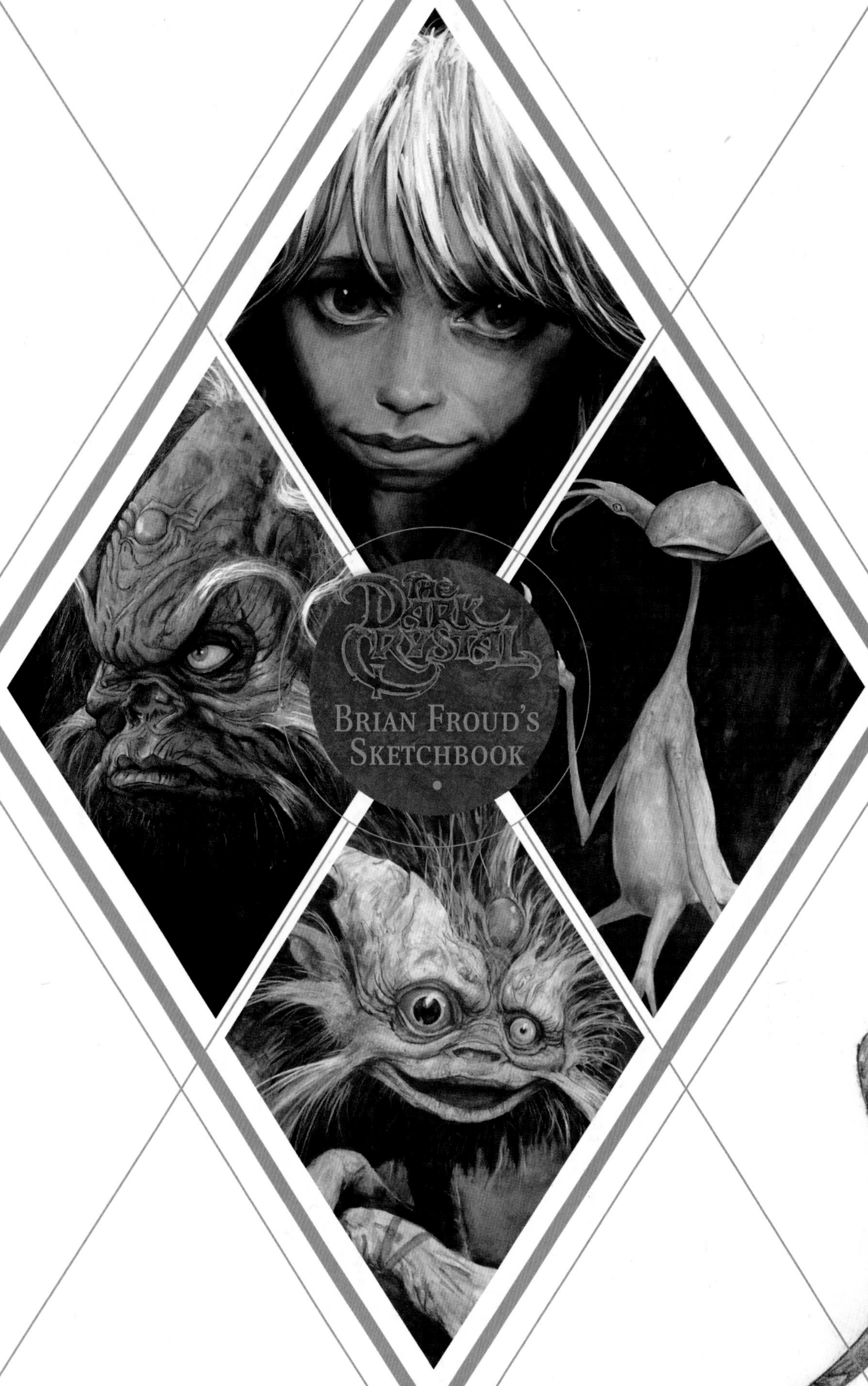
The Dark Crystal
Brian Froud's
Sketchbook

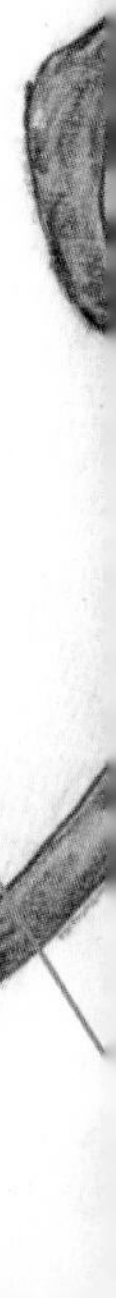

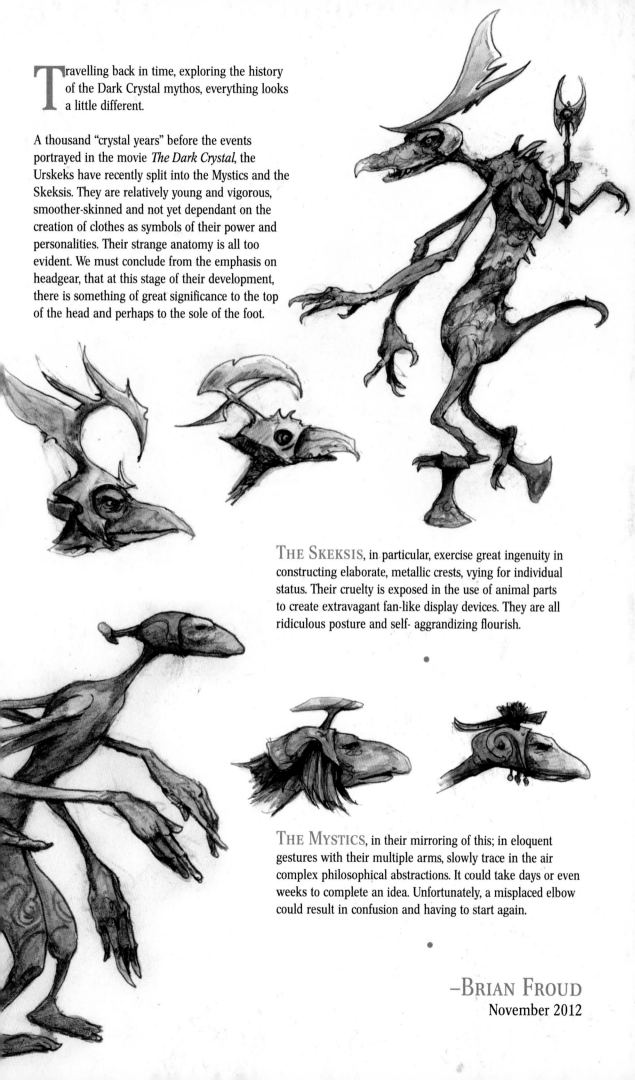

Travelling back in time, exploring the history of the Dark Crystal mythos, everything looks a little different.

A thousand "crystal years" before the events portrayed in the movie *The Dark Crystal*, the Urskeks have recently split into the Mystics and the Skeksis. They are relatively young and vigorous, smoother-skinned and not yet dependant on the creation of clothes as symbols of their power and personalities. Their strange anatomy is all too evident. We must conclude from the emphasis on headgear, that at this stage of their development, there is something of great significance to the top of the head and perhaps to the sole of the foot.

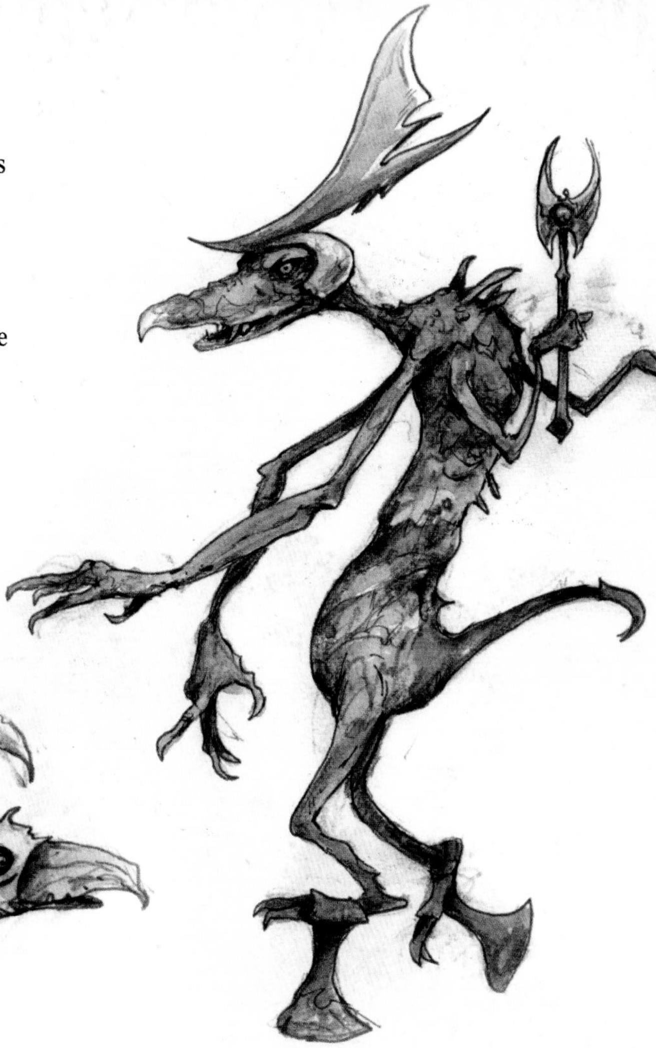

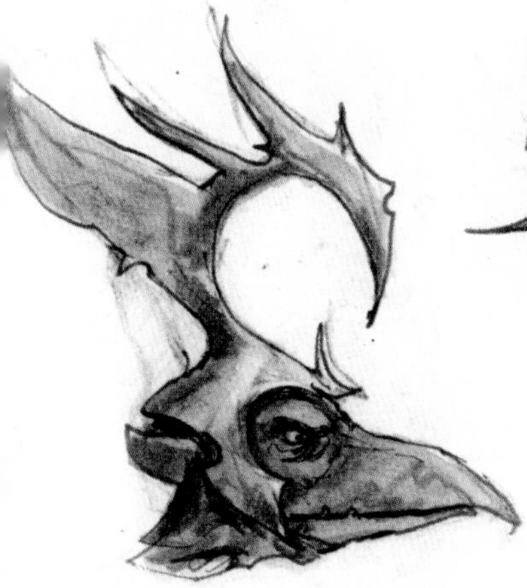

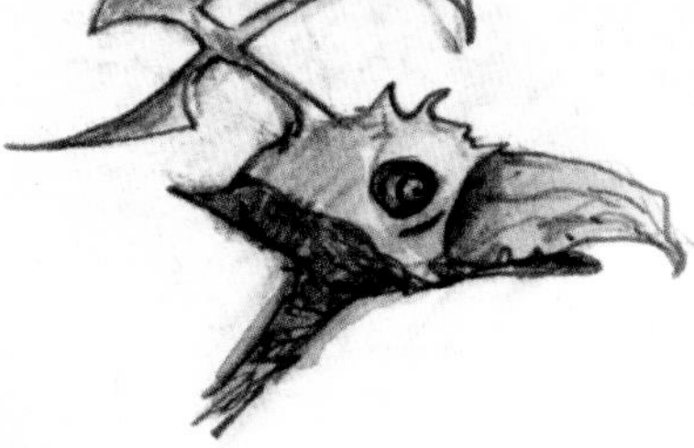

THE SKEKSIS, in particular, exercise great ingenuity in constructing elaborate, metallic crests, vying for individual status. Their cruelty is exposed in the use of animal parts to create extravagant fan-like display devices. They are all ridiculous posture and self- aggrandizing flourish.

•

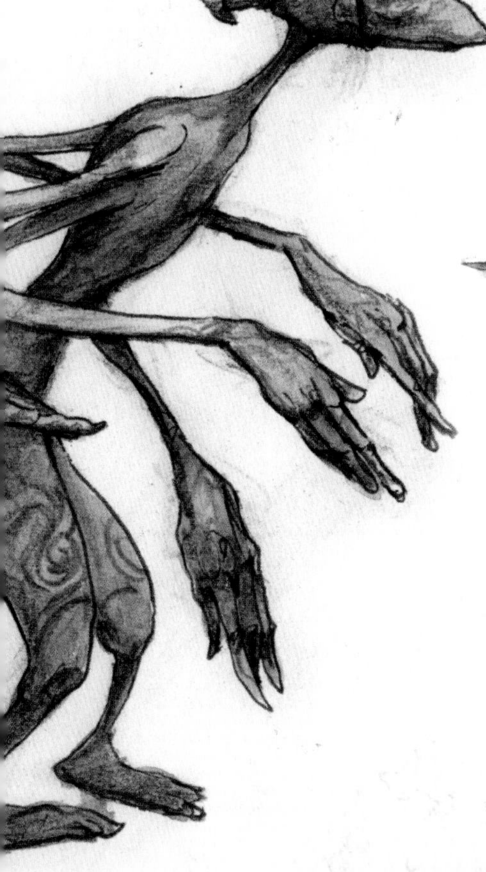

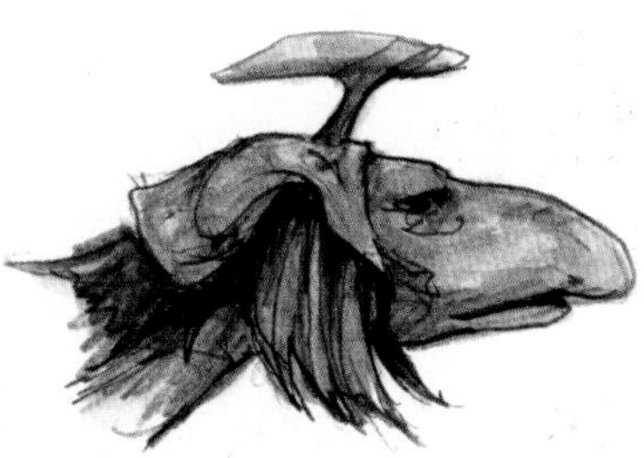

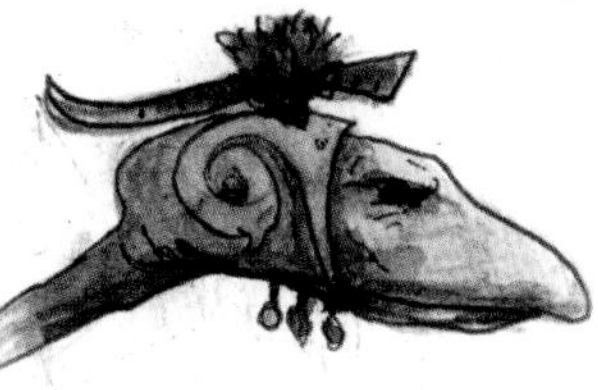

THE MYSTICS, in their mirroring of this; in eloquent gestures with their multiple arms, slowly trace in the air complex philosophical abstractions. It could take days or even weeks to complete an idea. Unfortunately, a misplaced elbow could result in confusion and having to start again.

•

–BRIAN FROUD
November 2012

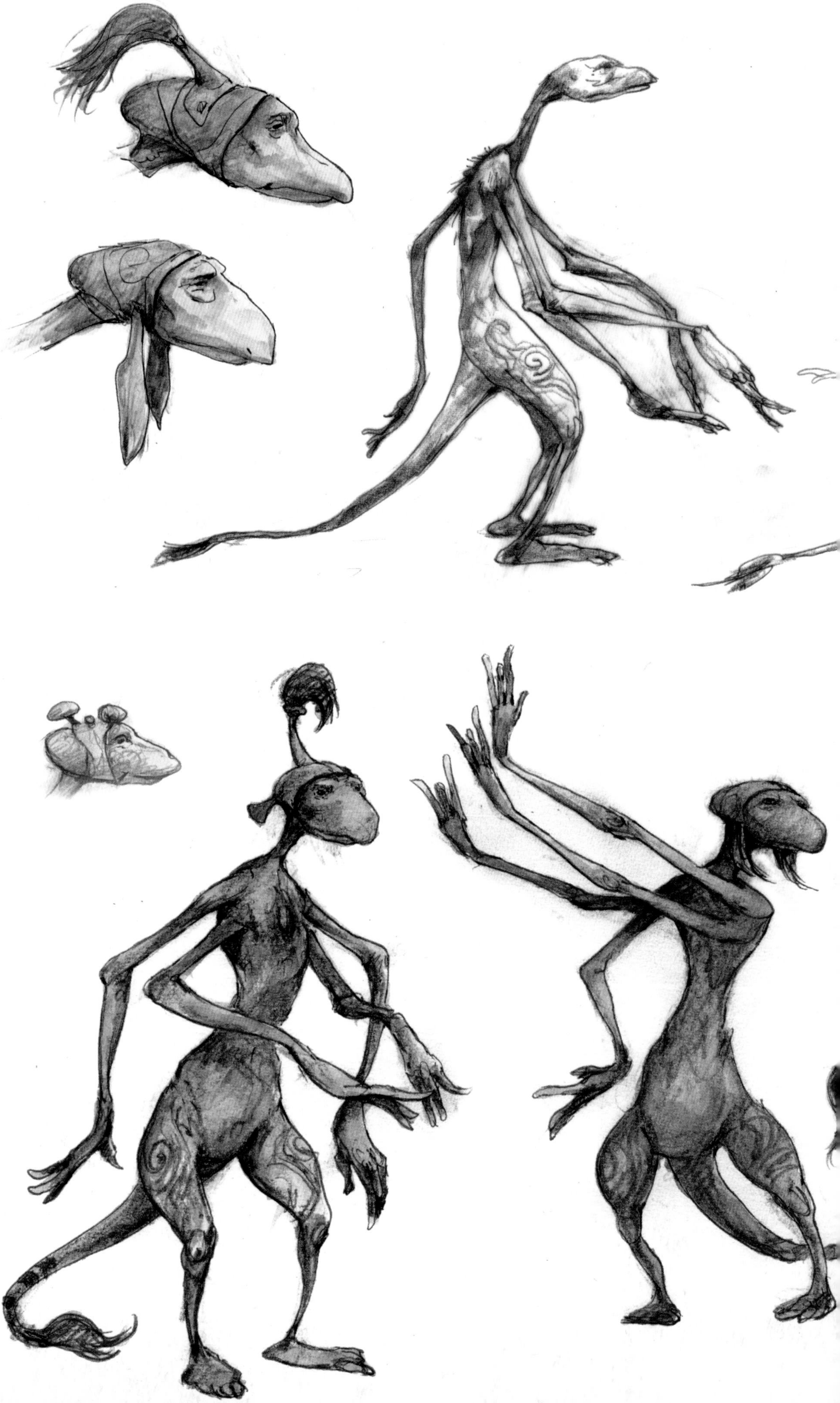

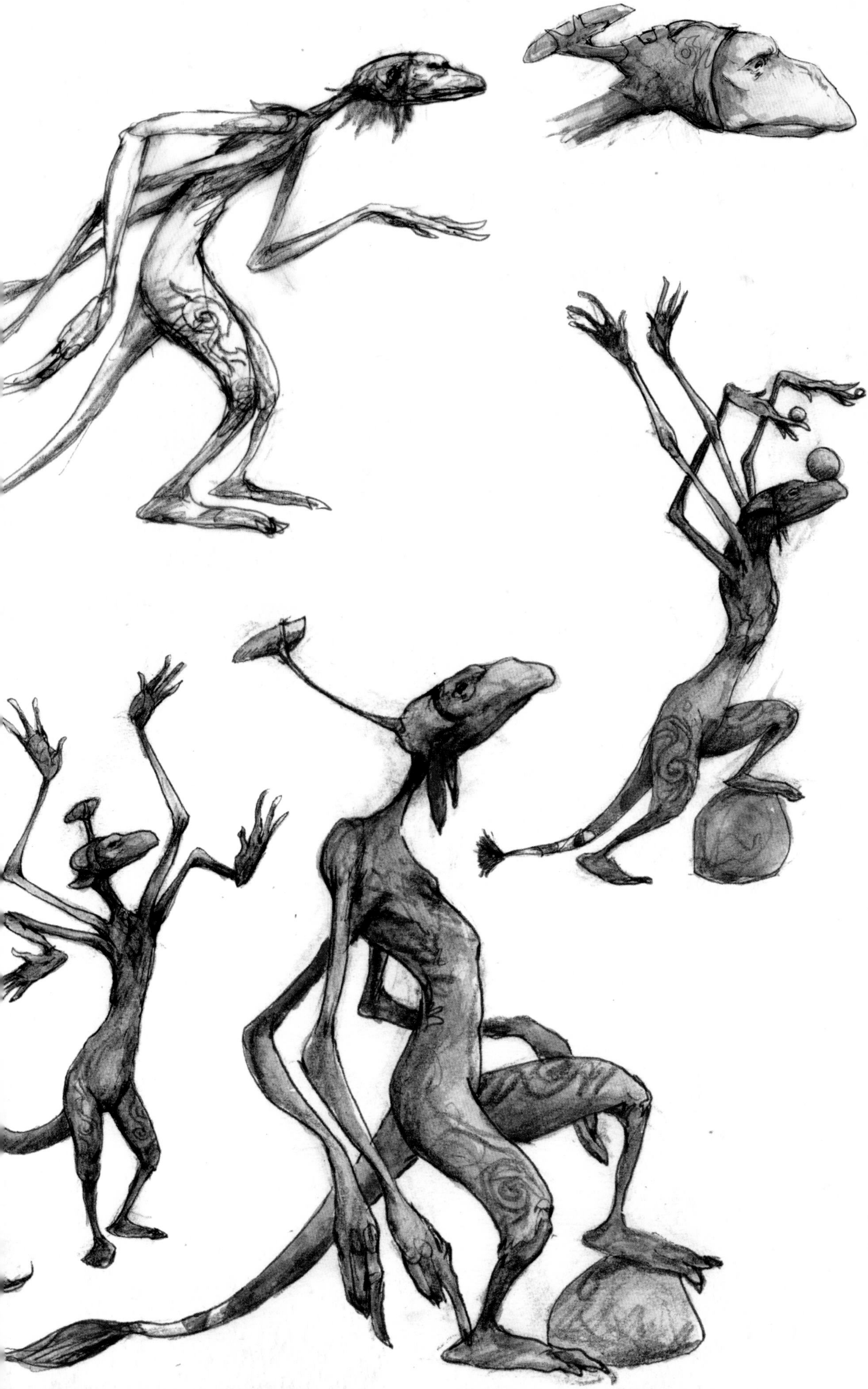

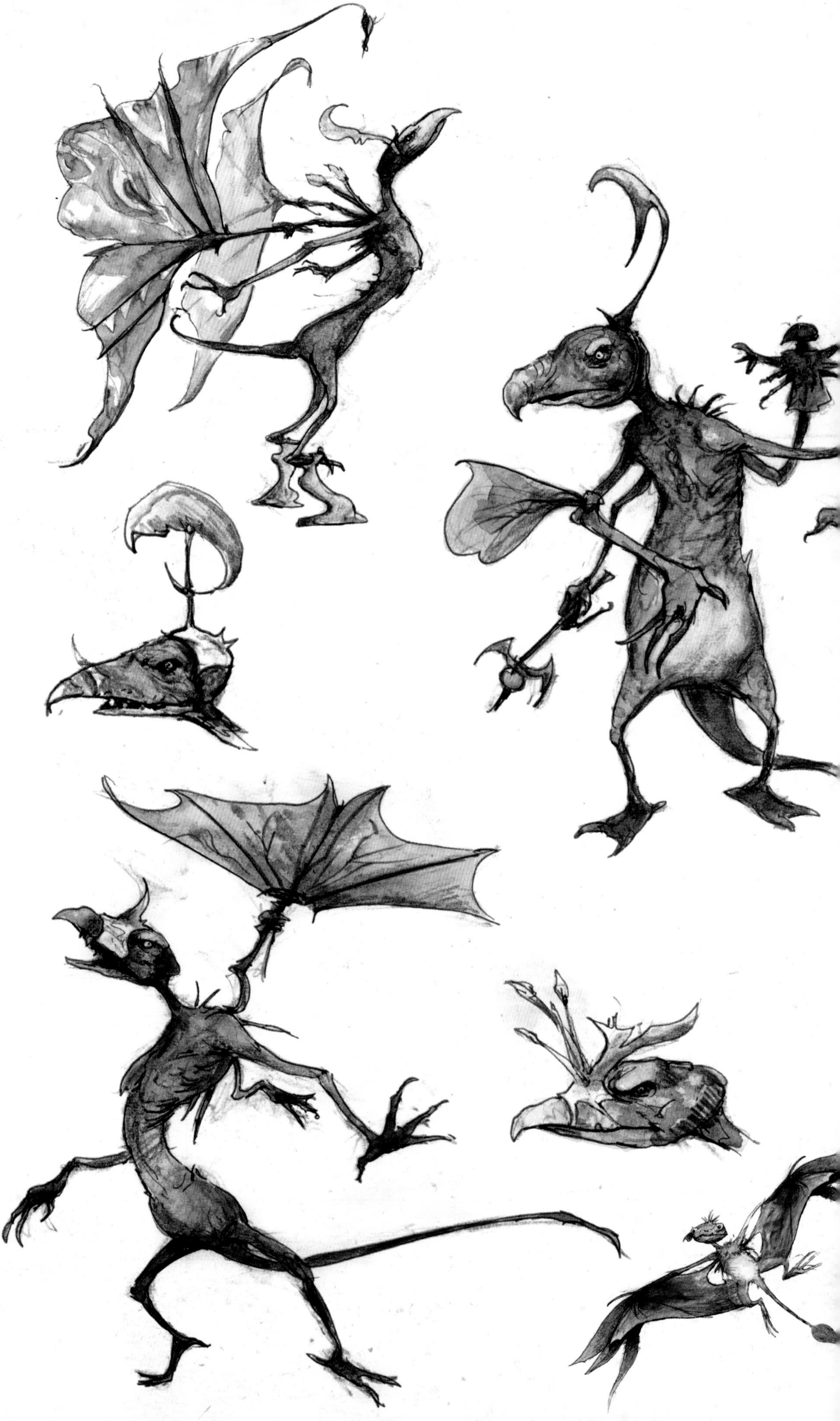

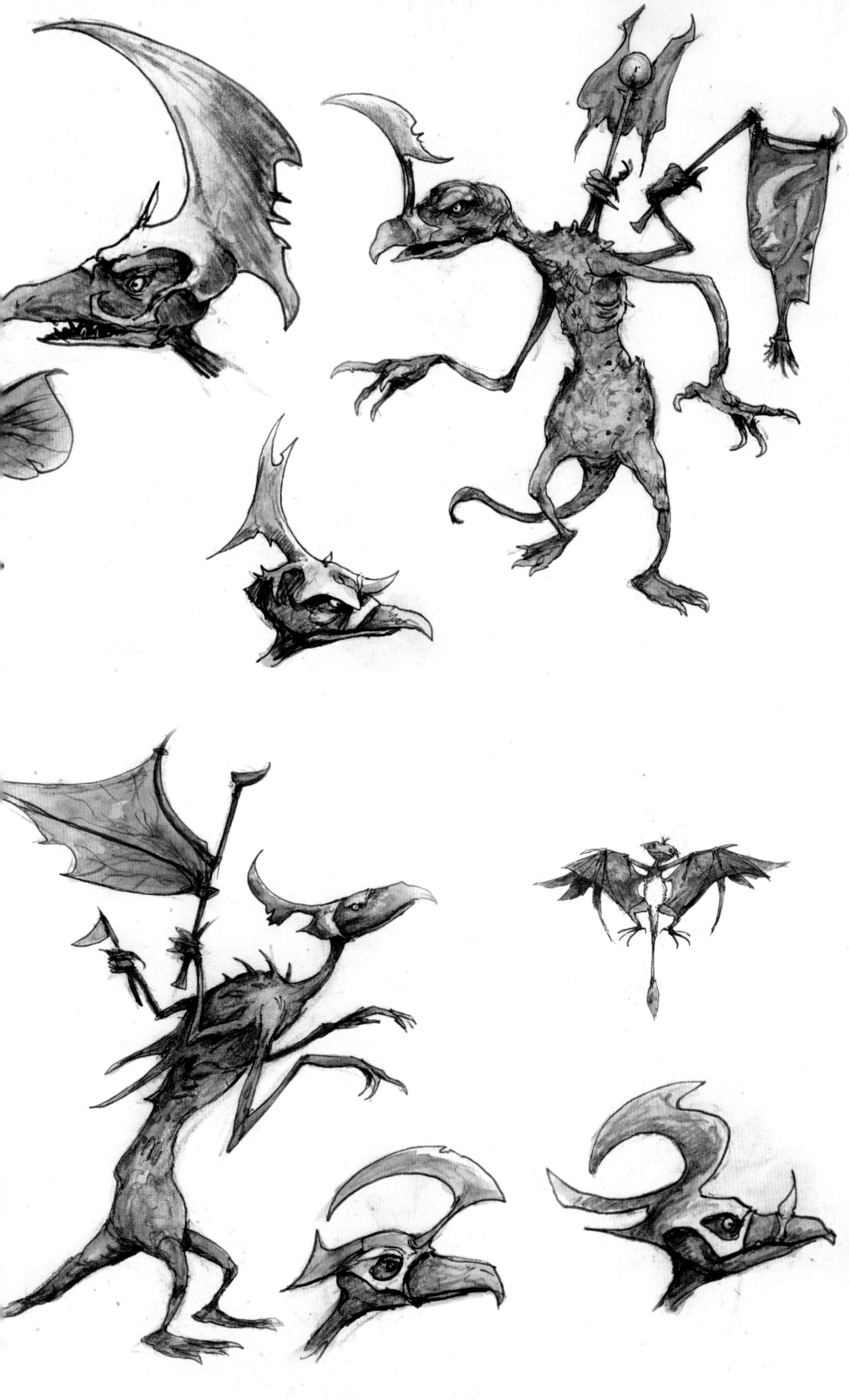

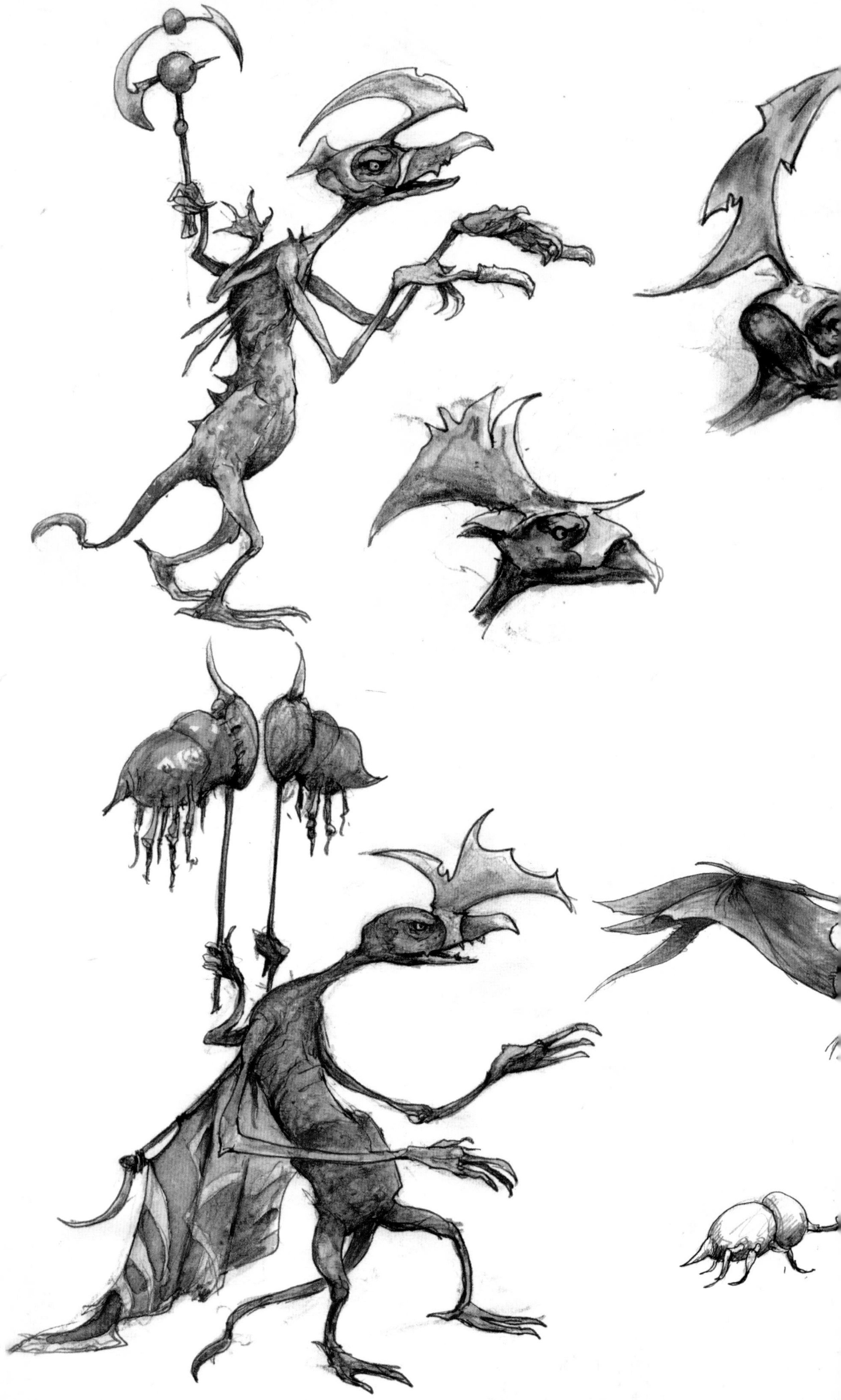

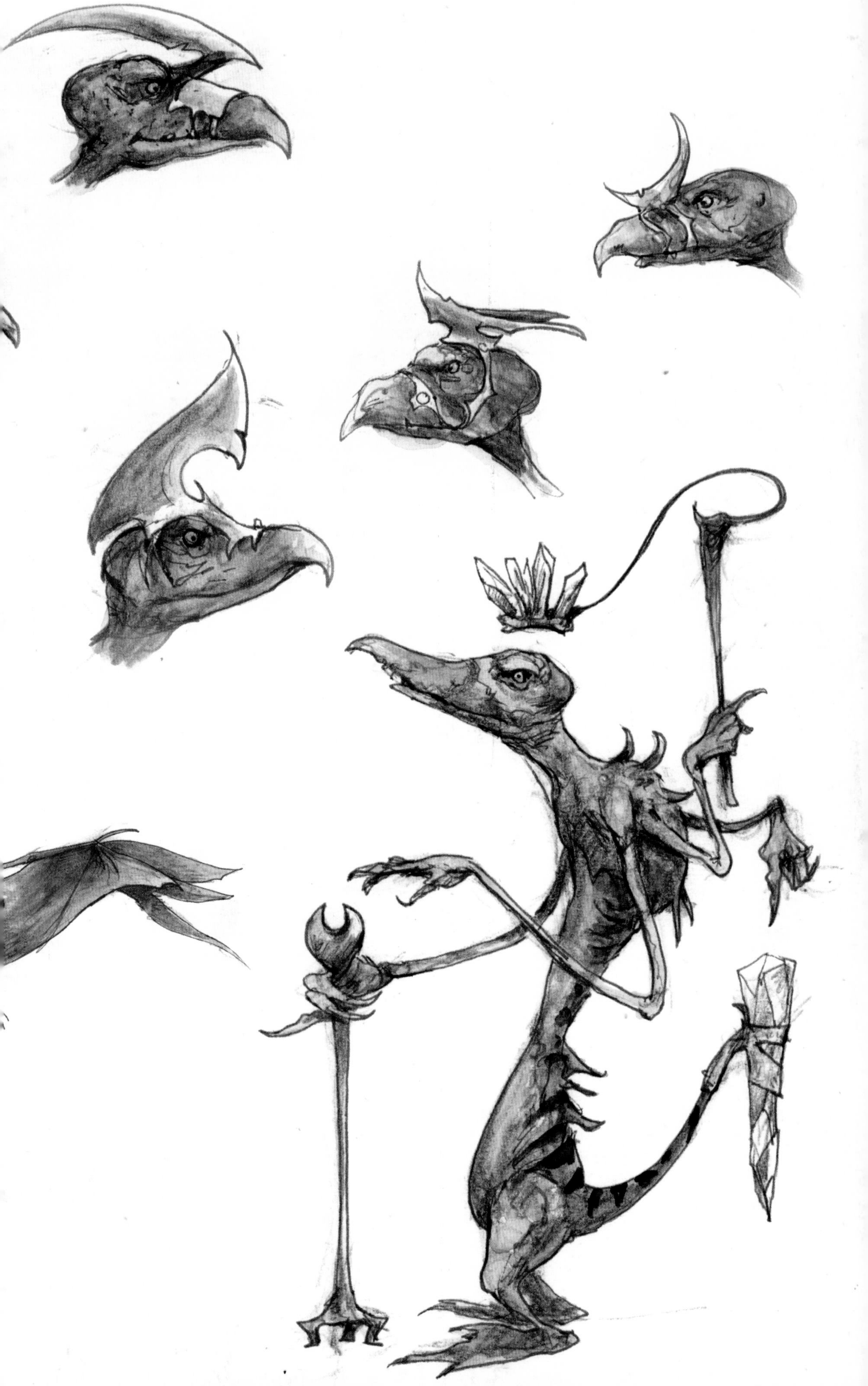

REFLECTIONS ON MAKING
THE DARK CRYSTAL

AND WORKING WITH
JIM HENSON

BY DAVID ODELL
SCREENWRITER OF *THE DARK CRYSTAL* AND *THE MUPPET MOVIE*

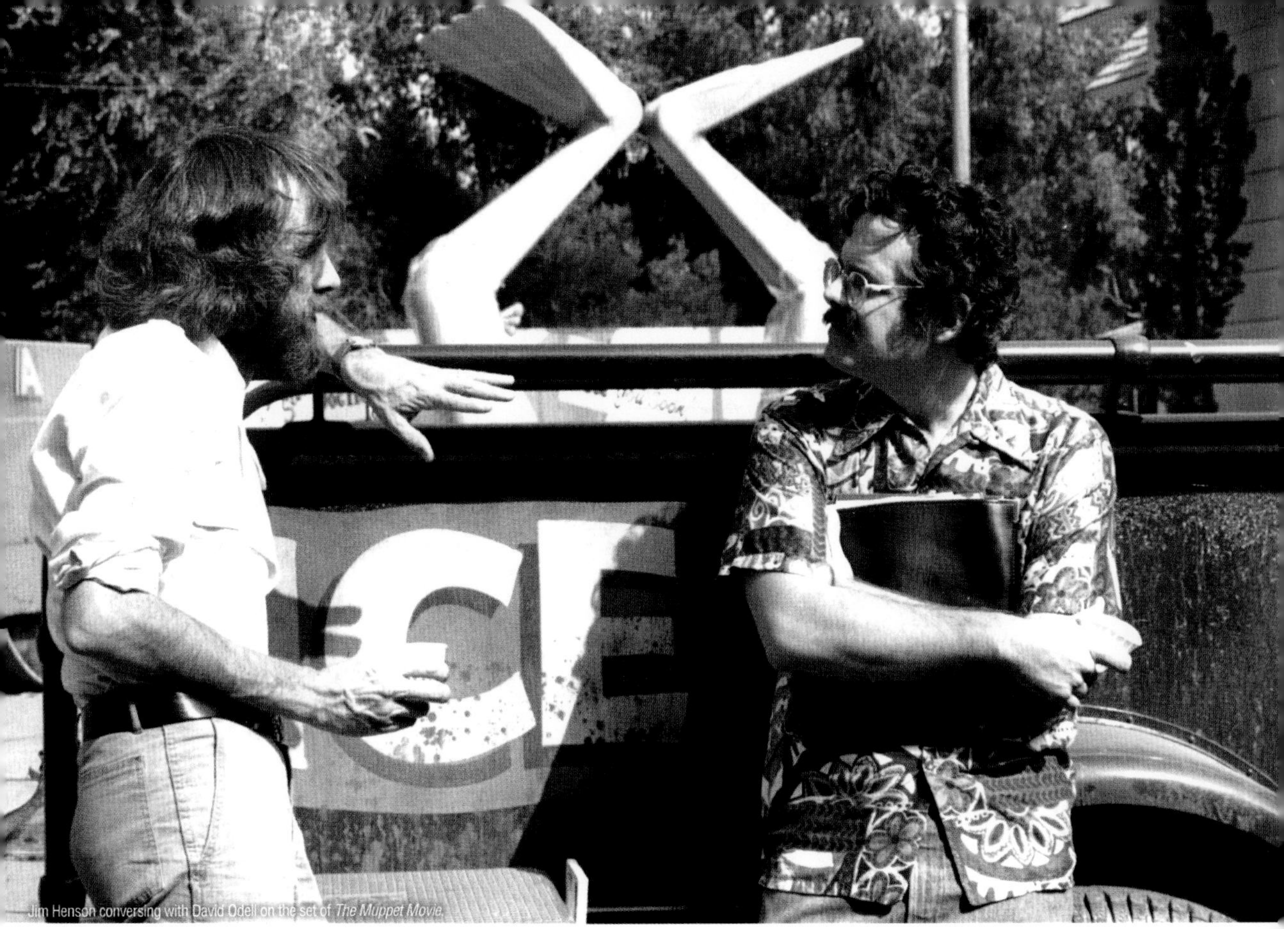

Jim Henson conversing with David Odell on the set of *The Muppet Movie*.

I worked with Jim Henson for five years on *The Muppet Movie, The Muppet Show,* and *The Dark Crystal.* He was the only genius I ever worked for. He was incredibly creative, astonishingly hard working, gentle, sensitive, kind, but with a wicked sense of humor. He was also unflappable. When disaster would strike, as it occasionally does in film and TV, he was invariably the calmest person on the set. He was a great leader, good at getting his collaborators to give him their best. I've never known anyone who inspired so much love in the people around him.

When I first started working with him I asked him what puppets could do. He launched into a great pep talk. "We can do anything with puppets," he said. "The possibilities are limitless. They can swim, they can fly, they can do karate, they can eat things..." Then he paused, and started to chuckle. "They can do anything, except walk and talk." It was true. Walking consisted of the puppeteer jiggling his arm up and down while the puppet moved across the stage. Talking consisted of flapping the puppet's lips open and shut in a rough approximation of the syllables of the dialogue. To me, that conversation symbolizes a thing about Jim's character: he was wildly enthusiastic and tended to ignore obstacles, thinking there was always a work-around. At the same time he was very practical and realistic and able to laugh at his excessive flights of fancy.

He was also a spiritual searcher. He had developed his own ideas that seemed to combine a little bit of theosophy, Hinduism, Taoism, and various new age philosophies. Before we started work on *The Dark Crystal,* he insisted I read a book called *Seth Speaks*. He had a lot of copies of this book and gave them away to people. (He also gave a copy to Brian Froud.) I was flattered that Jim wanted me to understand his spiritual insights before we collaborated. The book was written by Jane Roberts, a science fiction writer, who one day began channeling "Seth." Seth was a multi-dimensional male being, outside time and space, who dictated monologues on metaphysics through her when she was in a trance, while her husband wrote them down in shorthand. One of Jim's favorite lines that I wrote in *The Dark Crystal* script was when Aughra asks Jen where his master is, and Jen says he's dead. Aughra looks around suspiciously and mutters "He could be anywhere then." I couldn't have written that if I hadn't read the Seth book.

The spiritual kernel of *The Dark Crystal* is heavily influenced by Seth. I've always felt that the idea of perfect beings split into a good mystic part and an evil materialistic part which are reunited after a long separation is Jim's response to the teachings of that book. Jim admitted that he didn't understand the book himself, and that everyone would understand it -- or not understand it -- in their own way. But he thought it opened up a whole different way of looking at reality, which I think was one of his goals in making *The Dark Crystal.*

Another example of Jim's different take on reality is the strange conversation Kermit has with his ghostly double in the desert in the third act of *The Muppet Movie,* followed by a star falling from heaven. That scene implies the idea of multiple selves, as in reincarnation or the avatars of Hindu philosophy. (The priest at Jim's funeral, as Jim had requested, read a selection from the Hindu scriptures.)

I pointed out to Jim once the similarity in the endings of *The Dark Crystal* and *The Muppet Movie.* The roof falls away and the puppets are bathed in a blast of light from heaven, which seems to solve all their problems. I asked him if it was a personal symbol of something, like the Christian paraclete or the beginning of Genesis: "Let there be light." He said he had never connected the two scenes in his mind, but he found strange echoes of things were always turning

up in his work. Another time I pointed out to him that both *The Muppet Movie* and *The Dark Crystal* have torture scenes in them, one done for comedy (with Kermit and Mel Brooks) and the other darker and more disturbing. I asked if he wasn't a little bit into torture for some reason. He said, "I hate torture. It's so upsetting just to think about it. I think I must have been tortured in a previous life."

I came in to do the production rewrites on *The Muppet Movie.* The technology of the Muppets was new to feature filmmaking, and the film took longer to shoot than had been planned for. Since there were a lot of cameo appearances by hard-to-schedule stars, the script needed rewriting to bring in new cameos when others had to cancel.

Part of the technology of the Muppets is that each performer watches his performance on a small portable TV set. Each performer has a TV, a microphone, and a headset. (Some of the big life-size characters like Big Bird have a TV inside the puppet. In those days, before bluetooth and Wi-Fi, this meant that the big puppets had to trail wires behind them when they moved.) Add the video tap from the camera to feed the monitors, and you had a maze of wires under the stage. This made it very hard to keep hum out of the sound system. Jim explained to me that the ability of puppeteers to watch themselves from an audience P.O.V. while they acted gave an added reality to the puppets' performance, especially their eyelines. (Puppeteers' use of TV monitors was an innovation of Burr Tilstrom in Chicago whose show *Kukla, Fran and Ollie* was the first prime time network puppet show.)

Toward the end of shooting *The Muppet Movie,* the closing musical number still hadn't been written because Paul Williams, the lyricist, had come down with writer's block. Finally Jim took me aside and asked me to write some lyrics and block out a number. The only thing the script said was that under

Kermit's direction, the Muppets go onto a sound stage and put together a musical number, sort of a Busby Berkeley version of the film's plot so far. It all seems to be going well, until the Muppets' incompetence breaks out, and they end up destroying the scenery and the sound stage. But in the midst of the disaster a rainbow shines down through a hole in the roof onto the Muppets as they end with an optimistic reprise of the opening song of the film.

To shoot this we needed a script describing who would be doing what, how the set and props would look, how the incompetence would break out and destroy the stage, and how we'd create an emotionally satisfying sense of an ending. So I wrote a dummy lyric, and Jim and I sat down one Sunday beside his swimming pool to write and draw the shots and action of the finale. Hearing that the train was leaving the station without him, Paul Williams wrote his lyric the next day, and the sequence was shot a week later.

Jim must have liked my work on the finale, because after shooting was wrapped, he called me up and asked me to read his story of *The Dark Crystal* with a view to possibly writing the treatment and screenplay with him. The story was about twenty-five pages and roughed out the general shape of the world: the three different races, the double funeral at the beginning, Jen's quest, Jen meeting Kira, the three suns, the great conjunction, reuniting the shard with the crystal, and the merging of the two separated races at the end.

Jim had seen some drawings by an English illustrator of crocodiles wearing elaborate jewelry and they were the seed for his concept of the Skeksis. Jim began imagining a film about a world that would have such creatures in it, a world unlike any ever seen before, that not incidentally would push the art of puppetry into new areas. He called this world Mithra. In 1977 he ran across the work of Brian Froud in a book called *The Land of Froud*. Jim said he knew at once that Brian was the artist who could make Mithra come alive. In February 1978 Jim was snowed in at an airport hotel with his daughter Cheryl. He sat down and poured out ideas into his notebook in one intense burst of invention.

Originally Jim wanted all the creatures to speak different alien languages. The images and the acting would do all the exposition, as in a silent film, but with natural sounds and music. And the audience would learn the few necessary new words while watching the movie. Thinking of the man who was putting up the money, I asked, "How does Lew Grade feel about that?" "He doesn't know yet," Jim said with a mischievous grin.

After weeks of discussion, during which we learned we were both big fans of the gibberish-talk foreign films that Sid Caesar used to do on his TV show, we agreed that the Gelflings would mostly speak English and the Skeksis would speak Skexish. But Jim promised me that if the preview audiences found the Skexish too hard to follow, he would replace it with Skexish-accented English.

There was also the related problem of names. Jim had invented a character he called Habeetabat, a busy, curious little creature, sort of like Yoda in his first scene in *Star Wars*. Brian hated the name, because he said it reminded him too much of a modern furniture store in London called Habitat. (Brian hates modern furniture.) Jim and I liked the name Habeetabat, but I guess to Brian it sounded the way a character called Ikea-kea would today. The drawing Brian did of Habeetabat was of a hideous monster sort of like a one-eyed witch, and for a while she was called Ogra, but I told Jim I felt the name was too much like "Ogre," which might make the audience feel she was an evil monster rather than the wise and more sympathetic character who is revealed as the story goes on. So we compromised on spelling it Aughra, suggesting a seer or prophetess.

(After shooting was over Brian further developed Aughra's character in the books he wrote and illustrated, making her into a kind of earth-mother, or Mithra-mom.) People also criticized the name Mithra for the world, saying it was too much like the ancient Persian god. So we altered it to Nithra for a while. Then Brian shortened it in his book to Thra.

For the scene where Jen goes to Aughra's house I proposed that Aughra have an orrery, or clockwork astronomical model. I worked out an orbit for a planet with three suns where the three suns would line up in concentric circles overhead at rare intervals. Jim was very enthusiastic about it, and we were talking about having the orrery demonstrate the Great Conjunction while Jen is looking at Aughra's crystals. Jim wanted to put it in the background so Jen doesn't notice, but where the audience might notice it on a second viewing. When Harry Lange the art director did a first budget it came to almost enough money to make a whole movie with, so we had to settle for the one-sun orrery we got. I was knocked out when I finally saw it on the set, and I think it gave a nice boost of energy to the end of the first act. A number of people have remarked to me that the makers of *Smila's Sense of Snow* must have liked it too, because they seemed to have borrowed the orrery concept for their movie, though theirs is not as well motivated dramatically.

Planning for people to see *The Dark Crystal* more than once was one of the things Jim tried to design into it from the beginning. Producer Gary Kurtz had pointed out to him that one of Lucas' brilliant choices in *Star Wars* was cutting his movie a little bit too fast for audiences to take in everything at the first viewing, which made them want to see it more than once. One shot in *The Dark Crystal* that most people don't catch on the first viewing is in the final scene with the Urskeks in the throne room before they disappear. You can see that the fiery shaft underneath the Crystal has been filled in and is now paved with flat stones. Healing the Crystal has not only healed the rift between the two races, it has healed the wound in the planet. (This was not intentional, it was one of those happy accidents. The scene was one of the last scenes shot, the film was over budget and running out of time, and it would have taken too long to rig the fiery shaft.)

I invented a language for the Skeksis to speak, and a related language for the Mystics, using Indo-European roots. It demonstrated that Skexish was a cruder, uglier version of the Mystic language. But in the rush before principle photography started, nobody seemed interested in the performers learning a new language. They were mostly interested in whether the costumes would be inhabitable, if the characters would be able to move around without showing the cables connecting their TVs, and if the audience would be able to tell the different characters apart. So I stopped pushing the language, since I believed it would ultimately be replaced by English anyway. Some lines in the script were in Skexish with the English meaning in parentheses so the actors would know the subtext of the scene. But if the actors had to fill an awkward pause or felt the need to join in a crowd response, they would have to improvise. The only remnant of the original Skexish is in the judgment stone duel, when the Chamberlain shouts "Haakskeeka!" meaning "Judgment By Stone" or "Let the Stone Decide!"

Jim knew the Mystics and the Skeksis would move slowly (both for character reasons—they were very, very ancient—and for the practical necessity of moving the large, complex puppets), so Jim wanted to fill the frame with a lot of design detail, even in the scenes with the smaller, faster-moving characters. When the film was finished, he told me he loved watching it over and over, because "it was like a rich fruitcake, full of different ingredients, and every bite you discover something new and delicious." (Jim's high metabolism and active life allowed him to be a connoisseur of rich desserts, which he had with lunch and dinner every day.)

Jim's original name for the Mystics was the Ooo-urrrs, which he would pronounce very slowly and with a deep resonant voice. Looking at him you could sense his vision of how they would move and how their movement would have a hypnotic, spiritual quality. I changed the long spelling to a simple Ûr with a circumflex over it, and then Brian added a "u" at the end for the plural, making it more alien.

I tried to establish the rule that "Skesis" was singular, And the plural was "Skeksis," but that distinction fell by the wayside early in shooting.

I wrote a first draft of the treatment in the fall of 1978 based on conversations with Jim and his story notes from the snowed-in airport hotel. Meanwhile Jim was busy doing *Sesame Street*, post production

on *The Muppet Movie*, planning recordings, theme park rides, and video games, and gathering a crew of artists and puppet builders to create the creatures and the world of Thra. Then in February we all moved to London to do *The Muppet Show* at Boerum Wood studios. The TV show was done at Lew Grade's ATV studio, and across the street *The Dark Crystal* would be done at Elstree, where Kubrick had made *2001* and Spielberg had shot *Indiana Jones*. Gary Kurtz of *Star Wars* and *The Empire Strikes Back* would be co-producer. And Frank Oz would co-direct with Jim.

The puppet builders and designers were located in an abandoned post office that Jim had bought across the street from his house in Hampstead, up the block from the house where Keats had written the "Ode to a Nightingale." Because Jim worked sixteen hours a day seven days a week he found it convenient to have the workshop across the street from his house. There was also a gourmet restaurant across the street where Jim often ate (he was fond of their desserts).

I lived in Highgate across Hampstead Heath. I would walk across the Heath from my house to meet with Jim at his house or at the workshop. And there were lots of meetings, with thirty artists and costumers and puppet builders sitting around with Jim and Frank, arguing about tiny details of puppet design and story concepts, looking at set models, Brian's latest drawings, and Wendy Midener's character sculptures. I remember one two-hour meeting that was about how many warts there would be and their placement on the faces of some of the pod-people. I once complained to Jim about all the meetings, and he said "Well, don't forget, I've been running a crew of artists for years. You need to let them hash it all out, and then they go off and do their best work."

Fizzgig was a new character Frank invented for the movie. He had added a new character to *The Muppet Show* in the last season. He felt Miss Piggy was falling into a rut, being asked by the writers to be "too harsh" all the time, and he wanted to explore more of her soft feminine side. So he invented a little poodle, a lap dog for her to carry around, whom he called Poopsie. His idea was she could be sweet and loving to this dog that all the other characters hated, but she wouldn't accept any criticism of him. The character was built, but the English TV executives all agreed that the name was too scatological, so his name was changed to Foo-Foo. Frank liked the way Foo-Foo worked to give Piggy a foil, and he wanted a similar character for Kira in *The Dark Crystal.*

Frank came up with the name Fizzgig which was an obsolete 18th century term for "firecracker."

His concept was a character who could suddenly explode with rage but would be a pet or companion to Kira, which would help show her sensitive, nurturing side. Jim was not fond of the character at first because he saw a retread of Foo-Foo. (Jim hated to repeat himself. He wanted to do something different every time. It was part of his obsessive creativity.)

I asked Jim what he hated most about the character, and he said he didn't like Kira having to haul the creature around. And he was afraid they'd end up having to use a real animal to do walking shots as they had to with Foo-Foo. But a real animal would not fit with his desire to invent creatures you've never seen before. He was also afraid the creature would get between Kira and his character Jen. It's no secret that Jim identified with Jen, as he did with Kermit. (The first time I saw Wendy's sculpture of Jen in the workshop it looked to me a lot like Brian Henson, who was about sixteen at the time.) Jim had explained to me that one secret of the Muppets was that the characters the puppeteers identified with most strongly were often those that worked best for the audience. Remembering Willis, the Martian flatcat in Robert Heinlein's *Red Planet*, I suggested that if Fizzgig could move differently, in an alien way, then he wouldn't seem like a lap dog. After some discussion we came up with a character who was a ball of fur with just the eyes showing, who could roll or bounce to move around, and who would change to all mouth (and teeth!) when he was angry or frightened. Dave Goelz gave a stellar performance of the part.

Once the Habeetabat/Aughra scenes had been shot, Jim had a lot of trouble with casting the voice actor. In explaining how to write the part he told me his inspiration was the seagull in *Watership Down*, brilliantly done by Zero Mostel as a kind of insane bird struggling to overcome Tourette's syndrome. Frank's performance had been great as usual, but Jim felt he needed a female voice. He read a lot of actresses but nobody was good enough to match Frank's performance, until Jim found Billie Whitelaw, who nailed it.

When the movie was finished the distributor screened it for some test audiences in Washington D.C. and Detroit, Michigan. Whether as Gary Kurtz explained it, in their enthusiasm for the imagery Jim and Frank had cut out too much necessary exposition, or whether people had come expecting a light-hearted romp with Kermit and Piggy, audiences were bewildered and repulsed by the sight of grotesque lizards snarling at one another in meaningless shrieks. As soon as the movie started, people began walking out. The word quickly spread in Hollywood that Jim's movie was a disaster. But Jim didn't waver in his belief that he had made a good movie, and it was just a matter of tweaking it here and there. Jim was afraid that Lew Grade and his underlings did not believe it was a good movie, and would try to cut their losses by skimping on publicity and promotion.

So the opening was delayed, and it was decided to write narration over the first scene in the castle and to replace the Skeksis' guttural snarls with English. Alan Garner, a British sci-fi writer, came in and wrote the narration. And I was delegated to replace the Skeksis' dialogue with English.

I flew up to Toronto where Jim was shooting his new show *Fraggle Rock*, and we sat in a hotel room running a tape backwards and forwards, counting lip flaps to see where we could put dialogue that would sync with the action. (At that time VHS had to de-thread the tape to go backward and forward, so we used a Betamax which could jog-shuttle like a Moviola without losing picture.)

I'd put English dialogue in the shooting script so the actors would know the subtext of the scenes. I had written it in a literary kind of English in case we decided to use it as subtitles under the Skexish. But

since the performers had been speaking gibberish, my English dialogue didn't fit the puppets' mouth movements. Now it had to be replaced by whatever I could make fit.

But oddly the new dialogue was better, less literary, more...alien. The creatures were speaking a language never spoken by human beings. It fit well with Jim's concept of a world like none you have ever seen. The movie came together and started to work. (You can see a segment of the original with Skexish dialogue as an extra on the DVD release.)

While Jim was remixing the film, I got a call from my lawyer, Tom Pollock, who was also one of Jim's lawyers. Tom told me that Lew Grade had sold his company, and therefore *The Dark Crystal*, to an Australian named Robert Holmes a Court. I said Robert who? He said "Holmes a Court," and spelled it out for me. I said that's a strange name for an Australian. Tom said "It's a pretty strange name for anybody.

My heart sank. I had complete confidence that the new version worked as a movie, but would the new owner release it with the necessary care?

Jim started screening the film again, mainly to show Holmes a Court that this was actually a good movie and encourage him not to dump it for a write-off. But Holmes a Court's people couldn't seem to work up any enthusiasm. The bad previews, the need to revoice the soundtrack, and the film's delayed delivery had everyone in Hollywood saying it was a turkey.

But a strange thing happened when people outside the film business (civilians, as they are called) saw the new version. People could now follow the plot and found they could identify with the characters. Many confessed to being profoundly moved by the ending. People started calling the Henson Company asking when it would be released, because they wanted to take their friends, or their kids, or their parents. The movie was scheduled to open at Christmas. Jim still didn't feel it would get the right promotion, so he offered to buy back the film himself. Holmes a Court said "Sold!" and Jim was the proud owner of *The Dark Crystal*. Jim had broken the one rule they warn you about in Hollywood: never put your own money in your movie.

The picture opened well and made about $40 million in its first two months of release. It's since become a classic and a terrific seller on DVD, largely to people in their thirties who fell in love with it when they were kids. It's also won a new generation of fans, in midnight screenings and TV, and spawned a full array of books, games, toys, lunch boxes, manga, and the current series of graphic novel prequels published by Archaia. Every time I see a midnight screening advertised I think "Jim, you believed in it, and you were right, it really is a good movie."

David Odell has written TV and screenplays, and directed episodes of Tales From the Darkside. *In addition to* The Dark Crystal, *he wrote the screenplays for* Masters of the Universe, Supergirl, Nate and Hayes, War Lords of the 21st Century, Battletruck, Between Time and Timbuktu, Dealing, Cry Uncle, *and the treatment for* The Quiet Earth. *He won an Emmy for his work on* The Muppet Show, *and directed* Martians Go Home. *With Annette Duffy he wrote a yet-unproduced screenplay for a sequel to* The Dark Crystal.

BRIAN FROUD is known worldwide as the pre-eminent faery artist of our time. He has published over twenty-five books, including the best selling *Faeries*, *Lady Cottington's Pressed Faery Book*, and many more. Brian and his wife Wendy have just released *Trolls*, a major hardcover book published by Abrams Books. Brian worked with Jim Henson for many years and was the designer for the iconic films *The Dark Crystal* and *Labyrinth*. Brian's art is represented in collections throughout the world and can be seen at Animazing Fine Art in New York.

JOSHUA DYSART is the multiple Eisner Award-nominated, New York Times Bestselling author of 16 graphic novels. His work has been discussed on NPR, the BBC, CNBC Africa and the NYTimes.

Born in the USSR, ALEX SHEIKMAN immigrated to the US at the age of 12 and shortly thereafter discovered comic books. Since then, he has contributed illustrations to a variety of role playing games published by White Wolf, Holistic Design and Steve Jackson Games. He is also the writer and artist of *Robotika*, *Robotika: For A Few Rubles More*, *Moonstruck* and a number of short stories. He lives in Northern California.

LIZZY JOHN lives in Brooklyn and spends most of her days there drawing pretty pictures. Sometimes she gets paid for it.

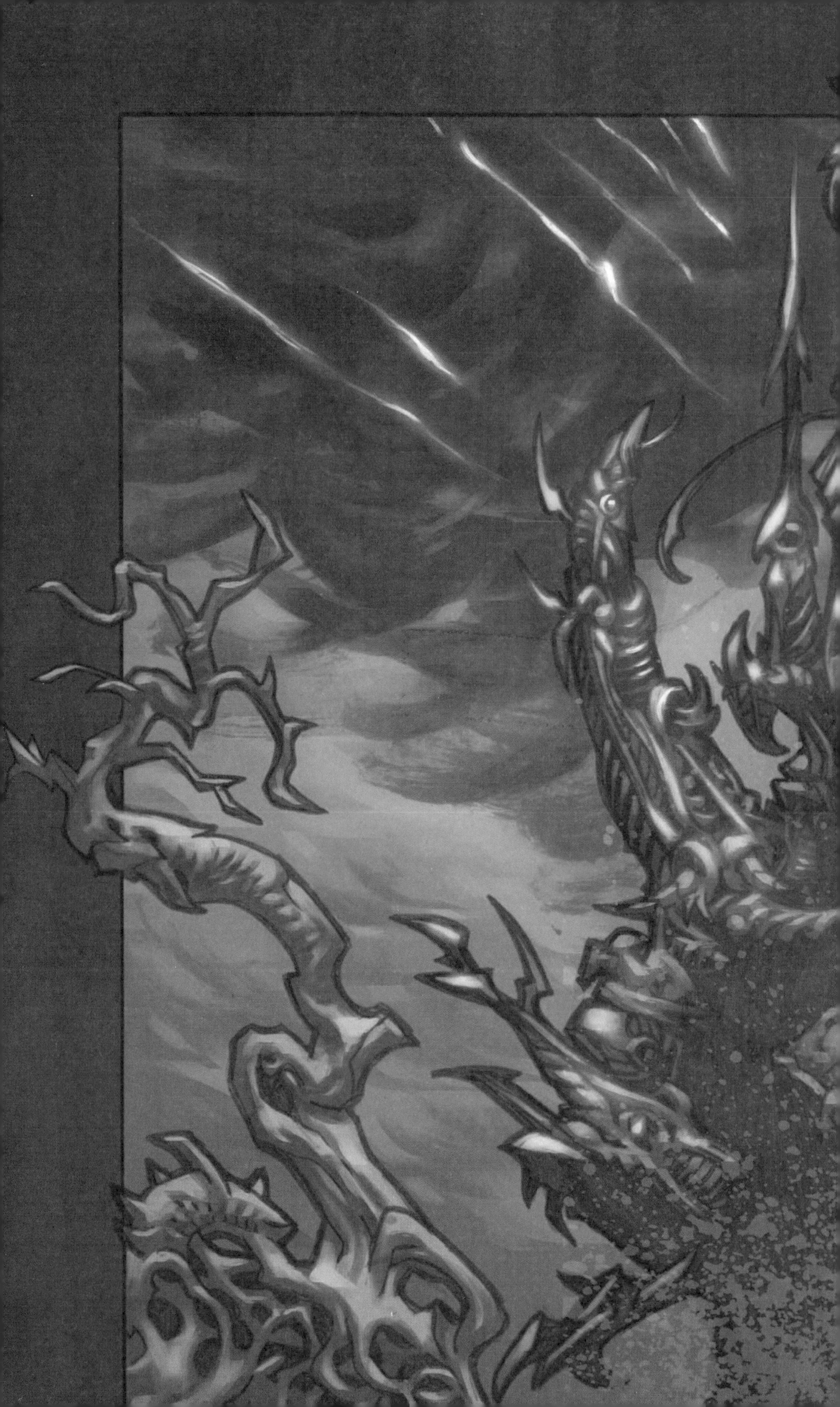